Praise for *PTSDr*

"An essential resource for psychotherapists to learn various modalities for helping clients... Clearly and beautifully written so that every reader can benefit from Linda's depth of experience." —**Lauren Schneider, MA, MFT, psychotherapist, creator of Tarotpy, and author of "Eco-Dreaming" included in *EcoTherapy***

"Through compelling case descriptions, thoughtful exercises, and a careful integration of clinical wisdom from the worlds of trauma treatment and dreamwork, Schiller skillfully introduces the reader to a wide range of strategies for addressing nightmares, transcending trauma, and finding relief." —**Deborah L. Korn, PsyD, faculty member at Trauma Research Foundation and EMDR Institute, psychotherapist, coauthor of *Every Memory Deserves Respect***

"Linda presents a delightful way of navigating through what might be one of our most terrifying experiences, post-traumatic nightmares." —**Bob Hoss, director and past president of IASD, director of the DreamScience Foundation, advisory board member of the National Institute for Integrative Healthcare, author of *Dream to Freedom***

"A cornucopia of techniques and wisdom that every therapist will find enlightening." —**Katharine Esty, LICSW, PhD, author of *EightySomethings***

"Schiller calls on a massive number of dreams and experiences collected from readers and clients to create one of the best new books on the subject of PTSD... Not only does she present a variety of techniques which can be used to work with PTSD dreams, but she also offers exercises which accompany and clarify each chapter.

There is no better book on the market today. You will want to buy this book and keep it nearby for all the support it offers." —**Jean Campbell, MA, past president of the International Association of Dreams and editor of IASD's** *DreamTime* **magazine**

"The warm and welcoming language, the holistic approach, and practical tips Schiller offers affirm that there is help and healing to be had—even from the scariest dreams." —**Tzivia Gover, certified dreamwork professional and author of** *The Mindful Way to a Good Night's Sleep*

"Beautifully written and full of important information on dreams, dreamwork, nightmares, and trauma." —**David Kahn, PhD, psychiatry instructor at Harvard Medical School, board member and past president of the International Association for the Study of Dreams**

"The breadth and depth of Linda's knowledge and how she weaves the tendrils of other healing modalities with dream work is stunning." —**Beth Rontal, MSW, LICSW, psychotherapist and founder of Documentation Wizard and creator of the Misery or Mastery documentation approach**

"This book is a must-have for anyone who dreams." —**Judith A. Swack, PhD, biochemist/immunologist, Master NLP practitioner, originator of Healing from the Body Level Up (HBLU) methodology, recipient of the 2015 ACEP award for major contribution to the field of energy psychology**

"Schiller has written a book that brings the gifts of a scientist, mystic, artist, and healer…[She makes] scary dreams a place we can walk toward rather than run from." —**Julie Leavitt, DMin, BC-DMT, LMHC, therapist, professor at Lesley University, spiritual director at Hebrew College**

"This book is bottled magic for the therapeutic treatment of nightmares." —**Jason DeBord, bestselling author of** *The Dream Interpretation Dictionary*, **lead operator of RedditDreams**

"Schiller expands the current dynamic conversation on trauma and dreams with clarity and brilliance…This book is a treasure for therapists and dreamers alike. "—**Kimberly Mascaro, PhD, author of** *Dream Medicine*

"*PTSDreams* does an elegant job of laying out the psychology and physiology of dreams and nightmares, the agony of trauma and post-traumatic stress disorder, and finally their intersection at PTSD nightmares." —**Deirdre Barrett, author of** *Pandemic Dreams*, **past president of the International Association for the Study of Dreams and of the Society for Psychological Hypnosis, dream researcher at Harvard University**

PTSDreams

· ·

About the Author

Linda Yael Schiller, MSW, LICSW (Watertown, MA), is a mind-body and spiritual psychotherapist, consultant, author, and international teacher. Linda facilitates group dream circles, provides individual, group, and corporate consultation, and trains professionals on working with dreams. She has designed several innovative methods for dreamwork. Linda is trained in numerous mind-body methods such as EMDR, EFT, energy psychology, Enneagram, and integrated trauma treatments. In addition to her professional work with dreams, she has been involved with her own dream-sharing group for more than thirty years.

PTSDreams

Transform Your Nightmares from Trauma through Healing Dreamwork

LINDA YAEL SCHILLER

AUTHOR OF *MODERN DREAMWORK*

Llewellyn Publications
Woodbury, Minnesota

First Edition
First Printing, 2022

Book design by Christine Ha
Cover design by Shannon McKuhen
Editing by Rhiannon Nelson

Llewellyn Publications is a registered trademark of Llewellyn Worldwide Ltd.

Library of Congress Cataloging-in-Publication Data (Pending)
ISBN: 978-0-7387-7047-5

Llewellyn Worldwide Ltd. does not participate in, endorse, or have any authority or responsibility concerning private business transactions between our authors and the public.

All mail addressed to the author is forwarded but the publisher cannot, unless specifically instructed by the author, give out an address or phone number.

Any internet references contained in this work are current at publication time, but the publisher cannot guarantee that a specific location will continue to be maintained. Please refer to the publisher's website for links to authors' websites and other sources.

Llewellyn Publications
A Division of Llewellyn Worldwide Ltd.
2143 Wooddale Drive
Woodbury, MN 55125-2989
www.llewellyn.com

Printed in the United States of America

Other Books by Linda Yael Schiller
Modern Dreamwork
New Tools for Decoding Your Soul's Wisdom

Contents

Exercises

Acknowledgments

My heartfelt appreciations to all my colleagues, friends, and clients who so generously shared their dreams and nightmares with me. Thank you for your trust. When I put out the APB that I was writing this book and looking for nightmares, I received countless dream missives containing your anxiety, fear, and distressing nightmares. I hope the act of sharing them with me and making them available to help others will also provide solace to these dreamers in their knowledge that they are furthering healing in the world. All client and colleague names have been changed to protect their anonymity unless they have specifically requested to use their own name, and personal information has also been altered for further privacy.

Big personal thank-yous to beloved friends and colleagues Jason DeBord, Julie Leavitt, Sara Levine, Betsy Magidson, and Jill Vetstein, for their dream-sharing. Additional special thank-yous to my long-term ongoing dream circle for their generosity and willing to share their dreams and our process over so many years: Joy Weider, Joyce Friedman, Marcia Post, Mia Woodworth, Ruth Silverstein, and Starr Potts. My other cheerleaders and supporters and dear sister/friends during this whole process include, as always, Diane Pardes, Beth Rontal, Lynn Roberson; all the Torah group women: Lorel Bar Kessler, Matia Angelou, Lynda Danzig, Julie Leavitt, Diane Pardes, Lori Silverstone, Joyce Friedman, Belle Halpern, Marilyn Stern, Janie Hodgetts, and Liza Stern; and my 35-year-long personal dream circle women: Lisa Kennedy, Marcia Lewin-Berlin, and Suzie Abu-Jabber.

IASD, the International Association for the Study of Dreams, has been my go-to place for all things dreamy for more than fifteen years. Special thanks to Jean Campbell, always a source of help and information and support; dear friend and dreamer Lauren Schneider, whose Taropy reading helped launch both my books; Jason DeBord and Steve Ernenwein for their wonderful podcast interview on *Dreaming My Daughter Home* on their podcast *Dreams That Shape Us*; and to colleagues Bob Hoss, David Kahn, Tzivia Glover, and Kim Mascaro for their support over the years.

Many thanks to Amy Glaser, Kat Neff, and all the staff at Llewellyn Publishing for their support, encouragement, and endorsement of my work. Big thank-yous to Rhiannon Nelson for her careful and thoughtful editing and her supportive comments along the way. Their patience, expertise, and warmth has made it a true pleasure to work with all of them.

Finally, love and thanks to my daughter Sara for giving me permission to share parts of her life, consulting on wording, and making me belly laugh. And this book could not have happened without my husband Steve being my first reader and wise editor, holding up the fort at home, feeding me, taking care of the infrastructure, and supporting my vision.

INTRODUCTION

It was a time of dark dreams. They washed in like flotsam on the night tide, slipping beneath doorways and window latches, rising through the streets and hills; and the little fishing-town of Scarlock foundered deep.
—J. A. Clement, On Dark Shores: The Lady

Our dreams slip in through the cracks in our consciousness every night, whether we recall them or not. Many of us have nightmares slip in too, some of us occasionally, and others all too often. On an average night of seven to eight hours of sleep we have five to six REM cycles (Rapid Eye Movements), the part of our sleep cycle where most of the dreams are generated.[1] We tend to only remember those we have just before waking, however. Nightmares are generally vividly realistic, disturbing dreams that frequently jar us awake. Our natural tendency is to want to look away from them, to put them back to sleep, if you will. Marcia, one of my colleagues, says that while she is a fairly faithful recorder of her dreams, she knows that she sometimes consciously chooses not to write down some of the scary ones because she just isn't ready to deal with them. This is valid. We might not yet be ready to deal with our ghosts and demons; we need to respect our need to go slowly.

---

1. "What Are REM and Non-REM Sleep?" WebMD, October 16, 2020, https://www.webmd.com/sleep-disorders/sleep-101.

However, when unaddressed, these dark dreams can follow us around in other forms, sneaking in through the cracks and fissures of our consciousness until they are finally faced, comforted, and healed. Psychologist Michael Conforti[2] cites his mentor Dr. Yoram Kaufman from an unpublished paper, "The Way of the Image," who taught that an inability to find a place for these memories can keep us shackled to a constrained, Sisyphean world. In this world, our movement into the future is thwarted by these "forgotten" memories which keep pushing us back down the hill. He states that while retrieving these memories is a psychological issue, learning to live with what we remember is a spiritual process. That is part of the premise of this book: that healing from our nightmares allows us deep healing at a psychospiritual level.[3]

The purpose of this book is to help you to heal from your nightmares in an integrated body/mind/spiritual approach so you can return to enjoying a good night's sleep, or perhaps be able to do so for the first time. Even if you have been a habitual lifetime nightmare sufferer, there is something here to help you find peace in the night, and as a bonus, greater healing from the upsetting or traumatic events that generated your nightmares in the first place. It may take some time, particularly if you have been having them for a long time, but it is possible. You can find peace and healing to replace the fear and grief and pain.

Nightmare sufferers oftentimes despair of ever finding relief or ending the emotional hijacking of what should be their peaceful, restorative sleep. Some even develop fears or phobias of going to sleep at all, as the anticipatory anxiety that they may have yet another

---

2. Michael Conforti, *Field, Form, and Fate: Patterns in Mind, Nature, and Psyche* (New Orleans, LA: Spring Journal, Inc., 2013).

3. Yoram Kaufmann, *The Way of the Image: The Orientational Approach to the Psyche* (New York: Zahav Books, 2009).

nightmare keeps them from feeling safe enough to relax into asleep. They sometimes develop elaborate rituals to stave off sleep and the concurrent terrifying dreams. You yourself may have tried many solutions: medications, therapy, guided imagery, TV or social media, alcohol or other drugs, tiring yourself out through exercise, or putting a night-light in your room. Some may have worked temporarily, only to have the same or a different nightmare return to seep into your sleep and bring new dangers or dilemmas to your dreamscape. It may be helpful to remind yourself that above all else, nightmares come to us to help us process information. This somewhat neutral statement can actually be a great source of comfort and relief if you wake with a nightmare in the middle of the night. Simply telling yourself, "Oh, okay I am processing some information here" can help you catch your breath and ground yourself until you have the time to deal with this information that you are processing.

Carl Jung hints at inherited and archetypical as well as personal memory, and Freud tells us that we need to make conscious our forgotten memories otherwise we tend to "repeat what we do not remember." Our nightmares actually contain within them the seeds of hope and transformation. Our dreams hold, as does our life, what Zorba called the full catastrophe; the whole range of our emotions and our experiences from the glorious and wonderous to the terrifying and enraging. If we don't engage with and resolve our nightmares, we also miss out on the joy and larger possibilities for our life.

Our nightmares are also biologically adaptive. They provide a threat simulation rehearsal to help us gain skills and perspective in case we ever have to face that threat again. They also provide an evolutionary perspective: We have to keep remembering so that we don't forget. Dissociated memories can reoccur in dreams because of the biological imperative of remembering.

The nightmares that we experience may disturb not only our nights but linger with sticky tenacity into our subsequent days as well. They may contain consciously known griefs and frights, such as the pain of the loss of a loved one, the helpless feeling of experiencing a natural disaster, the dull depression of living during an isolating pandemic, or the shame- and blame-filled traumas of an abusive past. Also appearing in our dreamscapes are those woundings that we are as-of-yet unconscious to in our waking minds. They are claiming the space they need to emerge during the night when the waking "day censor" parts of our brain are asleep. These, too, the unknown ghosts of our past, our present, or even our future, can haunt our dreams with their icy fingers. Charles Dickens touched on this concept with Ebenezer Scrooge's powerful dream apparitions of Christmas Past, Present, and Future. That might be the bad news. But there is also good news.

The Shadow Healed Becomes the Gift Revealed

Here is the good news. We are not meant to stay wounded—we are designed to heal. Our psyche wants to move us toward healing and wholeness. Psychotherapist Diana Fosha frequently tells us that the movement toward healing is in our hard wiring, in our very DNA.[4]

PTSDreams can help you access your own internal healing powers, and with gentle guidance and abundant resources resolve your nightmares once and for all. The goal is to transform both the heart pounding and the uneasy nocturnal missives into a new story, one of hope, of healing, and life-affirming images. Although it is not possible to live in this world or in these bodies and not experience pain or suffering at times, the good news about nightmares is that healing is

---

4. Diana Fosha, *The Transforming Power of Affect: A Model for Accelerated Change.* (New York: Basic Books, 2001).

possible. Even for our most long-standing or repetitive and terrifying ones. Trauma touches our spirits as well as our body and minds, so we need to carry the healing there as well. Full healing includes our bodies and our spirits as well as our minds and hearts. Our soul can feel separated from our body during trauma, and deep dreamwork helps us to restore soul loss and become re-ensouled.

How do we know when we have resolved the issues that contribute to our nightmares? The short answer is: when the scary dreams stop, or we feel at such a great distance from them that they no longer have an upsetting emotional impact. When our suffering ends, we have resolved the trauma. It is not as if it never happened, but the events no longer interfere with our life or sleep or functioning. Sometimes the nightmares are short-lived and cease quickly, but more often they gradually decrease in frequency and intensity. As we engage directly with the dream images and stories and do our personal work to resolve the underlying issues as well, the dreams become less and less frequent, contain less and less emotional intensity, and ultimately the frightening dream story is transformed, and we can then harvest the gift of the night. If you don't already have one, buy a dream journal and record your nightmares and your dreams so you can keep track of this progress.

I remember vividly one nightmare story line from my adult life and one from my childhood. In my recent dream the understanding and resolution came relatively quickly. The childhood one had lost its power over the years but was not fully resolved until several decades later. In my adult nightmare I dream:

I am underwater and trying to swim up to the light. I am holding my breath and hoping I will reach the surface before I run out of air. I finally manage to surface with a big gasp.

And then wake up panting. "Whew," I realize with relief. "That was a dream." And yet a lingering sense of uneasiness stalks me from my bedroom and out into my day. I know that I need to pay attention to this, especially since it was so much outside of my usual style of dreaming.

It was clear to me from the dream that something in my life was overwhelming and threatening to pull me under, but I didn't know what. Even as a professional dreamworker and psychotherapist, I still needed some help to figure it out. We all have our own blind spots, and no one can see the back of their own head without two mirrors. Carl Jung famously said that he always needed help to get to the bottom of his own dreams. So, I brought it to my dream circle, a small group of friends who have been meeting regularly to share our dreams for many years. They helped me figure out where in my waking life I needed to "get my head above water," stop to take that much-needed breath, and how to respond proactively with real-world action to resolve the nightmare. The goal of this book is help you to do the same with your own nightmares: to understand, to heal, and to resolve them.

My childhood nightmare was a repeating dream with the same story line:

I am being taken up in a helicopter with my dad and brother and some bad men threaten to cut all of us into pieces.

I remember that this dream was quite distressing as a child, but by the time I was an adult the emotional part of the dream had dissipated, and I just remembered the story line. One day in dream circle I didn't have a recent dream to work on, so I brought this old one in with the hopes of understanding it more fully. Fifty years later, I made the connection that I started having this nightmare during the time of my parents' divorce, when our family was being "cut into pieces."

The emotional resonance of the nightmare had long since faded with time, maturation, and some good therapy, but I never forgot the content. I was pleased to figure out, even many years later, what the play on words and imagery meant. I could then put it to rest even more completely.

The Power of Repair

As paradoxical as it may sound, the Talmud tells us that nightmares come bearing gifts, and can ultimately empower us. The power of repair in your dreams will ripple out into your life as well. We can then transform the fear in the nightmare into the gift from the dream, and then make a gift to the world from our own history of suffering and healing.

Embedded in Scrooge's journey in *A Christmas Carol* and in our own dreaming is the rich potential of transformation and joy, that we too can engage with and heal and learn the lessons from our dreams, and thus change our lives. Scary dreams and nightmares don't just come out of nowhere. Something has happened to us, to our family, to our ancestors, or to our society that has seeded in us the fears that "haunted [our] midnight pillow," as Mary Shelly observed. As the title of this book indicates, some of our dreams are embedded in post-traumatic stress disorder, the unresolved traumas we have experienced in our lives. As we address these traumas both large and small, both the personal and the global, with the dreamwork and trauma treatment tools contained in this book, we can access our highest potentiality and manifest it in our lives. That is the main thrust of this book. The first half will address the relationship between trauma and nightmares, and the second half will offer a wide and varied toolbox for transformation. Each chapter will include case studies of dreams and dreamers, some as one-off dreams; other dream stories will follow a dreamer's progress over time with repetitive dreams and themes as they work on their nightmares and trauma. Also included in each chapter are experiential exercises that you can do on your own, with a therapist or guide, or as a health or mental healthcare professional to use with your clients. Therapists, clergy, and medical practitioners may all find something here that resonates with their practice.

The first half of the book will orient us to the relationship between trauma and nightmares. We will examine how the story line of the dream connects with the emotional narrative in the dream, which is what differentiates a dream from a nightmare. Next, by closely examining the complex and varied nature of trauma, and how it is experienced, we make the connections between our nightmares and our traumatic experiences. The protective autonomic response of dissociation, which is often responsible for compartmentalizing the memories until such time as we are safe and grounded enough in our life to address and heal them, gets special attention. One aspect of dreaming is re-membering things that we knew but have buried. To "re-member" is to put ourselves back together again, to literally put our body "members" (our limbs) back together.

Careful self-pacing is part of the essence of healing from trauma. Only go as fast as the slowest part of you is comfortable going. So, if you feel that you are not ready to take a deep dive into the dynamics of trauma and dissociation yet, don't stop there! Just read these two chapters lightly and move on to the more dream- and nightmare-focused chapters. Come back to them later when you are ready for a closer read.

The remainder of the book will focus on a variety of dreamwork methods and offer a large toolkit to safely work with healing post-traumatic nightmares, while reducing the likelihood of re-traumatizing the nightmare sufferer in the process. We will review the GAIA Method (Guided Active Imagination Approach) I developed with its two-part methodology based on best-practice trauma treatment and

Jungian active imagination principles. The subsequent chapters focus on integrated and embodied dreamwork techniques as well as somatic, energy psychology, narrative, and psycho-spiritual approaches to healing from trauma. The final chapter offers a framework for the main goals of healing—that of post-traumatic growth and the opportunity to give back to others through the archetype of Chiron, the wounded healer. I add one more letter to the framework of PTSDreams to get PTSG-Dreams: Post-Traumatic Spiritual Growth Dreams.

Through active specialized dreamwork and trauma treatment techniques you can resolve your nightmares, transform them into healing resources, and ultimately end them altogether. You will notice that I use the word *dreamwork* rather than *dream interpretation* throughout this book. This is a purposeful choice. Most of us want to know what our dreams mean. How can we interpret this symbol or that metaphor? If I dream of a cat—what does that mean? If I dream of my hometown where I grew up—what does that mean? This is a valid and very human response. Off the top of my head, I can give you several possible answers, without even knowing who you are, based on my knowledge of potential meanings of dream symbols. They may or may not be true for your dream though, as your dream is contextualized within the specifics of your own life.

In addition, this is not the only purpose of dreams. Dreams come to us with messages and meanings and their own internal structure and story. Ofttimes we need to first stay inside of the dream story itself and work directly with the metaphors of the dream to glean their reasons for coming to us. If we rush too quickly into "this means that," we may miss both the beauty and power of the dream story and miss out on the message it may be sending us in its own language.

Dreams have a language of their own, and as we know, translation from any language into another is imperfect. Staying first with the language of the dream itself, in the way it has come through to us, gives us a chance to get the full flavor in its own language. So, as we move into the dreamwork in this book, you will notice that we often first work within the dream itself, and let the dream tell its own story as we expand or continue it or add more resources to a scary dream. Only after that do we move into what each symbol may mean—if we still need to. Sometimes we don't because we have extracted the messages and our marching orders for what to do in our life because of the dream without parsing out every image into a waking sensibility.

You can use the dreamwork techniques and skills you'll learn here on your own, or in a dream group, often called a dream circle. The additional guidance of a therapist or counselor is recommended if you know or think that you may have a history of trauma.

Integrating Dreamwork and Trauma Treatment

My own experience includes more than 40 years of practicing psychotherapy, clinical supervision, consultation, teaching university classes and workshops, and extensive writing as both a trauma therapist and a dreamworker. During this time, I have studied and practiced integrated trauma treatment and dreamwork and created a variety of approaches and protocols to prepare to guide you on this journey. My nightmare protocol, the GAIA Method: Guided Active Imagination Approach, is grounded in best practice trauma treatment and Jungian active imagination. With dreamwork training in Jungian, psycho-dynamic, Gestalt, expressive, archetypical, Image Rehearsal Therapy, body-based, energetic, and spiritual and shamanic disciplines, I incorporate all of these in my approach to dreamwork.

As a psychotherapist, I am also trained in trauma-specific methodologies, such as EMDR (Eye Movement Desensitization and Reprocessing), IFS (Internal Family Systems), EFT (Emotional Freedom

Technique, colloquially known as "tapping"), hypnotherapy, NLP (Neuro-Linguistic Programming), Enneagram, energy medicine, and Somatic Experiencing. I am a professor emeritus at Boston University School of Social Work with scholarship in relational group work theory and practice and taught in the Post-Graduate Trauma Certificate Programs at both Boston University and Simmons College.

I have been a student of Kabbalah for many years, and my original work on the Kabbalah of Dreams has been taught at Hebrew College, Boston, and many other spiritual and educational venues. I combine all these methods to specifically target the resolution of nightmares. This integrated body / mind / spiritual and trauma-informed approach to dreamwork and nightmares offers you many options on your path toward sweeter dreams.

ONE

THE DIFFERENCE BETWEEN A DREAM AND A NIGHTMARE:
The Narrative and the Emotional Stories

So, the beauty of the dream is that it can't create a rosy, make-believe picture of your life. And underneath the edginess and fear and helplessness of the dream, that's good news. It means you can trust your dreams. They may be unpleasant, as the truth can be, but they won't attempt to falsely soothe you.
> **—David Jenkins, "The Nightmare and the Narrative"**

The difference between a dream and a nightmare is contained in the emotional story that accompanies the dream narrative. The feeling of the dream; or in other words, the emotions that are experienced both within the dream itself and upon waking are what change our story from dream to nightmare. Dr. Ernest Hartmann, noted dream researcher, makes the case that the connection between dreams and waking life is through the cross section or the net of consciousness between the two.[5] He argues that the dominant emotions in the dream are what should guide the exploration of the dreamer. In his research on thousands of dreams, he found

---

5. Ernest Hartmann, *Dreams and Nightmares: The New Theory on the Origin and Meaning of Dreams* (New York: Plenum Trade, 1998), 4.

that the emotional concerns of the dreamer guide the dream imagery and story line. Dream journaling may be our own Jacob's ladder between the worlds above and the worlds below. Our journal provides the rungs or scaffolding to hang our dreams on to be able to carry them with us into waking consciousness, and thus honor them and carry their healing potential into our lives.

EXERCISE
Journaling Your Dreams and Nightmares

Purchase a journal to record your dreams if you don't already have one. If you have dreams or nightmares you recall from your past, write those down to start with, and date them as closely as you can recall. Try to write the oldest dreams you remember first so you have a beginning log for your dream progression. Notice if the general direction of your dreams is toward greater or fewer nightmares. Once you have captured your past dreams as much as you can recall, you can continue to record your dreams as often as possible, remembering to date them in your journal. Begin to notice if you find any themes or dreams or images that repeat and highlight them to keep track. Write, draw, or sketch your dream. Finally, make a note in your journal that you intend to bring healing and resolution to your nightmares and bad dreams. Setting that intention and writing it down in your journal will start to point you in the direction of healing even before you work more actively on it.

Tracking the Emotional Dream Story

Some of my psychotherapy clients tell me that certain dreams should come with a trigger warning. Rick's nightmares are full throttle terrorist chases through twisting dark alleys, right up to the edge of a cliff, often with the sound of gunfire coming increasingly closer. Merrel frequently wakes with a panicked gasp, her heart in her throat and an icy feeling of anxiety shivering in her limbs, but she doesn't recall any pictures or stories—just the embodied emotions. The physical and emotional feelings she wakes with are all that remain of her dream, so for all practical purposes, they are her dream. She doesn't yet know why, since her daily life is reasonably safe. Robin screams "F…k you" to her dream characters, something she would never dream of doing while awake, and her husband tells her she screams this out loud in her sleep too. Jay relives his assault over and over in his dreams. Anne dreams of a creepy, murky river that she needs to navigate. Larissa dreamed of an alligator crawling out of the swamp and approaching her with its mouth wide open, exposing his large, pointed, threatening teeth.

My own adult nightmare occurred during the COVID-19 pandemic. I simply screamed out loud in my sleep, and then woke up. I had no memory of any content, just the emotion that generated the scream. I needed no help figuring out what that meant this time; we were all living with various degrees of panic and fear as the waking nightmare of the virus unfolded.

Tracing the emotional narrative as it changes within the dream, and as we work on it after we awake, are the magic keys to understanding and unpacking the meaning of a dream and to know when a nightmare is resolving. Keeping a record of your dream life over time is imperative to knowing if you are making progress toward resolving an issue that shows up in your dreams. Really write in that journal you started. Otherwise, you won't know if the nightmares are changing, getting less frequent, or less intense—or not. A dream journal, whether written, typed, or dictated, where you record all of your dreams (not only the nightmarish ones), with a date for each dream, is the best way to track your progress.

The strength or intensity of the emotions inside the dream, as well as the emotions we experience upon waking and recalling it, are what constitute the barometer that takes the pulse of our dreams and should be part of the focus of your dream journal. A change in the emotional story line in a dream can take the same scene, the same actions, and alter their meaning for us as our reaction to them varies.

Different people can have similar dreams, but the meaning may be wildly different for each depending on the emotional resonance they have with the dream figures and actions. If I meet a panther in the woods of my dream, I might be delighted to run into my totem animal and expect that he has come to bring me some advice or insight. You, however, who does not have a panther as a totem, or has not encountered the idea of helpful totem creatures in your life or dreams yet, may feel terrified. We can also experience intensity variations in the same emotional arena. Anger, for example, can range from fury to rage to mad to upset to irritated to annoyed. (Your specific progression may vary, but you get the idea.) All are forms of anger, but one end of the spectrum is intense while the other end is mild. Notice how your emotional barometer changes on varied emotional bandwidths of the same feeling state, and if it changes to different emotions with the same narrative story for clues to the soothing of your distress.

When we experience a dream, what are the emotions at the beginning, the middle, and the end of the dream? A sign of progress is when we feel better by the end of the dream than we did in the beginning.

Are we feeling anxious, delighted, or angry? Do the feeling states change as we move about various parts of the dream? And like in the doctor's office when you are asked to rate your pain on a scale of 0–10, how big is the feeling? High numbers for pleasant feelings have us wake feeling grand, but an 8 or 9 on the fear barometer indicates that this is a nightmare. In both energy medicine and trauma treatment this rating scale is called the *SUDS* scale, or *Subjective Unit of Distress*. It is primarily used to rate our level of upset, and the treatment goal is to get that number as close to zero as possible when recalling the trauma in present time. We can also use this rating scale in our dreamwork to get very concrete and quantifiable information on our progress. If we started working on our dream of being chased by that panther and our fear SUDS level was an 8, and by the time we had squeezed as much juice out of it as we could we now rated it a 4, then we have a quantifiable measure of our progress, not only on resolving the nightmare, but also with reverberations to the underlying issue that generated it.

Questions about the type and the intensity of emotion are profoundly important for nightmare healing. They provide us with feedback as to where we are vis-à-vis the problem or issue that the dream is highlighting. We also get feedback from which emotions are found at the beginning, the middle, and the end of our dreams. If we start out feeling anxious but are able to resolve the dream problem inside the dream and end up feeling calm by the end, we know that we are already making real headway in our healing. However, if the dream ends with the same anxiety, or worse yet, escalates into abject fear, that too is information for us. It is telling us that what we have been doing thus far is not what our psyche needs to resolve the problem, and we had best find other resources, other help, other ideas or solutions, or ways of holding the problem gently until such time as we can bring greater healing to it. We may need to move more slowly. There is a timelessness to both trauma and our dreams that needs to be addressed. We need to slowly unfreeze the frozen-in-time aspects of trauma that still show up as "now" in our soul and in our dreams. Then, in our dreams, where it is always now, we have the opportunity to rework and thaw the state of frozen terror.

These kinds of explorations of the dream comprise part of the template for healing from nightmares. Working with a guide, be it a therapist, a wise friend, this book, or your own internal highest best self, we bring fresh ideas, alternate emotional response options, and potential solutions to the dream and the dream characters. Once the SUDS is lowered and the emotions have calmed, we can find a better resolution to the threat than the one that appeared in the original nightmare. We keep doing this as many times as we need to until the nightmares cease or transform.

Swimming to the Light or Drowning?

To give you a taste of the relationship between story and affect, as well as a taste of the many layers embedded in each of our dreams, here is an example of a waking dream that connects to a nighttime dream. A waking dream is not the same as daydreaming or losing our attention to a fantasy or thought. Rather, a waking dream may be defined as an event or reoccurring series of events that seem to be more than coincidence; or, alternately, an image, a symbol, or a synchronistic experience that contains something of the numinous in it. Jung has often described synchronicity as a meaningful coincidence.[6] Déjà vu and intuitive knowledge are both aspects of waking dream states. When something catches our attention in this way, we can bring our dreamwork skills and curious mind to examine it for deeper meanings.

---

6. Carl Jung, *Synchronicity: An Acausal Connecting Principle. (From Vol. 8. of the Collected Works of C. G. Jung)*, ed. Sonu Shamdasani (Princeton, New Jersey: Princeton University Press, 2010).

Here's my waking dream. I have a picture hanging in my office of a woman swimming upward underwater in a luminous blue-green pool or river. She is swimming up through tall reeds toward brilliant sunlight that we can see shining overhead above the water. The reeds are wrapped around her legs as she swims, and it is not clear from the picture if she will successfully clear the surface as she tries to swim, or be pulled down by the reeds and the undertow. We can't really see the expression on her face, which might give us a clue. Looking at it one way, with the emotional resonance of anxiety or panic filling our chest, it would be the nightmare of potential drowning. If we were to rate the SUDS in the drowning version, it could be an 8, "I can't do this, I can't breathe, I could die," or a maybe a 4, "This is so hard, but I think I can get there." Looking at the same picture from another perspective, that of a strong swimmer enjoying the water and confident in that element who just needs to make a few strong kicks to surface, it becomes a picture of joyful personal strength and emerging into the light. The level of upset would then be zero, and the feeling would be one of empowerment and delight. Two very different dreams of the same picture.

A few weeks later I see the connection between this picture that has been hanging on my office wall for years while I work with trauma survivors and my own dream of swimming underwater and just making it to the surface before waking. In truth, I actually love the picture—it is a print of the Celtic goddess Boann that was painted by a friend of mine on one of the cards in her goddess deck of the Tarot. I used it frequently as a sort of Rorschach test to assess progress in the treatment. When I looked up how to correctly spell her name, I found this description: "Boann, herself a water goddess approached a sacred and forbidden well. Because of this transgression, the well became a raging river, which then pursued her. In some versions of the story she drowned, and in others she managed to outrun the current. But in either case, she became the presiding deity of the river Boyne."[7]

I had no idea—even the mythic stories about this goddess contain two possible endings. Here we find yet another layer to the dream and the dreamish picture—the resonance with deep archetypical forces and mythos. Ancient myths and legends and holy books also seep into our dreams, sometimes at a layer beyond our conscious awareness. This too becomes part of the dreamworld we will explore for resources when we look at uncovering the layers of meaning in our dreams and nightmares in chapter 5.

My own personal association to the picture on my wall in waking life had always been that it is beautiful and hopeful. However, I had my swimming and "just-getting-my-head-above-water" dream in the early months of the COVID-19 pandemic. No wonder I could just barely surface. In addition, my daughter had just completed some surgery and was on crutches, so it was like being in a double quarantine for us for a few months until she got her mobility back. The good news for me was that I did gulp the air and breathe before waking, signifying my hope and confidence that we would all breathe easy again. And, if we continue the associations, which are one of the keys to strong dreamwork, the most distressing symptom of this virus is respiratory distress. Yet another layer of potential meaning to take into account.

A Change in Perspective

It is this way with our dreams and nightmares too—sometimes a change in perspective, or how we look at something, can mean the difference between a heart-pounding dream of terror or a hidden gift.

---

7. "Boann (also Board, Boyne, Boannan)," LiveJournal, October 18, 2004, https://the-goddesses.livejournal.com/9019.html.

Motivational speaker Wayne Dyer tells us, "When you change the way you look at things, the things you look at change."[8] Does she drown, or shake off the offending reeds and breathe freely? If this were my dream (as we say in the dreamwork world), my imagined outcome would depend on my emotion. If I woke panic stricken, I might worry about drowning, but if I woke feeling confident that I had plenty of air to reach the surface and I was having fun swimming, then that is a different dream altogether. Active dreamwork allows us to work with the images that may have started out as nightmares and transform them from a traumatic dream to one of safety and empowerment.

This is the same principle that holds true for trauma treatment. When the actual traumatic events are in the past and are no longer currently happening, then it is our memory of the event, rather than the event itself, that is wreaking havoc in our psyche. We can then move in our healing work from the experienced memory of fear into the present moment of now with safety and empowerment. However, when the traumatic events have very recently occurred, or are still occurring, we may need a different approach that considers the reality of our current situation; perhaps by finding small moments of empowerment or of safety or self-efficacy and control within the larger scope of the ongoing events. Both dreamwork and trauma work also allow us to widen our perspectives. We can use both the telescope lens of clearer far-seeing and the microscope lens of enlarging our close-up seeing to broaden and highlight time and space and get different perspectives on what happened to us.

Here is one more association to this dream that some of you may have already gotten to ahead of me: George Floyd. "I can't breathe."

---

8. Wayne Dyer, *Change Your Thoughts, Change Your Life—Living the Wisdom of the Tao,* read by Wayne Dyer (Carlsbad, CA: Hay House, 2009), Audiobook recording, 9 hours and 9 minutes.

I don't remember if I had the dream before or after that tragic event, but either I was resonating with it at a visceral level or had a glimpse of prescience or pre-cognitive insight into an upcoming event. This is a collective layer of my little personal dream that we can all grapple with: the breath of justice for all in our country and in our world. We see that sometimes the work on our own dream can take us far afield from the original dream content alone. We can dream for ourselves, we can dream for our families, and we can dream for our world—and the same dream may contain all these layers simultaneously. We'll come back to this idea again when we learn the *PARDES* method of layers of a dream in chapter 5. The gifts buried in even the darkest nightmares may contain gifts for the world as well as ourselves.

Big-T and Small-t Traumas and Nightmares

Some milder nightmares signal the presence of the little run-of-the-mill daily slings and arrows of life (such as when we were cut off on the highway or when we were endlessly kept on hold while trying to make an important call). In addition, some nightmares represent normal hallmarks of traversing a developmental life stage (especially in childhood: weaning, starting day care or school, first losses, such as a friend moving away). These types of traumatic events are what we might call the small-t traumas; upsetting, but not blocking our life force or dysregulating. The other more intense type of nightmare represents the big-T traumas, alerting us to large-scale, life-threatening, or life-changing events. They may have happened in the past and we have not yet fully processed them, or they may still be occurring. These big-T nightmares generally have to do with violence, abuse, childhood neglect, disasters, and/or traumatic losses. War veterans, domestic violence survivors, childhood abuse, and living during a time of global crises and pandemic are a few examples of big-T traumatic events that may infiltrate our dreams.

Other nightmares still may contain the fingerprints of intergenerational traumas. The relatively new science of epigenetics informs us that events from generations past can still affect us for generations after the traumatic events occurred. While extreme stress or trauma may not change our actual DNA structure, scientific studies have now shown that it does make chemical changes or leave marks on our genes in a process called methylation. That affects how these genes are expressed and may affect the function of the gene itself. These generational ghosts can show up in our nightmares, demanding their due.

Our Vulnerabilities

Trauma theory informs us that we may become vulnerable in certain areas of our life because of traumatic experiences, even when these experiences have ended or been fairly resolved. This heightened vulnerability may then get re-triggered in later periods in our life when we face a similar situation or similar emotional state, and then the nightmares resurface. Think of the veteran of war who still ducks and covers when a plane flies low overhead or a car backfires. Or the survivor of childhood sexual trauma who has nightmares resurface after years of dormancy when her child reaches the age she was when the abuse happened. We will address these nightmare re-triggers as well in the second part of the book.

We need strong dreamers now more than ever.

EXERCISE
Finding Your Emotional and Narrative Stories in the Dream

Go back and look at some of the dreams you have recorded in your dream journal. Now write down the emotional story line that accompanies the narrative or image. One way to do this is to write down the emotion you felt in the dream next to the section of the dream that you experienced it. If there is no room on the page, use arrows to indicate which feelings went with which parts of the dream, and next time when you record your dream, simply leave a little space alongside it. (My dream journal is full of these little arrows.) By doing so you will have constructed an emotional narrative to go along with the dream. Now you can more easily see whether you are already moving in the direction of resolution and healing if the nightmare ends on a more positive note than it began, or that you are still as stuck in distress by the end as you were in the beginning of it. This insight will help to inform you as to what direction you need to go in next as you work on the dream: more of the same, or something else; different or more resources are needed before you can resolve it. Then you will use the resources from subsequent chapters to move on.

* * *

EXERCISE
Bridging Your Waking and Sleeping Dreams

Think about the relationship between your waking dreams and your sleeping dreams. If you haven't already done so, begin to pay attention to the synchronicities, the déjà vu, and the meaningful coincidences in your waking life. How do they relate to your dreaming life? Can you begin to build a bridge between the two? If you are struggling with nightmares, are there themes that continue to surface for you? Can you find a connection between your nightmare themes and waking life issues or concerns in your current life or in your past? If you turn the prism around, twist the end of the kaleidoscope, the telescope, or the microscope to get a different configuration or look at it differently, can you get a different perspective?

· · · · · · · · ·

TWO

"ORDINARY" NIGHTMARES
(NOT ONLY FROM TRAUMA)

Though we seem to be sleeping, there is an inner wakefulness that directs the dream, and that will eventually startle us back to the truth of who we are.

—Jalaluddin Rumi (translated by Coleman Barks)

Before taking a deep dive into the effects of trauma and PTSD (Post-Traumatic Stress Disorder) in our lives and in our dreams, let's take a brief look at other factors that may generate nightmares. Our approach to dream and nightmare work will vary depending on the etiology or source of the problem. These other factors may include hormonal changes, developmental life changes, food and drink, and illness.

The Role of Biology and Hormones

This next section takes a close look at our endocrine system and some of its interaction with the limbic system, where our emotional trauma responses are mediated. Both of these brain/body systems are involved in the production of dreams and nightmares. Perhaps because I am so interested in the body/mind connection and healing at that intersection, I have a fascination with the neurobiology of trauma and dreams.

Some dreams are biologically or hormonally based. An example of this are the wild dreams that many pregnant women report that are frequently like nothing they have ever had before. They are often quite vivid and seem to be generated by the hormonal surges of pregnancy as it progresses, rather than specific life events. Hormones are our chemical messengers, and our hormonal production can also be profoundly affected by trauma and stress. It makes sense that changes in our biochemistry may effect changes in our dream life as well.

Many of the components of our endocrine system affect our sleep/wake cycles. Several of these endocrine glands are located in the brain. They are the pituitary gland, the hypothalamus, and the pineal gland. The other parts of our endocrine system are the thyroid and para-thyroid located in our neck, the thymus between our lungs, the adrenals on top of our kidneys, the pancreas behind our stomach, and the ovaries and testes in our pelvis. Together these hormones control mood, growth and development, metabolism, and reproduction. Our sleep and wake waves and cycles are part of our metabolism. If our body is making too much or too little of a neurotransmitter or hormone, our moods, both in waking and dreaming life, may also be affected.

The pineal gland is located deep in the center of the brain and produces the melatonin that regulates our circadian rhythms and aids in sleep. It has been known as the third eye for its reactivity to light, and many esoteric and spiritual traditions see it as a metaphysical connection between the physical and spiritual worlds. Also, deep in the center of our brain is our limbic system; our reptilian or emotional brain. The limbic system is the seat of our emotional brain and houses the famous fight/flight/freeze response system well known to trauma. We can begin to hypothesize as to the relationship between these two such proximal structures. For example, the brain exerts executive control over the endocrine system via the hypothalamus, which is one of the structures in the limbic system where our emotions are sourced both in waking and dreaming life.

Dr. Sandra Nagel instructs us about the overlap between the biology of our nervous and endocrine systems when we experience both stress and trauma. "The interaction of the nervous system and endocrine system is most evident in the sympathetic response of the autonomic nervous system." (Our autonomic nervous system is what controls our automatic, or autonomous functions, such as blood pressure, heart rate, digestion, and respiration.) "The hypothalamus, a part of our emotional limbic system … integrates autonomic functions … through two separate pathways. Each pathway stimulates the adrenal glands to secrete substances that prepare the entire body for an emergency." (Note how nicely our body comes to our defense during times of stress.) "In general, the response of the nervous system to environmental change is quicker than the response of the endocrine system … [while] the changes affected by the endocrine system and hormones are in general more long-term and widespread."[9]

In summary, loosely translated, our nervous system acts more quickly in response to threat, including the reactivity in our dream life immediately following a disturbing event; but it is our endocrine system that may carry that response to a more permanent state. This then results, among other things, in those repetitive and long-lasting nightmares we experience even many years later.

---

9. "Tutorial 12: The Endocrine System," Introductory Biological Psychology Tutorials, https://psych.athabascau.ca/html/Psych289/Biotutorials/12/part1.shtml.

Developmental Changes and Effects on Dream Life

As mentioned earlier, our hormonal balance can also change due to normative developmental life passages, such as starting daycare or school, or the onset of adolescence, pregnancy, or lactation. Small and young people (children) experience the world as bigger and more powerful than it is, because at that time in their life, it is. They are told what to do, for better or for worse, by parents, teachers, other adults, and older children. It is no wonder that they frequently have dreams and nightmares of large monsters and wild animals! These dreams may be metaphorically expressing their sense of vulnerability in the world. In addition, it seems that there is a period of time developmentally, somewhere in early latency age (approximately ages five to nine), when children begin to realize that their parents are not infallible. This comes as a terrific shock to them either when they catch their parents in a lie (e.g., having seen mommy and daddy fighting but being told that there is no problem, it is just their imagination), or when there is a loss or upset that dad or mom can't fix. "What do you mean that Sparky my pet hamster died? Why can't you bring him back to life? Maybe he just needs a Band-Aid or some Pepto-Bismol!"

When real life rears its head in these ways, it is common for children to experience nightmares until their inner and outer worlds are again more in balance, and their internal reality matches more closely with what their parents actually can and can't do in the outside world. This is a normative period in childhood, and most often the bad dreams resolve by themselves with good parenting, nighttime rituals, and soothing. If they don't, that may be time to seek some consultation to be sure there is nothing else amiss in their life. Chapter 9 will include an exploration of working children's nightmares.

Also developmental in nature, yet with a twist, is adolescence. Teenagers are infamously fearless and think they are omnipotent.

Add to this belief system the very real hormonal flooding of puberty, coupled with the fact that their prefrontal cortex, our thinking and reasoning brain, doesn't fully come online until about age twenty-five. We can therefore see fertile ground for all manner of dreams and nightmares as their unconscious tries to sort out the differences between what they think they can do and what they actually can do, and the inherent frustrations therein. Again, this is a normative period in life for strange dreams and nightmares as our teens begin to stretch their wings in the world and have so much more to navigate. Many teens (dare I say most) could benefit from even a short course of some good therapy to help them sort things out, and most of them love to talk about their dreams. In fact, dreamwork can be a secret back door into the real issues they are struggling with, as the famous teen resistance to therapy is circumvented by focus on dreams.

When adolescents are exposed to trauma, it is held in their nervous system and brains differently than adults. For example, there were several differences between World War II veterans and Vietnam veterans. In addition to the war theater itself, the purpose of the fighting, and how the soldiers were or were not welcomed back home, the average age of the recruits varied. WWII vets were an average of twenty-two years old, and Vietnam vets were an average of only eighteen. This significant four-year age gap in part accounts for the exponentially larger amounts of intrusive nightmares and the greater development of PTSD in the Vietnam-era vets. The eighteen-year-old soldiers did not have the reserves or resources developmentally that the twenty-two-year-old soldiers did.

Any major life changes in adulthood can also generate mild to moderate nightmares regardless of whether the change itself is traumatic or not. Moving, graduating from college and embarking on "real life," or a large weight change can disrupt our self-image. Even a positive change, such as a promotion, getting married, or exotic travel causes a disruption in our lives that our dreaming self may respond to and try to sort out and regain equilibrium.

Food, Drugs, and Illness

What else can affect our dream life? Some categories of sleep disorders may also affect or contribute to nightmares. Sleep apnea can be a major culprit, since if it's hard for us to breathe fully while we are asleep, then we are not getting enough oxygen to our bodies or our brains and our dreams may symbolically alert us to this. Nightmares, fuzzy headedness, and "brain fog" when waking can also be warning signs. Dreamworker Jason DeBord, on his Dreams 1-2-3 website, enumerates dream themes that may be pointing to apnea, including nightmares of strangulation, choking, trying to breathe in outer space or underwater, and dreams of clogged pipes or chimneys. If you or a loved one suspect you have sleep apnea, please get a sleep study to ascertain if you need an assisted breathing device, such as a CPAP, as too little oxygen to the brain can be dangerous over time. To start with, if you live or sleep alone, set up a recording device at night to record your snoring. "Normal" snoring and sleep apnea can sound very different, with the latter including noisy machine-gun like sounds of sudden breath intake, interspersed with periods of silence where you are not breathing at all. At the very least, try lying on your side rather than your back to keep your airways more open and see it that improves your sleep, your daytime fatigue, and your nightmare and dream themes.

Food has long been known as a culprit—that spicy pizza or bad oyster we ate last night can reverberate in our dreams. Eating too close to bedtime can trick our metabolism into thinking it should be awake and digesting. Too much or too little food can also have an effect on our dreams. The media and print "food" we feed our brains can also cause nightmares. We can still become traumatized even if the trauma is media-induced rather than from events we have experienced or food we have eaten. Scary books, movies, and video games can show up in our nightmares either directly or indirectly. So can the news feed. Personally, I never watch the news. I know that I am a thin-boundaried person and that it will seep into my sleep and potentially cause nightmares. I stay informed, but not with a visual news feed. Same goes for bloody, violent, or horror films—they will never be on my playlist. If you are prone to nightmares or know that you are an empath who feels things deeply, try a diet of milder stuff to avoid some of those bad dreams.

Alcohol acts a depressant to our nervous system. It affects our decision-making and impulse control as well as offering some relaxation after a stressful day. It certainly may affect our dream content or emotion as well, for better or worse. Detoxing from alcohol abuse can create DTs—delirium tremens—and recovering addicts describe hallucinatory day and nightmares as their system rids itself of the drug. Coming off any medication, including prescription pain medicine and SSRIs (selective serotonin reuptake inhibitors such as Prozac), can also contribute to strange and uncomfortable dreams.

Taking various prescription and non-prescription drugs for blood pressure regulation, depression, anxiety, or sleep can similarly affect our dreams. Some come with warning labels of this as a side effect. The prescription sleep aide Ambien is famous (or infamous) for this. And, of course, people have been taking mind-altering drugs for centuries in religious or spiritual ceremonies or just for fun. The altered states may happen both while awake or while asleep, and not being able to tell the difference between these two is one of the hallmarks of an altered state. We are familiar with the phrases a "good trip" or a "bad trip"; these hallucinatory states also show up in our dreams, and a sleeping bad trip is what we might call a nightmare.

Finally, illness may affect our dream life. Upsetting fever dreams are well known to parents of a fevering child, and adults with high fevers may also experience strange and unusual dreams. In addition to sleep apnea, other nighttime disturbances such as restless leg syndrome, sleep paralysis, and other sleep disorders may also contribute. The physical and emotional aspects of our illness can burrow their way into our dream life either as literal or metaphoric images. One friend of mine suffers from scoliosis, and over time her ribs are slowly closing in on her lungs and beginning to constrict her breathing. She may need surgical intervention at some point. She dreamt:

I feel like my body is filling up with shredded paper. This is an uncomfortable but tolerable sensation. Then it changes to concrete or metal that locks me up so I can barely move.

A category of dreams known as "prodromal dreams" give us windows into our body's metabolic processes and potential illness before we even have symptoms. Aristotle proposed that, "The beginnings of diseases and other distempers which are about to visit the body…must be more evident in the sleeping state."[10] This idea seems less far-fetched when we remember that the body can produce detectable changes even before we have symptoms that can be picked up by various diagnostic tests. Being alert to this potential layer of the early warning system of our dreams may allow us to stave off or catch early what could be a more serious symptom if it progressed. Marilyn had been feeling not just tired, but exhausted, for years and kept having nightly vivid dreams of being lost and not being able to find her cell phone with the phrase, "Where is my cell?" repeating through her dreams. When she found a suspicious lump in her breast, which turned out to be cancer, she reported, "So that was

---

10. Robert Van de Castle, *Our Dreaming Mind* (New York: Ballantine Books, 1994), chapter 13, 364.

why I kept losing my cell phone—my cells had lost control." Wanda Burch paid attention to her own dreams of cancer and believes that they guided her toward treatments and wellness. She described being able to access and utilize several healing resources to survive her ordeal of breast cancer and its treatment, and then gifted us with her book which shares her journey.[11]

I coined the phrase, "What we don't metabolize, we are at risk for metastasizing." Dreamwork helps us to metabolize or digest our upsets and traumas and emotional states so that there is less risk of experiencing them at the physical level. This is emphatically not to place any blame on a person suffering from a physical illness or symptom, but simply to recognize the inter-relationship of our minds and our bodies, and how healing in one arena can affect healing in the other.

EXERCISE
Identifying Non-Trauma Nightmare Sources
Review the last few dreams and nightmares you have recorded, or that your child has shared with you. Can you identify any developmental life stages that may be influencing the content or emotions? How about hormonal changes, including but not limited to pregnancy, onset of puberty, or in relationship to your menstrual cycle? Have you or your child recently started or stopped taking a medication? See if you can track any relationship between your nightmares and your news and media intake. If you find a connection, please take appropriate steps to titrate your news input, and at the very least, set aside a

---

11. Wanda Burch, *She Who Dreams: A Journey into Healing Through Dreamwork* (Novato, CA: New World Library, 2003).

news- and media-free zone for the hour before bedtime. Instead, fill that time with calming and soothing activities that won't trick your limbic system into thinking that danger is imminently lurking.

· · · · · · · · · ·

THREE

THE EFFECTS OF TRAUMA AND STRESS ON OUR LIVES AND OUR DREAMS

If you bring forth what is within you, what you bring forth will save you. If you do not bring forth what is within you, what you do not bring forth will destroy you.

—The Gnostic Gospel

We all experience upsetting events, losses, and distress from time to time. Sometimes these life circumstances are stressful enough to reach the threshold to be to be categorized as trauma. In this chapter we will identify the difference between stress and trauma, how each affects our dream life, and what exactly is PTSD (Post-Traumatic Stress Disorder). One of the many hallmarks of PTSD is the presence of reoccurring and intrusive nightmares. Both general stress and anxiety, as well as trauma, can affect our dreaming lives and create upsetting dreams and nightmares. When our innate dreaming functions are working well, our dreams provide us with mood regulation. However, with PTSD dreams, the opposite occurs—rather than helping us to metabolize and digest the material or events from waking life as non-traumatic dreams do, the high emotional valence in these dreams without the restoration of balance makes the upset worse. We become chronically reactivated rather than calmed and restored in these looping nightmares. This is when we need to get some help to restore our balance and health.

What Is Trauma?

Trauma is defined as an injury to our physical, emotional, spiritual, or energetic bodies or all of the above. It may be a result of experiencing the injury ourselves, or witnessing it happen to another. It is often sudden and unexpected, and frequently invokes the emotions of fear, anxiety, vulnerability, overwhelm, and intrusion. The traumatic events we are dealing with may have occurred recently or some time ago. They may have happened to us directly or we may have experienced them or learned about them secondhand, which is then called vicarious trauma.

Caregivers and medical professionals who witness and care for people who are suffering can experience the trauma as if it was their own as they interact with and bear witness to the suffering on a daily basis. Trauma can also be experienced as "Big T" traumas or "little t" traumas: large, life-altering events that rent space in our minds and bodies for years to come, or smaller upsets that affected our short-term quality of life but not our overall or long-term functioning.

We also know that loss pulls loss, and trauma pulls trauma. A current traumatic event may trigger, reactivate, or rekindle the memories of previous traumatic situations involving the same or similar emotions both in our daily life and in our dreams. So, a field hospital set up to treat COVID-19 patients in a football stadium may rekindle battle memories for a war veteran of the field hospitals set up on the edges of the war zone. Similar emotional memories of threat, vulnerability, terror, and helplessness may reemerge even though they are now safe.

A Buddhist philosophy often attributed to the Dalai Lama says that in life pain is inevitable, but that suffering is optional. This speaks volumes to what we do and don't have control over in our lives. Our reactions and responses to the pain, stress, and traumas that we inevitably experience make all the difference in the subsequent quality of our lives. Deep dreamwork can resource and heal us to be able to move through the pain and release the grip of the suffering. Much of the suffering we experience happens when we are re-triggered to an older trauma from a recent event, and then feel both in spades.

What Is Triggering?

Being triggered happens when we have an emotional response to a current situation that is out of balance to the event itself, more than one might expect from just the situation itself, or larger than life. In effect, being triggered is unconsciously combining a current loss or trauma or even an echo or a reminder of one, with previous unresolved events in life that have a similar emotional landscape or valence. If not sufficiently resolved, the original emotional upset keeps recurring; even accumulating force, much as a snowball rolling down a hill picks up more and more snow until it becomes a massive snowball or even an avalanche. I recently saw a Facebook meme that showed a character holding a big sack on his back containing rocks labeled pandemic fatigue, climate change fears of fire and floods, loss of job, and political unrest. He then stubs his toe, trips, falls to his knees, and breaks down sobbing in complete collapse. The caption read, "Don't you think you are overreacting a bit?"

Both the waking and the sleeping response to these triggers is often the re-experiencing of the emotional state that accompanied the original trauma. So, a feeling of panic or overwhelm in a seemingly neutral situation or waking up with that self-same feeling of panic, but not knowing why, can be a sign of being triggered. In fact, waking up with strong emotions out of the blue, not necessarily even with any dream imagery or content can be the dream itself. The emotion itself is the dream, or all that remains on waking. Record these in your dream journals as well. You can simply write the date, and then write, "Woke feeling anxiety" or "Waves of sadness overwhelm me on waking." That is the part of your dream that you remember.

Triggering or Reactivation Example: In the Trenches

Jeanette was an emergency nurse during the COVID-19 pandemic crises. She showed up for work daily like a trouper until she began to experience symptoms of overwhelm and PTSD, such as recurrent nightmares, high anxiety, irritability, and loss of focus. She was referred by her supervisor to her HR department for crisis intervention therapy. While seeing her therapist, she disclosed that she had lost a child to suicide six years ago, and that her family had been singularly unsupportive and unhelpful during that crisis. She felt that period of time was reactivated in her with her current daily stress and pain of caring for the suffering Covid victims, and the inability of the family members to be there with them. This older, multi-layered trauma was triggered by her current work environment; both the physical and emotional pain and the lack of support the victims and survivors received. It was a double dose for her: the vicarious trauma in the field, and a rekindling of her own personal traumas of the loss of her child and her family's lack of support around the circumstances of her death. She became consumed by negative beliefs about herself, including "I am always alone" and "No one will help me."

This sense of darkness and aloneness permeated her dream life as well. We will return to Jeanette's story in chapter 8 when we look at the shadow in dreams. By using a powerful method of trauma treatment, Eye Movement Desensitization and Reprocessing (EMDR), her therapist was able to help Jeanette to metabolize both her current and previous trauma using imagery, metaphor, and body-based practice.

EMDR is an integrated body/mind therapy developed in 1987 by Dr. Francine Shapiro.[12] A large part of the protocol mimics the eye movements found in REM sleep. The premise of EMDR is based on bilateral stimulation of the brain: right/left, right/left, as the eyes follow this back-and-forth motion and the client simultaneously follows the cognitive protocol that accompanies the eye movements.

Ancestors, Epigenetics, and Trauma

Trauma can also be a part of the emotional and energetic field that we live in inside of our family systems. The traumatic experiences may be a part of our larger family system. This is called a legacy burden in the therapeutic modality of IFS, Internal Family Systems, and we are learning more about it through the new science of epigenetics.[13] Through epigenetic research we are discovering that we can inherit trauma both through learned behavior and through our actual DNA. For example, our grandparents may have been subject to violence or extreme poverty in their country of origin, which led to their emigration to America, and traces of these traumas can show up in our own lives even though we have not personally experienced the trauma. Deborah reported that her grandmother was molested by her father. While parenting Deborah's mother, this grandmother passed on the messages not to trust men, and that to be beautiful was a curse and put her at risk of harm. Deborah herself then got this coded message passed on from her own mother and developed both an overeating disorder to hide her body, and a fear of her own sexuality and femininity. This became a generational

---

12. Francine Shapiro and Margot Silk Forrest, *EMDR: The Breakthrough Therapy for Overcoming Anxiety, Stress, and Trauma* (New York: Basic Books, 2016).

13. Richard Schwartz and Martha Sweezy, *Internal Family Systems Therapy* (New York: Guilford Press, 2019).

response, and she luckily discovered it in her own dreams and therapy before passing it onto her daughter as well.

Meagan's grandparents survived the great Irish potato famine. To this day, her mother and Meagan are very careful never to waste any food and to save all leftovers. Meagan sometimes dreams of little potato eyes winking at her. When we unpacked this dream message, she decided that they were winking at her to let her know that she and her family did in fact survive, and the wink was a green light to go forward in her life without fear of starvation. It is also fun to find humor and puns in our dreams and nightmares.

In Holocaust studies, Dr. Rachel Yehuda and others have been doing research on second- and third-generation survivors, many of whom exhibit the same types of intrusive and violent nightmares that their parents or grandparents experience, even though they themselves did not experience concentration camp life. Although our parents, and we ourselves, may not have experienced the violence or starvation, the memory traces of that history remain in our energetic field through the epigenetic imprinting in our DNA called methylation. They are also passed on through the repetition of the reactions and responses of the subsequent generations that may have been actual coping styles during the original traumas. Both Meagan's and Deborah's stories are examples of this. Parenting styles, such as being suspicious of outsiders or never wasting even a drop of food, evolved from being parented by trauma survivors, and then the next generation of parents passes on both direct and indirect messages about safety, food, or trust, to name a few. This then becomes a learned response for us and can show up in our dreams and nightmares, even though we ourselves did not go through the original traumatic event that started this chain of reactions.

Trauma dysregulates our ability to cope and function optimally in our lives. Our trauma response may also cause us to react to historical events as if they were happening right now. The past and the present become entangled and confused, much as in a dream state. Martha, one of my clients who is an author, was recently asked to appear on television to promote her book. Her knee-jerk response of panic to that invitation went way beyond typical performance anxiety. The next night she dreamt:

> As I make my way to the television studio for my interview, I know that I will be killed if I go through with it. The only recourse is to run home immediately and cancel the show.

As we unpacked her dream and her reaction, she traced it back to generations of family history where she got the message, "Don't be visible, it isn't safe. The only safety is in hiding who you are." While processing this dream she was able to remember numerous messages about assimilation, "passing," and not standing out that she received from her parents and grandparents. Her family had fled pogroms in Eastern Europe at the turn of the previous century. Living in the United States in the twenty-first century, this was not Martha's current reality, but it registered as such in her unconscious until we could identify the sources. Then we could use active dreamwork to upgrade the operating system of her unconscious and dreaming mind as to what was in the past and what was in the present, what belonged in her own life, and what belonged in generations past. We will see later how to use dreamwork from both outside and inside the dream to add information and resources to heal and soothe both the dreamer and her ancestral family.

Fight, Flight, Freeze and Beyond

The *events* of traumatic experiences are often confused with our *reaction* or *response* to trauma. Our reactions include behaviors like the fight, flight, and freeze responses and emotions like panic, fear, overwhelm, helplessness, powerlessness, vulnerability, etc. When faced by a threat or danger, our nervous system quickly assesses the situation and gives us several possible responses. If we choose the right one for that threat, we escape the danger and survive. If not, the consequences can be painful or even fatal.

Peter Levine, creator of the body/mind healing modality of Somatic Experiencing, describes this in relation to his studies of animals in the wild.[14] If the hawk is tracking the rabbit for its dinner, turning and fighting the hawk is not going to be a successful choice for the rabbit. Rather, it may be able to outrun the hawk and get to the safety of the bush. If cover is not an option, it may be able to freeze in its tracks and thus escape the notice of the hawk who tracks prey by their movement. In other cases, when cornered, even a smaller animal may turn to fight a larger one if there is no other option. Rats, for example, will often turn to face their attacker, and because of their arsenal of teeth and claws they may have a fighting chance at survival and escape even from larger predators. The deer will try to outrun the wolf, but the boar may turn and face it and attack back. Another key to healing that Somatic Experiencing offers us is how to avoid developing PTSD, as we will examine more in detail in the chapter on embodied dreamwork.

Additional responses to trauma have been more recently delineated in the fields of trauma treatment and Polyvagal Theory. According to Stephen Porges PhD, polyvagal theory states that not only does the body remember a traumatic experience, but it can actually get stuck in the trauma response mode. So even when the threat is gone, the body still perceives danger, and its defenses stay engaged. This psycho-biological phenomenon may also add an additional

---

14. Peter Levine, *Waking the Tiger: Healing Trauma* (Berkeley, CA: North Atlantic Books, 1987), 15–17, 85–94.

explanation to recurring nightmares, where the dreaming mind is stuck in trauma response mode. In addition to the more commonly recognized fight, flight, and freeze responses, humans can also experience responses to chronic trauma in three additional states: 1) the collapse/submit state of chronic helplessness, 2) the disorganized attachment/cry for help response of an inability to be soothed, or 3) a please/appease response that is close to what is known as the Stockholm syndrome of bonding with captors or jailors to achieve greater safety or protection.

Types of Trauma

Trauma itself can be a single incident, several ongoing incidents, or years of repetitive exposure to extremely stressful events. It can further be broken down into acute trauma, chronic trauma, and complex trauma. Acute trauma refers to current dangerous or highly stressful event or events. Chronic trauma is repeated and prolonged exposure to dangerous or highly stressful events, such as living with domestic violence or in a war zone. Complex trauma occurs when a person is exposed to multiple types of trauma, generally over an extended period of time, and of an invasive and interpersonal nature.

Trauma can further be examined through the lens of public or private trauma, with similarities and differences between the two. Public trauma refers to traumatic events that occur in the public arena and are visible and recognized by others. There are witnesses or pictures that can verify that the traumatic events occurred. This category includes events like natural disasters, car accidents, or terror attacks. Common to these experiences is that the traumatic event is seen and accepted by the general public, and the event not questioned as to the veracity of the report. There is generally little, if any, subjective sense of shame attached to experiencing this type of trauma.

Private trauma refers to traumatic events that take place out of the public eye, often in the privacy of a home or family, and away from other witnesses, such as within an institution, team, or religious setting. This includes experiences like growing up in abusive or addictive families or subtler forms of trauma like emotional abuse or neglect. In private trauma, the additional burden of being believed and then supported in a "he said, she said" scenario compounds the original traumatic events. The responses of the caregiver or the person who receives the disclosure become intricately connected to the healing of the trauma, as well as how long it takes before the child or adult gets to a safe place. Addressing this latter part as well is crucial to healing.

I am postulating that there is a third ambiguous type of trauma category that I have recently identified. It occurs when traumatic events happen in a public arena, but not everyone agrees as to what they have seen or witnessed. Thus, we have in the public sphere the type of questioning of reality or validity that is so often seen in private trauma, with the lack of an agreed-upon narrative by all parties involved. This phenomenon often takes place during a general zeitgeist in society of dissonance and fearmongering. The category might include events like witnessed bullying, fat shaming, racial profiling, street and community violence, the behavior of law enforcement officers, or the multiple sides of many conspiracy theories. While there may not be a question of whether or not a shooting or injury has occurred, especially in this era of cell phone videos, there may be disagreement as to who is at fault or responsible. For example, what happened on January 6, 2021, in Washington, DC, has been interpreted differently by different people despite video footage.

Knowing who is responsible for the traumatic events is a key part of healing and creates much of the concurrent emotional narrative in life and in dreams. Being believed and supported after a trauma accelerates the healing process. So, in addition to clear cut public or private traumas, this third category is an indisputable public event that is cloaked in the ambiguity more often associated with private hidden trauma. Thus, it contains traumatic responses associated with both the public and private types of trauma. We might call this new category "ambiguous public trauma."

Correct attribution of blame and responsibility is key to the resolution of many types of trauma. Knowing what we truly are and are not responsible for affects our healing process. Many trauma survivors take undue responsibility for events or actions beyond their control, and the subsequent misplaced guilt, a subset of survivor's guilt, can wreak havoc with their dreams and their life. How others respond to the event also affects our healing process. If we are believed and our report of what we have experienced is validated, then we are much less likely to develop long-standing or complex PTSD. The nightmares that may follow trauma have a different flavor if we are not in a position if trying to convince others of the veracity of our experience while we are simultaneously trying to heal from it.

What Is PTSD?

PTSD refers to Post-Traumatic Stress Disorder. It has almost become a colloquial expression these days, so it is useful to explore what it actually is. It has been defined as a mental health condition that may occur in people who have either witnessed or experienced a traumatic event, such as a terrorist act, a natural disaster, a sudden death, a rape, or who have been threatened with death, violence, or injury. The first thing to notice about the term is that it is called Post-Traumatic, which means that it is a series of symptoms and reactions that occur after the event, not necessarily during. Acute trauma response would be the set of symptoms commonly found during and immediately following a traumatic event.

Just as important to know is that experiencing PTSD is not a given following trauma. Not everyone develops it. Whether or not someone develops it depends on the nature of the trauma itself, its duration, what kind of supports the trauma survivor does or does not receive, and what is called their "pre-morbid" personality (which simply means what was their personality style and usual way of coping before the trauma occurred). Also noteworthy is the "D" part: Disorder. For something to become entrenched enough in our body/mind system to become a disorder, it needs to have a duration of about six months or more. If our nightmares and other symptoms resolve on their own, then it does not become a disorder. That is, the pre-trauma life, coping skills, mood states, and dreaming style of a survivor return on their own pretty much to what they were before the trauma. If the symptoms do not resolve, or worsen, then we are looking at possible PTSD. Survivors will hopefully experience some relief after the first few months.

PTSD can affect mood, physical health, relationships, coping abilities, and a sense of self and safety in the world. The *DSM-5*, the *Diagnostic and Statistical Manual of Mental Disorders*, lists five categories and symptom clusters needed to make the diagnosis. They need to be present for at least a month following the events to be categorized as PTSD. They are as follows:

1. A person has been exposed to actual or threatened death or injury or to the threatened physical integrity of themselves or has been indirectly exposed in a chronic fashion (such as emergency room doctors or firefighters). It is also now recognized that individuals have different

thresholds of response to the same stimuli, so there is a subjective component to this criterion as well.

2. They experience intrusive symptoms like flashbacks and nightmares that can generate the mental images and the emotional and physiological responses associated with the original traumatic events.

3. There is an avoidance criterion whereby people develop behavioral strategies to avoid exposing themselves to actual or similar trauma-related events in an attempt to minimize their upset and distress responses. This can perhaps best be understood when examining phobias, and can manifest in more extreme cases as agoraphobia, where the sufferer cannot even leave their house for fear of being triggered.

4. Negative cognitions and moods reflect an altered state of self-assessment and unrealistic self-blame and shame for the events that occurred and the responses to them. In addition to negative self-cognitions like "I am powerless" or "I don't deserve to be happy," there are marked mood disorders of anxiety or depression or inability to feel joy known as anhedonia.

5. Alterations in arousal or reactivity can show up as increased irritability, anger outbursts, difficulty sleeping, hypervigilance, and heighted startle response. This heightened reactivity may also show up in reckless behaviors, lack of impulse control, and self-destructive behaviors. A great variety of sleep and dream reactions to trauma include difficulty falling or staying asleep, nightmares, sleep paralysis, sleep walking, and talking or screaming out in the

night. Since being asleep is one of our most vulnerable and unprotected states of being, it is no wonder that this area in our life is often so affected by stress and trauma.

Here is one example of nightmares following trauma and the emergence of PTSD. For most of her childhood, Robin lived with a clinically depressed mother who was periodically hospitalized for severe depression. As an adult, Robin's husband tells her that she screams out loud in the night, "F...k You" to unseen figures in her dreams. This is very out of character for her adult persona. In Robin's case, her anger outbursts occur primarily in her dream life. She also has chronic dreams of her mouth being filled by taffy or gluey foods and needing to pull them out to clear her mouth to breathe and talk. We will follow Robin's healing journey to be able to access both her voice and her power in chapter 6.

Core Components of PTSD

Somatic therapist Peter Levine breaks down four core components that could evolve into PTSD if they persist. Frequently occurring during and immediately following trauma, they are hyperarousal, constriction, dissociation, and freezing.[15] These states can also show up in our dreams.

Hyperarousal can include rapid heartbeat and breathing, hypervigilance, intrusive thoughts and nightmares, agitation, tight muscles, difficulty sleeping, and anxiety or panic attacks. Waking and sleeping flashbacks (a sudden intrusive recollection of the events that often occur in a neutral setting) are common post-trauma features. When Marybeth was young, her alcoholic and neglectful mother locked her out of the house in a snowstorm. Only eight years old,

15. Peter Levine, *Waking the Tiger: Healing Trauma* (Berkeley, CA: North Atlantic Books, 1987), 132–144.

she was stuck outside for several hours until her father came home from work and let her in. Years later as an adult, Marybeth began having anxiety attacks that escalated whenever there was a snowstorm. Her dream images often contained the sensations of shivering or being lost and not being able to find her way home. Intrusive nightmares can be replays of the actual event or symbolic in content. In other examples the overwhelming emotions of the sudden loss of a loved one can show up in dreams as a tidal wave, or a tsunami or flood (think of the metaphor of being flooded by emotion).

The response of constriction can also result in tight musculature and a drawing-in of the self as the system conserves its energy to deal with the threat. Perception of the environment can also take on a hyper-focus or tunnel vision so that full attention is directed at the threat. This hyper-focus is a useful response during the trauma, but it becomes problematic if it continues once the threat is no longer present. It cuts off our engagement with the world and limits our relationships. In dreams, this may be hinted at by dreams of being stuck or trapped or a "falling-down-the-rabbit-hole" sense of tunnel vision. David described a dream image of looking at something through a keyhole and the feeling in the dream that the rest of the world fell away and just what he could see through the keyhole remained. (This reminds me of *Alice in Wonderland*: After she fell down the rabbit hole and drank the potion that made her so big that she couldn't get through the door; she was reduced to peering through a keyhole until she found the potion that made her smaller again.) David's dreams metaphorically recreated the idea of "tunnel vision" that was his only focus.

Dissociation is a breakdown in the continuity of a person's sense of time and space. Ideally, it is just a temporary rending or separation between the events and our emotional responses that can buy us time and allow a neutral space from which to react. If this state is temporary, it can be adaptive and protect one from overwhelming feelings. It can feel like an out-of-body experience and later show up as spaciness or an inability to connect events and normative feeling responses. Depersonalization is a variation on this, where the trauma survivor feels that they do not inhabit their own body. A survivor of childhood sexual abuse once drew a picture that contained several childlike drawings of bodies with their heads floating a few inches above the bodies, completely detached. Tracking the progress in her healing was in part determined by the changes in her drawings over time, as the heads and the bodies gradually became reattached in subsequent pictures. We will examine the role of dissociation in nightmares and dreams and how it may be resolved.

Freezing is a primitive biological response related to feelings of helplessness. The body automatically applies the brakes, so to speak, and shuts everything down hoping that will enhance their chances of survival. This is manifest as a sense of paralysis, stuckness, or immobility that can be felt both in waking life as an inability to get ahead or move forward in life, and in two forms of what is called sleep paralysis. This sense of paralysis is related to the trauma spectrum of speechless terror, whereby our voice as well as our body feels frozen. The first form occurs inside of the dreams with images of being stuck or frozen or trapped within the story line of the dreamscape itself. My client Denise dreamt of a large ocean liner that got stuck in an ice flow. In her dream, the enormous boat became surrounded by thick ice and could not move an inch either forward or backward. In her active dreamwork she slowly rocked the boat back and forth to open up a bit of space and room for the boat to begin to break up the ice and move again.

The second form of sleep paralysis is the waking phenomenon. It occurs when we wake up from sleep and dreams, and our mind is now fully awake, but our body is still immobilized. This state is frequently quite terrifying to the dreamer as they know that they are awake but can't move. I only experienced this partially in the half lucid state of my swimming-up-from-underwater dream, but I also can compare it to the feeling I had when I woke up once while under anesthesia during an endoscopy procedure. I couldn't talk or move, just was able to grunt, and luckily I grunted loudly enough so that I heard the doctor say, "She's awake, give her more ..." and that was all I knew until I later awoke in the recovery room. The physiological condition of muscle atonia as well as psychological and spiritual belief systems all may play a part in this phenomenon. We are literally frozen in fear when we experience some forms of sleep paralysis. Fear plays a big part in this, and how we respond to our fears helps us to regain mobility in both dreams and waking life.

Good Dream Digestion

One of the primary functions of dreams is that of memory consolidation. This happens when our short-term memories of recent experiences are transformed into more permanent long-term memories. In his article on our "Wake-Centric Society," Dr. Rubin Naiman states that our bodies and our minds "go their separate ways" during REM dreaming.[16] The body gets a break from our ego-driven mind, and our mind gets liberated from the physical limitations and constraints of our body. During REM sleep our upper executive functions become separated from our lower somatic functions, and if all goes well, our dreaming mind can then act as a second gut and digest the events of our day. If our body/mind system is functioning smoothly, then our dreams can metabolize and process the events that have occurred during the day or past weeks. They help us to analyze and consolidate

---

16. Rubin Naiman, "In exile from the dreamscape," Aeon, December 24, 2020, https://aeon.co/essays/we-live-in-a-wake-centric-world-losing-touch-with -our-dreams.

our memories and provide a mood regulation function. By doing this over time, the dreams can then reduce the emotional intensity and negative valence of the memories. This has also been referred to as a rinsing out of our day while we sleep.

Healthy dream digestion helps us to sort through our memory networks and determine what will be released and what will be assimilated into our long-term memory storage. Ideally, we keep the memories that feed and nourish us and release those that cause us distress or are toxic to our system. However, if we are struggling with an overload of difficult experiences or trauma in our lives, then this dream healing function may not be able to do its job, and we end up with unresolved and/or repetitive nightmares.

Neurologist and sleep specialist Dr. Guy Leschziner proposed that because of the extreme emotions of some dream experiences, people wake up during their dream before being able to finish it.[17] Leschziner therefore hypothesized that this means that the dreaming process is never truly completed, and that the emotional memory is never fully processed. Since one of the main tasks of our dreams is to help us process and metabolize things that have happened to us in our waking life, we can see that if the brain keeps getting interrupted in this process, it will keep trying to finish its nocturnal job. In addition, during normal REM sleep the anxiety-triggering chemical of noradrenaline shuts off so that we can revisit upsetting life events in a neurochemically calm environment. Neuroscientist Dr. Matthew Walker hypothesizes that PTSD sufferers have reoccurring nightmares because their brains produce an abnormal amount of noradrenaline, preventing their dreams from having their usual

---

17. Guy Leschziner, *The Nocturnal Brain: Nightmares, Neuroscience, and the Secret World of Sleep* (New York: St. Martin's Press, 2019).

sorting and rinsing and healing effect.[18] When the dreaming brain is not able to reduce the emotional intensity attached to a traumatic memory, it will keep trying and return to the scene of the crime night after night.

This is when we may need to attend more closely to working directly with our dreams, either on our own or with a guide or therapist. In line with Leschziner's theory of the unfinished dream, one suggestion that I often make to a dreamer when working with a nightmare is to remind them that this isn't necessarily where the dream ended, but that this is just where they woke up. I continue, "Let's see how you can dream it forward or continue the dream now to get a different ending or resolution."

Dreams, Memory, and Emotions

Memory *re*-consolidation is a recent neuroscience discovery that has revealed how to heal trauma at its roots by recalling a memory and then updating it with new information. Traumatic memories can then be paired with current non-traumatic cognitions, beliefs, and life circumstances. Our more ordinary dreams themselves help us with non-traumatic memory consolidation, sorting into long- and short-term memories, and making nocturnal connections between things that we may not have been able to while awake. Part of dreamwork with our nightmares involves a form of active memory re-consolidation. We will trace several ongoing series of nightmares throughout the book to see how this works. As is the nature of nightmares, some of these stories are graphic, some are distressing, and some are just weird. The dreams and nightmares I share may contain upsetting themes or images, but as the dreamwork with

---

18. Matthew Walker, *Why We Sleep: Unlocking the Power of Sleep and Dreams* (New York: Scribner, 2017).

them unfolds from chapter to chapter, using a variety of dreamwork and trauma treatment methods, you will be able to join in the healing journey and see how they resolve.

Many dreams come couched in metaphor, but some are simply replaying the trauma over and over. Vietnam veterans often report this kind of nightmare: They return to the war theater over and over in their dreams and repeat the traumatic and soul-shattering experiences they were forced to participate in, sometimes against their own moral code. By many definitions, trauma is soul shattering, even more so when during the traumatic events we are forced to do something that is morally abhorrent to us. If we have the resources in our life necessary to heal, then ultimately these dreams fade away on their own. If we don't however, they get stuck on replay without any relief or resolution.

My client Jay had this event-replay experience in his nightmares. As a young adult he was sexually assaulted while at a party. Away at college, a shy young man to begin with, from a family that did not "do feelings," he told no one of this experience. After several weeks of deep depression, he pulled himself back together, finished his schooling, and thought he had put the incident behind him. Years later, with a solid marriage, two grown children, and a successful business in high tech, he began to re-experience chronic nightmares. An avid runner, he was near the finish line when the Boston Marathon bombing took place, and that traumatic event triggered his memories of his assault. After that they were often triggered by a movie or TV show with similar themes of rape or other story lines of vulnerability, helplessness, and victimization. (Sadly, these themes are all too easy to find in our media "entertainment.")

In Jay's nightmares, the original event simply replayed over and over, night after night, and he would wake up in a panic and a sweat. He finally told his wife what was happening, the first person he ever told, and began therapy. He worked with a therapist for several years being heard, believed, and supported. The nightmares diminished in frequency but did not stop entirely. A few years later he watched the movie *A Star Is Born*, and the suicide of one of the characters re-triggered his own memories of his deep-seated depression and suicidal thoughts of that earlier time. This time he returned to dream therapy to explicitly work on resolving these nightmare replays of his trauma. We will follow Jay's dreamwork journey to healing in chapters that follow as we explore nightmare resolution methods and learn how he is now turning his own history of trauma into a source of healing for others.

Dreams store memories of emotional experiences, be they positive or negative. Our sleeping brain picks out the events in our life that have most strongly registered with us emotionally to provide our dreamscape with related themes and images. During REM sleep the hippocampus, the part of our brain involved in short-term memory storage, moves the experiences and emotional material into long-term memory storage in the neocortex. The hippocampus is part of the limbic system, which is our emotional brain. This will become important to remember when we are working to alleviate emotionally upsetting dreams and nightmares. Another part of the limbic system is the amygdala. This structure processes emotion. One metaphor or mnemonic for remembering which is which, is that the amygdala is the accelerator of our limbic system, and the hippocampus is the brakes. We need both the "go" and the "stop" pedals to be working well in our vehicles and in our lives!

Problem-Solving from an Anxiety Dream: Which Group Is Which?

Dr. Ernest Hartmann, a dream and nightmare research pioneer who studied hundreds of dreams and dreamers, found that in general our distressing dreams follow emotionally charged life events.[19] Our mind picks out the issues that we are grappling with and gives us an opportunity to get more information and resolution through our dreams. Our wise unconscious may then shift things around in the dream, add in dream-created characters, actions, and places, and thus dilute and mitigate the effects of the stress. Other dream functions include problem-solving and inspiring creativity. By contextualizing the trauma in metaphor, or by simulating waking life but adding in their own unique dream-crafted elements, our dreams help us to practice and rehearse new coping and survival strategies.

This contextualization allows us to experience mastery without having to encounter the saber-toothed tiger or the difficult boss or the intrusive relative in the flesh. According to Hartmann, this dream function helps us to adapt and heal. It surpasses the dream function of memory consolidation alone by broadening the memories through these neural cross-connections and weaving old and new experiences together, thus repairing and reorganizing our neural circuits and "knitting up the raveled sleeve of care." Neurologist Daniel Amen wrote a book on healing our brains from depression, anxiety, obsessions, and anger and titled it: *Change Your Brain, Change Your Life*.[20] The title captures the essence of strong dreamwork. We will learn to do this purposefully with your own dreams and could paraphrase his title to read, Change Your Dream, Change Your Life.

Here's an example of how the problem-solving and cross-connections might work with a mild stressor that stimulated an anxiety dream. While writing this chapter I had the following dream:

---

19. Ernest Hartmann, *Dreams and Nightmares: The New Theory on the Origin and Meaning of Dreams* (New York: Plenum Trade, 1998), 25–31.

20. Daniel Amen, *Change Your Brain, Change Your Life (Revised and Expanded): The Breakthrough Program for Conquering Anxiety, Depression, Obsessiveness, Lack of Focus, Anger, and Memory Problems*, (New York: Harmony Press, 2015).

I have gone down to my office and found that both groups I facilitate, the dream group and the supervision group, were there at the same time waiting to begin. I immediately feel a great deal of anxiety and worry that I might have made a scheduling error. Clearly one group had made a mistake and had come at the wrong day and time (each group meets on opposite days and weeks). I say to them, "I think that today is the turn of the supervision group, I'll go check my datebook to make sure." I realize that I had left the datebook upstairs and go back up for it. I find it and I am correct; it is the week of the supervision group. I start back down to my office, and then realize to my dismay that I am naked. I quickly throw on a dress and go down with the news. The dream group has meanwhile taken up squatter's rights in the office while the supervision group members are milling anxiously about in the waiting room. I inform them all whose week it is, and the dream group reluctantly leaves. One dream group member who clearly wants to stay keeps asking me, "Are you sure?" and I show her the groups' days marked off in my datebook before she is appeased. It gets sorted out and we begin the supervision group.

I woke up with my anxiety quite intact, but even as I recorded the dream, I began to have some glimmers to its meaning. By the time I finished recording it, I knew what action step I needed to resolve the anxiety. When our uncomfortable emotions dissipate this quickly, we can be pretty sure that they are situationally stress related, and not deep trauma. Here is the background information to help you to contextualize this dream in my waking life: I facilitate two professional groups; one of them is a dream work group and the other is a supervision group for other psychotherapists. The second group often consults on clients of the members who have experienced trauma in their lives and how to best help them.

Here's what I figured out by reviewing the dream: In waking life, I was having a dilemma with this chapter as to how to weave together enough dreamwork into the explanation of trauma and its properties to tie the two themes together. I hadn't resolved how to do it yet when I went to bed that night. But the dream showed me that even though those two topics, represented by my two groups, were competing for space, I needed to give more priority to the "trauma group" for this chapter. My anxiety turned into a big grin as I thanked my unconscious for the tip. Although the supervision group does not deal exclusively with trauma, it was close enough for my dreaming mind to make the easy connection and find a solution. The naked thing, well, that is a common metaphor for feeling exposed or vulnerable. It can, of course, have many other meanings as well, but this time the shoe fits. I didn't want to be "exposed" by making the wrong choice in primacy. As to the dream group member who is reluctant to leave, in waking life this group is very important to her, and she often expresses how much she misses the group when we are on break. In the dream I believe it has to do with reassuring this part of myself, as well as my author and trauma worker selves, that no part is getting shortchanged.

Healing the Past and the Future in the Present

Our responses to trauma are individualized. They depend in part on the event itself, but also on the personal history and the absence or presence of support systems of the person who is experiencing it. It is our reaction and response to the events once we are no longer living through them that causes our distress. This is where we can intervene both in active dreamwork and in life. While we can't change what has already occurred in the past, we can change our reaction and response to it. By our understanding and healing in the present and taking actions in the future based on this new awareness, we can redeem the past and make meaning out of it in our lives. Psychiatrist and Holocaust survivor Viktor Frankl chose to title his book *Man's Search for Meaning* with this theme in mind.

Making meaning and finding redemption may be other words for paying it forward. We are hardwired for growth and healing, so with proper support in resolving our nightmares and the sources of them, we can move forward to healing and wholeness. Dr. Eduardo Duran, a Native healer as well as a psychologist, speaks of the need to make amends consciously and purposefully as an integral part of dream healing to both the land and the people if we have harmed them in any way, including if we have harmed ourselves.[21] This intentional give back then becomes a gift rather than a loss.

Rabbi Jonathan Sacks has a fascinating interpretation of this concept of healing the past via the future as he discusses the biblical character of Joseph the Dreamer.[22] In Genesis, following his incarceration, Joseph is promoted to Pharaoh's right-hand man by virtue of his dream interpretation skills. Later in the story, Joseph's brother's journey into Egypt to ask the Pharaoh for help during the time of famine over the land. They are brought before their brother Joseph, but don't recognize him in his new role as advisor to Pharaoh and in his new life. After their pleas for food supplies, Joseph finally reveals his identity to them. His brothers then become afraid that Joseph will want to take revenge on them for their very bad behavior toward him. If you recall, their treatment of him culminated in throwing him into a pit, and then deciding to sell him off

21. Eduardo Duran, *Native American Dreamwork Traditions*. Keynote Speech, IASD International Conference, 2021.

22. Jonathan Sacks, "The Future of the Past." December 2018. Covenant and Conversation, www.rabbisacks.org.

into slavery instead of just killing him because of their jealousy of him and his bodacious dreaming. By the time of this encounter years later, Joseph himself has made peace and meaning out of these traumatizing events in large part through his dream interpretation skills. He now has a different response to them.

His brothers' betrayal and his many years in an Egyptian prison could have become life-defining traumas for Joseph. Instead, according to Sacks, Joseph was able to overcome and transcend them with the dreamwork that ultimately brought him to Pharaoh's attention. He reassures his brothers that although they had meant to harm him, in the larger scheme of things, their actions turned out for the good, saying to them, "You intended to harm me, but God intended it for good." As Pharaoh's steward, he is now in a position to save them and his father by inviting them to Egypt where abundant food has been stored as a direct result of Joseph's dream interpretation skills. Joseph had been promoted out of prison when he correctly interpreted Pharaoh's dreams of the seven fat cows and the seven lean cows, foreshadowing the famine and the need to stockpile grain in silos for the seven lean years that were coming. Paradoxically, because of all that happened in the past, even the traumas of expulsion from his home and family and years in jail, Joseph is now able to help his father and brothers. This new interpretation of their past actions helps to relieve the guilt the brothers feel over their actions and saves their family and their tribe.

Sacks points out that Joseph's re-interpretation of the brothers' history, and thus their memories of it, "changes one of our most fundamental associations about time, namely its asymmetry."[23] The commonly held belief about time is that we can change the

---

23. Jonathan Sacks, "The Future of the Past." December 2018. Covenant and Conversation, www.rabbisacks.org.

future, not the past. But Sacks argues that in changing our understanding of the past, we can look back with new eyes and see how it all turned out. In doing so, we are no longer held captive by the past. He continues, "By action in the future, we can redeem much of the pain of the past," which is a very similar message to that of indigenous healer Duran. When we can understand the events of our past with new eyes, new resources, and additional knowledge as Joseph did by unpacking our own dreams and nightmares to find new meaning and make potential redemptive actions, then in effect we too have transformed the pain of the past. This is an important insight to keep in mind as we work through our nightmares.

Healing from trauma needs to incorporate all the elements of healing of the mind, the body, the emotions, and the spirit to be complete. We need to quiet our bodies to reduce the agitation so that our conscious and unconscious dreaming minds and hearts have a calm resting place in which to be held. Traditional therapeutic approaches may excel at attending to the mind and the emotions, but often neglect the body and the spiritual aspects of healing. To fully heal, we need to add these dimensions on as well. We do so in the integrated embodied approach to dreamwork.

EXERCISE
Bridges to Life

Think about any nightmares you or your children are having. Make a list in your journal. Are they repetitive? Do any themes, events, or emotions reoccur? Notice how big the emotional upset is in the dreams, and if it seems to be getting less, staying the same, or getting worse. Write that down as well to keep track.

Now see if you can make what dreamworker Robert Moss calls a bridge to life, a form of dreamwork that invites us to make the associations directly from our dreams to our life and see if they seem connected. Are your dreams connected to any traumatic or upsetting events that you can think of? See if there are any "ahas" here. Without judgment, notice if the events that come to mind are recent, from your past, or from your family history. Think also about the concept of epigenetics and comb your family history for any stories that seem relevant. You might ask your parents or grandparents for more family stories of ancestors that you may not know about. Begin to make a list of all the events or stories that somehow seem connected to your nightmares or anxiety dreams, even if you are not yet sure why. Trust your intuition as you begin to explore the threads of connection. Also take note of whether these traumatic events were private hidden traumas that happened without witnesses, public traumas that were verifiable, or in the third category of ambiguous public trauma that happened in a public space but may contain disagreement about who is to blame, who is responsible, or the sequence of events. Take note if there are any ancestors who can be helpers or healers for you now.

* * *

EXERCISE

Starting Your Resource Files

As we are now thinking about trauma, it is important to also think about the resources you have in your life before moving forward. When working with your nightmares, it is important to feel grounded, supported, and protected before going into dark places. Who or what could you turn to for support if you felt the need? Make a list in your dream journal. List any people (alive or passed over, real or imaginary), pets, safe places, or divine or angelic beings. Do the same for important objects or favorite stuffed animals.

Who and what are the people, objects, and places that help you to feel safe, secure, and loved? What characteristics or traits do you possess that you can rely on as a resource to help you get through tough times? For example, is your creativity or sense of humor or your ability to persevere a strong suit? Know that if you are coping with nightmares or trauma that you can now call on these beings, places, and traits in your mind's eye and begin the journey by feeling safe, grounded, accompanied, and no longer alone. This is part of the beginning stage of the GAIA method, which we will explore in detail in chapter 6.

FOUR

· · · · · · · · ·

DREAMS, DISSOCIATION, FRAGMENTATION, AND MEMORY

I wonder sometimes if the thoughts that flock my nightmares are abandoned memories coming home to roost.
—*Danielle Teller,* **All the Ever Afters:**
The Untold Story of Cinderella's Stepmother

In this chapter we will more closely examine the phenomenon of dissociation and its function to appreciate how our dreams can help us to re-integrate the fragmented self that dissociation can create. This can then help us knit up the lost pieces of our dreams and of our souls that the dissociative process has shredded and unraveled.

Pierre Janet, the grandfather of trauma treatment, in 1889 said, "Traumatic stress is an illness of not being able to be fully alive in the present."[24] Dissociation is a complex topic and one of the most misunderstood and undertreated aspects of trauma. It refers to a compartmentalization of experiences and a splitting of awareness, and it is a break in the continuity of how our minds handle information. When we are overwhelmed by a dangerous situation, or one that

---

24. Bessel van der Kolk, *The Body Keeps the Score: Brain, Mind, and Body in the Healing of Trauma* (Westminster, London: Penguin Publishing Group, 2015), 314.

we perceive as dangerous, or one from which there is no escape, our mind in effect creates the escape by splitting off our consciousness from what is happening in our current environment.

Post-Trauma Memory Encoding

Post-trauma dreams have some unique characteristics that differentiate them from non-trauma dreams. These dreams frequently activate the content and/or the emotional elements of the traumatic life events or circumstances. The trauma memories that are embedded in our neural networks are carried into our dream life and contain the difficult events that we have not yet fully metabolized or sufficiently processed. In a sense, these memories are still undigested by our psyche. In addition, they may bring into dreams the emotions that were originally connected to events that have been un-remembered or hidden from consciousness. The disembodied emotions that we learned about in chapter 1 may be a form of fragmented memory.

Sometimes traumatic events are so upsetting that we just cannot tolerate remembering them consciously. But the embedded memories of these events have to go somewhere. They may have been suppressed initially in the service of our ability to cope and function in life, and then later re-emerge in dreams as metaphors. These dream metaphors also have the emotions connected to them that were present in the original traumas (for example, a hurricane in our dream may be a metaphor of feeling overwhelmed, swept away, or flattened by something; a snarling dog may be a metaphor of anger or fear of someone who wants to "bite our head off"; falling into a deep hole may be a metaphor for shame—when we want to just disappear from view). In its wisdom, our unconscious seems to decide just how much we can cope with at once. Our dreams may also contain the unique phenomenon of memory bursts whereby previously occluded memories may resurface in the dreamscape. The phrase "memory bursts" always reminds me of the goddess Athena's birth—she burst straight from Zeus' head, a fully formed adult and the goddess of war and wisdom and crafts.

Understanding Dissociation and the Need for Embodied Work

Trauma expert Dr. Bessel van der Kolk says that dissociation is the key indicator of trauma. One of the ways he defines trauma is "overwhelmingly negative experiences which become lodged in the body beyond the reach of language."[25] As an expert on PTSD, he maintains that "The talking cure—the traditional psychoanalytic attempt to make a coherent narrative of one's trauma—cannot sufficiently help patients, but embodied work such as EMDR (Eye Movement Desensitization and Reprocessing therapy), mindfulness, and body-oriented methods such as yoga can. Dissociation implies that the memories of the event have been separated out from our conscious mind."[26]

As embodied beings, van der Kolk believes that trauma that is beyond the reach of language can be re-integrated into the wholeness of our beings when we engage with the body. This is a part of why an embodied approach to dreamwork is so important—our bodies hold clues that point us toward that wholeness both in our waking and sleeping life. Having a coherent narrative of the whole trajectory of our life is crucial so that our life hangs together as a unified whole, and all the parts of it are connected to each other.

---

25. Bessel van der Kolk, *The Body Keeps the Score: Brain, Mind, and Body in the Healing of Trauma* (Westminster, London: Penguin Publishing Group, 2015), 66, 100–101.

26. Bessel van der Kolk, *The Body Keeps the Score: Brain, Mind, and Body in the Healing of Trauma* (Westminster, London: Penguin Publishing Group, 2015), 250–263.

Re-creation of this coherent narrative is one of the core goals of trauma treatment, and therefore of PTSDreamwork as well.

People dissociate when they are in extreme pain or fear and no other recourse appears available. It is an autonomic process, not something that we decide to do. A long-term sense of overwhelm and unintegrated dissociation are two of the main impediments to healing from trauma. Untreated dissociation is strongly associated with vulnerability to the development of PTSD, and frequently is part of the source of PTSDreams or nightmares.

Here are five key reasons that dissociation may occur:

1. As a coping mechanism for protection and defense against the pain of remembering.

2. There is no picture memory available to the mind, that is, the events took place in the dark, or facedown, or with a blindfold, so all that remain are the sounds, smells, and sensations.

3. The trauma took place in a pre-verbal stage of life (prior to age two or three) where our brains are not yet encoding what happened to us in words, but rather in somatasensory memory.

4. In familial abuse or neglect, there is a family history of denial or gaslighting that leads to doubting one's own memories or impressions, so they become buried in defense.

5. The previously mentioned biological substrate of speechless terror generates a physiologically different encoding of the events in parts of the brain that are not wired to encode language or narrative memory.

Functional Dissociation

There is another form of short-term dissociation known as healthy or adaptive dissociation. Sometimes short-term dissociation can be adaptive. It can buy us some needed time to respond during the actual traumatic event. Many of us have had the experience of time slowing down as we watch an upsetting event unfolding, such as an impending car accident, or that out-of-body experience that allows us to feel as if we were floating on the ceiling above ourselves looking down. (Surgical patients frequently report this phenomenon.) If our felt experience of time slows down enough for us, then we might have the time we need to jump up, run away, or do something to get safe. One young mom reported that when she saw her toddler dash out into the street in front of an approaching car, she somehow found the time to rush out and grab him back to safety before the car hit him, even though he seemed too far away. However, when this response continues past short-term periods of time it can then affect our sense of identity, our sense of time (i.e., struggling to differentiate the past from the present) and interfere with our functioning.

Dr. Martin Lowenstein describes functional dissociation as a way of organizing information under extreme stress. As we learned in chapter 3, when the body is flooded with stress neurochemicals, such as cortisol, it can develop the hyper-focus necessary to be able to respond. This narrowing of perception is like tunnel vision that eliminates distractions and is one of the elements of dissociation. During extreme stress our emotions and our spirit frequently split off from our body, creating that sense of floating outside ourselves or feeling numb and frozen.

Shock is often our first response to sudden bad news and is itself a temporary form of dissociation. When we suddenly hear of the death of a loved one, for example, we may go numb, feel frozen, or like time has stopped for anywhere from a few moments to a few days. This initial avoidance of pain and overwhelm are necessary survival mechanisms; it only becomes a problem when they persist longer than is needed for that survival. It is a brilliant temporary solution for coping with overwhelm. I still remember that moment when I picked up the message from my voice mail several years ago that my husband had been hit by a car while on his bike. I had that rush of a freezing-hot flooding sensation throughout my body and was glued to the spot for several seconds before I could move. (The healing was a long haul, but we were lucky, and he recovered well.)

But if this numbing strategy becomes entrenched and keeps the trauma unprocessed, then the trauma goes underground, so to speak, into our unconscious self. If it lodges itself there it eventually sends us signals to both our waking life and our dreams: There are ghosts from the past that need to see the light of day to be liberated. These split off parts show up through nightmares, flashbacks, and intrusive memories. So, in a very real way, our split-off memories of past events may first come back to our consciousness in our dreams.

Understanding Dissociation from the Inside

It is always now in our dreams, never yesterday or tomorrow. We live our dreams in the present tense, so when memory emerges in dreams, whether it is consciously known or unknown to the waking mind, we re-experience it in the dream as a current reality. Quantum physics is now teaching us about the reality of this timelessness. Here is an exercise that will help to illustrate the concept of dissociation.

EXERCISE

Understanding Dissociation

Think about a mildly upsetting nightmare or bad dream, or if you prefer, a waking experience. For this practice, please do not pick one that is higher than 5 on the SUDS scale of upset from 0–10, with 0 being no distress, and 10 being the worst distress possible. This Subjective Unit of Distress (SUDS) barometer that we were introduced to previously is used to chart progress in several mind/body therapies. For example, my dream of anxiety about which group had the right day would be a good choice for me, since it only registered as about a 3 or 4 on the SUDS scale. Then, take a piece of paper and fold it in half. Write the dream on one half, and then write all the emotions connected with the dream on the other half. Also write where in your body you experience these feelings, such as "sadness as a lump in my throat" or "anxiety as a sense of pressure on my chest." Next take that paper and tear it in half and then rip up into tiny shreds the half that had the dream written on it. What is left on the other half of the paper are just the emotions and body sensations. This remaining half is an example of what a trauma survivor may feel if they have dissociated from their memory of the event. Just the somata-sensory memories are left, but not the narrative contents of the memory, or in this case, of the dream.

When trauma has occurred this biological phenomenon of splitting between the events and the emotions that accompany the events represents an adaptive separation of the memories and the feelings in waking life to prevent overwhelm. It may be the same with some dreams. We can wake with dream images and story lines intact but not have any idea what they mean—no sense of connection to them. For example, Deborah dreams:

Crystalized spiders keep pouring out of my mouth. They are sharp and stick to my tongue. Then I notice that they are actually Swarovski crystals, beautiful and valuable. I feel scared and disgusted at first, and then kind of awed when I see that they are crystals.

Deborah had many other dreams where things were stuck in or came out of her mouth, but as of yet had no connection to their meaning. These spiders were a strange stand-alone image, yet it also carried a repetitive theme. If it is a nightmare, then the emotions we wake with are unpleasant at best. Deborah's dream had elements both of a nightmare and contained a transformative quality, or at least appreciation of value, even though the spider crystals were uncomfortable. Our nightmares carry the seeds of redemption right inside themselves, not always this obvious, but it is there if we unpack the dream and look for it.

Sometimes we wake with emotions that have no story or images attached to them; these emotions and/or physical sensations are what remains of the dream. When I woke with a feeling of panic one day early on in the COVID-19 pandemic, there was no story line to my dream at all—just the raw emotion. Your feelings-only dreams may be pleasant or unpleasant. If you wake feeling inexplicably delighted, that was your dream. If you wake feeling inexplicably anxious, that too was your dream.

* * *

EXERCISE

Tracking the Somata-Sensory Aspects of Your Dream

Write down the date in your dream journal and record the emotions you wake with as a part of your dream log. Don't ignore or minimize the importance of these feelings-only dreams. They are just as valid as the big, long narrative ones. Also, if you wake with just one word, or just a sentence, that too is your dream. Record that as well. For example, you can write "Wednesday, January 22, woke with just the word *escape* in my mind." Or "Sunday, February 5, woke with a lump in my throat and feeling like I wanted to cry but didn't know why." Later you can go back and work on these shards of dreams to find the surprising layers of meaning they contain.

REM and EMDR

Many of our nightmares may represent a form of nocturnal dissociation. These dreams give us the time and space to use parts of our brain that are off-line when we are awake in order to gather resources and let the functions of our dreaming brain do their automatic work on our behalf. We get to access our deep limbic and right brain functions more fully to help us with problem-solving, consolidating memories, rehearsing for potential future similar threats, and practice in coping. Our natural REM dream state seems to mimic what happens in the brain when the trauma treatment method of EMDR is used. According to EMDR therapist Ricky Greenwald, "The EMDR procedure, although using a consciously selected starting point, can arguably be characterized as a focused, induced dream analogue."[27] Ricky makes the compelling argument that dreaming itself is a therapeutic process, in which disturbing material is meaningfully selected by our unconscious, which then repeats until the matter is fully processed and is no longer upsetting, much like the protocol of EMDR. Once metabolized, our nightmares can lead us to mastery both in our dreams and in our waking life.

The technique itself, created by Dr. Francine Shapiro, is predicated on bilateral stimulation of the two hemispheres of the brain, through purposeful guided back-and-forth eye movements while attending to the upset and the trauma.[28] The method was later expanded, adding to the use of bilateral eye movements the additional options of bilateral tapping or auditory sounds. When our dreaming brains are not able to perform their function of metabolizing our upset on their own, we need to step in with purposeful and active dreamwork and trauma treatment to assist.

The Dissociative Continuum: From Normative to a Disorder

In waking life, dissociation takes place on a spectrum from the type of normal everyday occurrences that most of us experience from time to time to a more serious disorder. Here is the range of the Dissociative Continuum from the mildest to the most severe:

1. *Normative brief lapses in time and space.* Think here about things like highway hypnosis, spacing out during a long lecture, and daydreaming. Your body is here, your mind is temporarily elsewhere.

---

27. Rick Greenwald, "Eye Movement Desensitization and Reprocessing (EMDR): A New Kind of Dreamwork?" *Dreaming*, no. 1, 1995.

28. Francine Shapiro and Margot Silk Forrest, *EMDR: The Breakthrough Therapy for Overcoming Anxiety, Stress, and Trauma* (New York: Basic Books, 2016).

2. *Temporary separation of feelings from events.* Being numb for some time while grieving, or consciously choosing to put something out of your mind for a while in order to focus on something else—like purposefully not thinking about your upcoming exciting date tonight so you can get your work done first.

3. *The event is remembered, but the expected feelings do not accompany it.* This begins to get into the realm of a trauma response. For example, one of my clients reported matter-of-factly that she grew up in an alcoholic family and had been subjected to periodic rage outbursts from her father. She and her siblings hid in the closet to avoid his wrath when he had been drinking. However, she initially had no emotions connected to these memories; it was as if it happened to someone else.

4. *No memory of the event, just the feelings remain.* This is closely connected with the exercise you may have just done and is the classic form of dissociation. The memory of the event has been walled off, but fragments return in the form of intrusive thoughts, feelings, or nightmares. Inexplicable feelings may seem to come out of nowhere. Under closer examination, they may have been triggered by a sound, a smell, or facial features on a passerby. It remains unclear to the person who experienced this why the sound of a drum or the smell of Old Spice aftershave should be upsetting.

Peggy felt an inexplicable urge to punch her boyfriend when he tried to kiss her after he had been drinking beer. In general, she really liked kissing him, but when the taste or smell of the beer was on his breath she had a viscerally negative response. One day she saw the can on the table and remarked offhandedly, "That was the kind of beer my father always drank." She woke up with a start that night and realized, "Oh my God. When he was drunk he used to give me these big, sloppy, gross kisses."

This same concept holds true for nightmares: They show up with impenetrable images, feelings, and events, but the dreamer can't initially connect it to anything that makes sense. Our work then becomes to follow the thread of knowledge both into and out of the dream to tie the fragmented pieces together.

5. *Fragmentation.* This is a sense of separation of the self into self-parts, rather than experiencing oneself as a unified whole. We all have different parts of ourselves that emerge, for example when we are parenting our children, teaching a class, exercising, or out on a date. Ideally these are all integrated into the unified whole of our Self. Trauma can prevent this sense of wholeness, and the trauma survivor can feel that there is no connection between these different aspects of themselves. In both waking and sleeping life, these parts sometimes represent different ages the person was when they experienced overwhelm or trauma and couldn't process what was happening to them. They may also represent metaphoric emotional states that are unintegrated and seem to take on a life of their own. In addition, depersonalization is a subset of this, where the dreamer or trauma survivor feels outside of their body altogether.

This type of dream dissociation can often be worked through with a Gestalt or an IFS (Internal Family Systems) perspective. When working in this way, we purposely look at the characters and even the objects in a dream as parts of oneself, sort of prescribing the symptom if you will, in the service of understanding the fragmentation and piecing the self back together. For example, my client Joann often dreamed of small children in various types of distress, and her job in the dream was to try to save them. Sometimes they were drowning, sometimes they were being chased by scary men or wild animals, sometimes they were wandering the streets and couldn't find their way home. This theme persisted over time, but in working from the Gestalt perspective, she became able to speak about the "three-year-old girl part of me" and the "ten-year-old part of me" in her dreams, and in doing so make the connection to what had been happening in her own life at ages three or ten that she needed saving from. Once she could make these connections, the dreams abated as she updated both her waking and her dreaming mind to the reality of her actual current life at age thirty-seven.

6. **Dissociative Identity Disorder.** At the far end of this dissociative spectrum is what used to be known as multiple personality disorder. In this state, the different parts of the self are so separated from each other that they do not know of each other's existence. They may be different ages, different genders, have completely different wardrobes, and even different eyeglass prescriptions. This disorder may occur following extreme and prolonged trauma that usually began in early childhood. The true story of Sybil, as described in both the book and the movie, depicts this multiplicity. A less well known but very powerful depiction of this phenomenon is the fictional television series *United States of Tara* where the self-parts are highly dramatized.

How Dreams May Reveal Dissociation

So, to review, dissociation is the splitting of awareness, a break in our conscious narrative when our system is overwhelmed by extreme physical or emotional stress and trauma. When these feelings and experiences overwhelm the body, mind, and spirit, our system automatically provides us with a way to slow down and take a step back, if you will, in order to contain them. When we dissociate, we lose the continuity of our narrative story line and the events we recall seem fragmented, out of order, missing in sequence. This is one of the reasons that we frequently get differing narratives about an event that occurred. In addition to seeing the mugging or the floodwaters bearing down from a different physical perspective (such as, I was on the right side of the street, and you were on the left), our memory under stress is often left with a non-coherent story. When our system is flooded with cortisol, the stress hormone, we get tunnel vision; some sights and sounds become exaggerated and some fade into the background. One person might say, "That man just came out of the alley," while another may say, "No, he clearly came out of that convenient store called Sam's Sundries."

Missing sequences, out-of-order narratives, exaggerated events: Sounds a lot like many of our dreams. In both our enjoyable dreams as well as our nightmares, things often don't make sense when we wake. We don't know how we got from here to there—we just did. Many dreams lack a coherent narrative. There are random events seemingly popping out of nowhere, and even when there is a clear narrative, there are often elements to the dreams that would be out of place if we encountered them in waking life. We might even say that our dreams frequently present us with information in a disso- ciated fashion. In part, this is simply the norm for the way in which our nonlinear right brain and limbic brain offer us information in the dreamscape. However, it may also be one way our system protects us from being overwhelmed with too much information at once following trauma. Van der Kolk and many other trauma experts tell us that trauma is not stored as a narrative with a well-ordered beginning, middle, and ending. Instead, it is usually stored in flashbacks, isolated images, and body sensations that have no context other than to give a voice of sorts to the unspeakable fears and terrors.

I propose that some dreams offer us dissociated memories in metaphoric or symbolic fashion, but also occasionally through memory bursts, those intrusive flashes of actual memory that may make their way fully formed into our dreams (hence my prior association to Athena who bursts fully formed from Zeus' head). Therefore, when doing dreamwork we want to also pay attention to the possibility that an actual memory of a prior event is being retrieved from its deep sleep in our unconscious in a Sleeping Beauty moment of our awakening. We then become our own prince who wakes our sleeping self from our slumber of unknowing with the kiss of a remembered dream.

This knowledge from dream memory can be useful information to have about our life and help with the reconstruction of a coherent and meaningful life narrative. I would caution to tread carefully though. While considering the possibility that something may be true as dreamed, we should not jump to conclusions that could be harmful to the dreamer or to others in their life. We know that memory can be fallible. Let the pieces and supporting facts emerge slowly and carefully. As always, it is up to the dreamer to decide if the dream resonates as true, not the guide. As a guide, be curious, not definitive.

During dissociation, events and emotions can become separated from each other; we lose pieces of time and space. We experience a sense of floating or being out of our bodies until our system cues us that it is now safe to reconnect. Childhood abuse and other unsafe conditions in the home, such as growing up with an alcohol- or substance-abusing parent, often leave the survivor with little or no other recourse but to "run away" in their minds, since there may be no other safe place to run to.

If we have experienced chronic ongoing trauma, there may not come a time until adulthood that feels safe enough to have all of our feelings and our memories in one place. In that case, either the feelings or the memories may become split off as we learned earlier. Years later we may still experience that sense of disconnect in our lives. However, in order to live our lives fully and with equanimity, we need to reconnect the disparate parts. Otherwise, the fragmented self-parts may continue to appear in an endless loop without a clear time sequence of past, present, and future. This occurs during intrusive, repetitive nightmares.

Healing Dissociation

One of the hallmarks of healing from trauma is that time is now re-ordered sequentially. When this sequential reordering occurs, both the past events and the feelings connected to them become properly relegated to distance memories, and we become free to live fully in present time and to hope, plan, and dream for the future. The mantra of "that was then and this is now" needs to become internalized as second nature when remembering past upsets and traumas.

When I am asked, "How do I know if this traumatic event is healed?" I respond, "When it is just a memory—nothing more." There is an energy healing protocol called TAT (Tapas Acupressure Technique). It uses a body/mind approach that combines a cognitive protocol of seven steps with hand or fingertip placement on key meridian points while simultaneously attending to the thoughts, sensations, and emotions that arise with each step. One step asks us to focus on the statements, "It happened, and it's over now. I can relax, I can heal, and I can move on." In other words, we know what happened, but it no longer has any hold on us or our emotions. It is in the past. When sufficiently metabolized, the dream or the memory is now neutral; no more rushes of anxiety or panic when recalling what happened. The AA slogan that it no longer rents space in our brain fits here.

When we are finally in a safe space and in safe relationships, the body begins to cue us that it is now time to put the pieces back together. The first signs of this may paradoxically be as nightmares. The presence of nightmares is actually a sign that our body is trying to move into healing, even though it may not feel like it at the moment. It is giving us signals, saying, "Listen up! We want to get your attention here, work to be done!" We need to clean out the muck at the bottom of the well for the water to run clean again. The shadow revealed can become the gift that heals.

We may start our remembrances and our dreams with emotions and metaphoric content that only hint at the actual events behind the dream content until we gradually become stronger and more ready to hold the coherent whole. This is one of the reasons it is so important to go slowly when working with nightmares. We don't want to re-traumatize the system and overload it again, sending those fragmented parts back into hiding in our deep unconscious. Please tread carefully, bit by bit with the big nightmares, and be sure that our dreamer has the resources needed to cope with what is uncovered. Chapter 6 on the GAIA method of nightmare healing is a system of careful yet active dreamwork that allows the dreamer to become well-resourced and safe before treading on the uneven or shaky ground of their nightmare narratives. First let's take a look at working with the layers of a dream.

EXERCISE
Noticing Life Experiences of Normative Dissociation

Think about times in your waking life when you experienced a sense of separation between yourself and your environment or your emotions. Have you ever had highway hypnosis or spaced out in a lecture? What happens when you re-integrate and come back to the present fully? What do you notice? Can you see any connections between these states of being and your dreaming states?

FIVE

· · · · · · · ·

THE LAYERS OF OUR DREAMS
The PARDES System

A dream is a microscope through which we look at the hidden occurrences in our soul.

—Erich Fromm

And like seeds dreaming beneath the snow your heart dreams of spring. Trust the dreams, for in them is hidden the gate to eternity.

—*Kahlil Gibran*

O ur dreams are multi-layered. Our nightmares alert us to something that needs to be addressed, and have meanings for us beyond the startle or the anxiety or the fear. Underneath the initial fear or monster may be messages and other meanings for ourselves and others. Sometimes the layers also reveal previously dissociated parts of ourselves that have now become available for healing. In order to mine the depths of creativity, healing, and problem-solving that are available to us through our dreaming, the more layers of our dreams that we can access, the deeper our resources. When we connect to the wisdom of our own unconscious and beyond, the more we can move into our fullest selves. We can then dream dreams not only for our own healing, but also dream for others and even for the planet. As we tap into this deep pool of wisdom we can then heal the parts of our lives that are troubled, traumatized, or cut off from our core Self. Previously cut off or dissociated parts may be willing to show themselves when invited out through dreamwork.

Dreams are not unilaterally determined; that is, they do not mean just one thing. The many layers are simultaneously true. It is not a case of either/or, but rather of both/and. To help us to organize our deep dive, I have created a system of dreamwork based on the mystical tradition of the Kabbalah called the PARDES system. I first introduced this method in my book *Modern Dreamwork: New Tools for Decoding Your Soul's Wisdom*. When we read the Torah and other sacred texts, the teachings of Kabbalah invite us to read them through four layers of ever-deepening understanding by utilizing the system of the PARDES. The word PARDES translates as orchard in Hebrew and is also an allegory for the Garden of Eden; our first orchard. In addition, the word itself is an acronym for the four layers at which we read the Torah. What follows is how I applied this system to dreamwork.

Unpacking the Word "PARDES"

The four-tiered system of the PARDES in Kabbalah corresponds to the first letters of each word in the acronym. "P" is the first letter of the word *P'shat*, which in Hebrew means simple or basic. Both in dreams and in sacred text, this is the literal story line. "R" is the first letter of the word *Remez*, which means hinted at. This layer is what we quickly associate to when recalling our dream or reading the text. "D" is for *Drash*, which comes from the root of the word *Lidrosh*, to chase after or pursue and may not be literally contained in the dream or text itself. It means to expound on. (A *Drash* is also the word used for the teachings or interpretation of the weekly Torah portion often given by the rabbi.) When we delve deep into the dream or the text, using a variety of methods of exploration, we are exploring on the Drash level. Metaphors, puns, or plays on words may be part of this layer. Finally, "S" is for *Sod*, which means secret or hidden. Here we may find layers of the dream that reference many sacred texts, sacred geometry, sacred landscapes, or connections with angelic beings or departed relatives. This also can be the transpersonal layer, where we dream not only for ourselves and for our world, but of worlds and dimensions of other time and space.

Applying the PARDES Method of Looking at Layers of a Dream

Let's first use an example of a simple nightmare to demonstrate how to delve into the potentially hidden depths of a nightmare, and then a more complex dream story. My client Joann had a dream *"My house is on fire."* That was the whole dream as she first reported it. She experienced, as expected with a dream image like this, fear and its henchmen panic and anxiety. That would comprise the first or simple layer of inquiry: The nightmare story and the accompanying emotions. Some well-placed questions help us get to the next layers.

To follow possible hints (Remez) to get to this second layer, I ask for more detail and inquire if she is inside or outside the house in the nightmare, and if she recognizes the house from anytime in her life or not. It will make a difference as to the meaning of the dream if this is her current home, her college apartment, a childhood home, or something else. Each option will have a different layer of meaning and association for her. Her perspective and relative safety also change if she is inside or outside of the house. At this level I am checking in with the dreamer about things that were already contained in the dream, but that they forgot to mention or didn't notice when they first reported it. When she told me that she was inside the house and that it reminded her of her college apartment, we could then place some of the roots of the dream into that period of her life. As we move into the third layer of pursuit (Drash) and examine potential meanings of a house on fire in her late teens and early twenties, the questions become oriented around that time of her life and its connection to her current life.

At this third layer we look for deeper associations, metaphors, puns, and plays on words. We follow the associations to elements that were not necessarily contained in the original dream, but that the dream may have been pointing toward and help us to connect that period of her life with her present-day life. I ask if the possibilities of burning with love or burning with passion for something resonated. Was she burning mad about something then? At this time in her life in college, was she learning of something new that lit her up, that caught fire in her imagination? By stretching out the possible metaphors, Joann was able to access meaning and emotion beyond her initial responses. She had studied anthropology in school and was lit up by the idea of ancient connections of peoples across time and distance and recalled learning how the acquisition of fire helped to change the lives of hunter-gatherers to farmer-householders. She did not however go on in her career to pursue this work as an adult and missed the sensation of being fired up by her work or studies. So, in one way a house on fire was a positive for Joann, something she missed feeling. So, although she woke with a fear response, that was not the only truth for her in the dream. Fire is often a two-edged sword, both a tool and a danger.

This thought brought her to a transpersonal layer as well (Sod), and she resonated with current issues of climate change, the heating up of the planet, and the danger to current and subsequent generations. Now she was full circle to her studies of people and civilizations. A final question for her to ponder about this dream was then, "What does this dream want from you? What is the dream asking of you?" Sometimes the dream or nightmare comes with a message or an invitation for us and is inviting us to do something for ourselves or our planet. She went home to think about where she needed to re-engage with her passions and get fired up to take action in her life.

When Fairy Tales Come True

Here is an example of parsing a more complex dream through the PARDES method using a dream from Dina, who had this dream as a young woman in her twenties. She is in her sixties today, so we will have the benefit of hindsight at the end.

The dream itself, or P'shat level, is this:

> I am in a village, like the ones from European fairy tales. Thatched houses and leafy trees and a road that goes in a circle around the village. I am being chased by a giant down this road. I run around and around, and he is right behind me. I am terrified he is going to get me and kill me or hurt me in a terrible way. I keep running. No one else is around but I hear a voice that says, "Look into the eye of the giant." I am confused and surprised by this and finally turn around to see the big brown eyes of the giant right behind me. His eyes are so kind. I stop running and turn around. He picks me up and we look at each other and then he dances with me. I feel so happy, relieved, and so safe in his arms.

At the simple P'shat layer we see the village, the encircling road, the dreamer herself, and the giant. The dreamer is chased by the giant. We hear an disembodied voice speak to her. We see her running scared, then stop, turn around, see kind eyes, and get lifted up and twirled around. This is the simple story line. We get the setting, the characters, and the action.

On the next level, the Remez layer, we begin to wonder about this dream to see what our first associations to it are. What might it be hinting at? I am immediately struck by the fairy tale motif; it is unusual and commands my interest. We know that fairy tales may hint at a collective layer of mythos in our dreams. This village is circumvented by a circular road. I wonder about circles, what is encircled, or going in circles. Next, I am struck by the CI, or Central Image, (a phrase coined by Ernest Hartmann) in this dream, which seems to be the giant. (The CI is the giant "if it were my dream," as we say in the dreamwork world, to respect the integrity of the dreamer and not superimpose our own projections on the dream.) At this level, the dream continues first with a chase and a nightmarish, terrifying quality, but then the dreamer hears a voice and is instructed to turn around and look into the eye of the giant, which seems to then change everything. I am so curious about this transformation of affect and story right in the middle of this dream. I now also notice that this change comes after she has been picked up by the now-kind giant who proceeds to dance with her. The dream spontaneously changes from a nightmare of terror into a dream of relief and safety.

On the Drash level, I want to pursue the associations I had on the Remez level. I spoke briefly with this dreamer and asked her if she had any associations to the meaning of the dream. She replied that it was so long ago that she had few memories, except for the fact that it was at a time in her life when she felt lost, not knowing where to go next, and was frightened to do anything. She also reported that she had three fairy tale dreams that summer. So, with this information I have an association to "going in circles" in her life, feeling aimless and purposeless. I also happen to know that she had spent time in Greece at this in-between time in her life, which had a wonderful fairy-tale-like quality in many ways, full of myth and legend and even some small villages with thatched roofs. It was a nice break for her to be there for a year but may or may not have helped her with her life direction. She was still going in circles when she returned.

The giant. Here is where the core of the action is. I wonder what she was running from that was so terrifying at that time in her life. Clearly something so big and gigantic that it became personified as a giant who could either kill her or harm her terribly. Often our dreams present our emotions in a personified form, fear showing up as a monster, sadness showing up as a blue whale, or confusion showing up as a trickster image. She tries to outrun this giant fear (the flight response to terror or trauma) but cannot. Instead, she gets a message from somewhere beyond to try a different tack: Turn and face the giant. This is a common choice to try while doing active waking dreamwork when confronted by a scary monster or someone chasing us in a dream. If Dina hadn't already done it herself, I would have suggested it as a dream-working option. However, she was empowered enough and tuned in enough in her life, even back in her twenties, that she could do it on her own in her dream.

Now the dream takes us into the realm of the Sod or mystical and spiritual level. For starters, this is a fairy tale dream. We know that myth and fairy tales tap into great collective unconscious worlds of wisdom and into an archetypical layer that may have meaning for the wider world as well as our personal one. Jung based much of his life's work on this premise, as did Clarissa Pinkola Estés. Who or what was that Voice? Her guardian angel, God, her Wise Self? Whoever it was, it came from beyond herself, from a place of higher consciousness. It told her to turn and face her fear and look into its eyes. She had enough trust in that voice to follow its direction, and in doing so found a deep source of kindness. Her big, bad giant transformed into the positive meaning of a giant, a person of great power and talent. Looking into the eyes of that which we fear is a powerful statement of trust, as looking directly into an animal's or person's eyes can be perceived as a threat. The eyes are also known as the windows to the soul, and when Dina looked within those eyes, she found happiness, infinite kindness, and safety.

Fast forward now to forty years later. This dream took place at a time in Dina's life when she was terrified and aimless and did not know in which direction to turn; she was "going round and round in circles." What ultimately happened in her life? For years now Dina has been practicing her life work as a healer, a spiritual director, and yes, a dancer! In the dream, the ultimate joy and healing came when the giant picked her up and danced with her. Her dissociated parts, or at least her separated parts of personified fear, her lost self, her spiritual wisdom voice, and ultimately her healing dancer, came forward to work together. She now helps others heal through dance and listening to their inner voice. Her fairy tale has come full circle.

Who or what is your giant? What do you need to do to transform your own gigantic inner or outer monster into a source of wisdom or healing or a hero in your story? Giants have always been with us, either as sources of evil or bullies or thugs, such as Goliath, or Blunderbore, who is killed by the appropriately named Jack the Giant Killer, or in modern times, Hitler. They can represent chaos or natural forces that frighten us. In the mythology of the Native American Lakota people, Waziya is a northern giant who blows the winter wind. They can also be positive giants in our lives of outstanding innovation or knowledge (think Einstein or Socrates or Ruth Bader Ginsburg). A giant of kindness may be the diminutive Mother Teresa. Working through the layers of your dreams and nightmares can help you find your own giant of humanity for yourself and for the world.

In this wonderful opportunity that Dina gave us to see how dreams may come true, we get a glimpse of the transformative process of the dream. As we peeled back the layers using the PARDES method, we get past the fear and confusion and into the "... kindness, relief, and safety." And if we keep track of our dreams, work through our nightmares, and look back at the stories our dream journals tell, then we too can see the record of our healing journeys.

Here is a summary of working with the layers to assist in your exploration:

1. **P'SHAT (Simple)**—This is the literal level, the dream itself. It contains the story, the landscape, and characters as they appear in the dream or nightmare. Your dream can be explored completely on the level of the narrative itself, without interpretive or associative elements. The content at this level is not added to or changed, simply journeyed through, and appreciated for what it is.

2. **REMEZ (Hinted at)**—This level contains our first mind and body associations to the dream or nightmare, and/or things that were there in our dream, but we didn't notice at first. This is the "Oh, I know what that means" layer. It may contain influences from things that happened in our lives yesterday or recently, and the events in our lives that show up only slightly disguised or encoded in symbology. We see beneath this veil rather quickly; the meaning for us is embedded just below the surface of the words and dreamscape itself. Our response may be cognitive or may be an emotional or physical reaction when we address this layer (e.g., we get cold, angry, a stomachache, giddy, tingling in our fingers, etc.), but we may not yet know why.

3. **DRASH (Pursued or Revealed)**—This is the subtler layer that is revealed to us when we work on the dream material through a variety of techniques that allow us to

go beyond what we know consciously, or even beyond what we think we know when we begin to work with the material. It is the symbolized layer, the layer of insight, of correlation, of deeper associations. We unravel the large and small details of the dream and pursue associations that may take us far past the dream itself. We use a variety of techniques, including active imagination, re-entry into the dream landscape, using energy techniques with the dream content, Gestalt work, embodiment techniques, and a variety of expressive modalities to reach the deeper layers.

4. **SOD (Secret)**—This is the deepest layer; it may contain mystical or spiritual guidance. It may be analogous to what Jung called big dreams, the understanding of which may have profound significance for our lives, and possibly the lives of others around us. It can often be accessed through dream re-entry and may provide us with passageways to other realms and alternate ways of knowing. This is the transpersonal, the mystical, the secret, our connection with other worlds, other time, other space, and our connection with the Divine. It can be a remembering of ancient wisdom from our spiritual ancestors that can show us a path, a vision, a hope. Sometimes this layer is in the manifest content of the dream; and of those dreams, we may just want to sit with them, rather than work with them further, and bask in the glow that is already manifest.

EXERCISE

Finding the Layers in Your Dream Through the PARDES Method

Choose a strong dream or nightmare you have had, one that is full enough to get a good amount of juice out of. Then see if you can peel back the layers of your dream using the PARDES method.

1. What is the simple layer (P'shat) of the story line itself?

2. What are your first hints or associations to the dream (the Remez or hinted-at layer)? Does some association or connection jump out quickly for you?

3. To access the Drash layer of pursued or realßed knowledge, try using a variety of methods to explore your dream. Use art, movement, dream re-entry, consult with other dreamers to get their associations, or go into a meditative state to see what emerges.

4. To explore the mystical or Sod layer, take note and tune in to see if there are transpersonal elements, visitations from departed loved ones or spiritual beings, or messages in this dream that have meaning beyond your own life, for your communityß, or the planet.

SIX

THE GAIA METHOD
The Guided Active Imagination Approach
for Careful Nightmare Healing

There is no coming to consciousness without pain. People will do anything, no matter how absurd, in order to avoid facing their own Soul.
One does not become enlightened by imagining figures of light, but
by making the darkness conscious.

—*Carl Jung*

The Guided Active Imagination Approach (GAIA) was created to
facilitate safe and careful work with nightmares. The name GAIA
is a fortuitous acronym for this method of work. As in dreams themselves, there are multiple layers of meaning in the word that reveal
themselves upon closer scrutiny, as well as a synchronicity I hadn't
realized when I originally designed this method. The word itself
contains associations to the earth-mother goddess Gaia. In addition,
it refers to our complete living planet itself as a complex organism,
as proposed by James Lovelock and Lynn Margulis in their Gaia theory in 1970. Now commonly accepted, they proposed that the earth
is a living, self-regulating being. We too are living, self-regulating
beings, and our dreams, including our nightmares, are one of the
ways that our own systems help us to come back into balance.

This nightmare intervention is based on two primary approaches: one from the world of dreamwork and one from the field of trauma treatment. It has its roots in Jungian depth psychology and in current best-practice trauma treatment. GAIA has two parts: Stage 1 is all about creating safety before venturing into the belly of the beast, and Stage 2 then allows us to take the resources we have generated and created in Stage 1 to move into working directly with the dream material.

The GAIA Method

Because trauma interferes with our ability to *be* safe, to *feel* safe, and to *create safety* both during and after the traumatic events, the creation of a safe enough environment in which to do the healing work is the first order of priority. We want to go gently into that dark night, with supports and resources that were not there either when the traumatic events took place or in the nightmares that occurred following the event. Overzealous attempts to move into the belly of the nightmare too quickly can result in re-traumatization. Treading carefully as we enter and exit this deep emotional territory allows us to avoid the extremes of getting too overwhelmed or becoming dissociated. In order to build up sufficient emotional musculature and resilience to be able to process the emotional residue, it is better to start building safety slowly and surely. We want to build in the capacity for the dreamer to be able to have emotional regulation as we approach the nightmare. The direct work on the dream itself that is done in Stage 2 of GAIA can wait as long as is necessary.

The two stages of the GAIA method are:

1. The pre-dreamwork preparation and ingathering of resources with the emphasis on the felt sense of safety in the present, both from outside the dream and possibly peeking into the dream from outside of it as well.

2. Utilizing the resources that have been generated in Stage 1 to work directly with the dream material, both from outside and inside the dream.

Working from outside the dream refers to examining various elements of the dream from the observer perspective, looking in at the story and the images from an eyes-wide-open in waking clock-time perspective. To work in this way, we use language such as, "When I think about my dream, I remember seeing myself in a dark forest. I remember that there seemed to be an animal lurking behind the trees." Working from inside the dream means to climb back inside of the dream while awake and wander around the dreamscape in real time, re-experiencing it in the now of the dream. Here we use language such as, "I am walking through a dark forest. I am chilly and can smell the vaguely rotten, damp matted leaves underfoot. The hair on the back of my neck rises as I sense an animal lurking behind the trees."

The first style is the external witness perspective, the other is the visceral felt sense of a lived experience. Neither is better or worse, just different styles of dreamwork. We can get different types of information about the dream from each method. Once the dreamer is ready and prepared, working from inside the dream also gives us access to the experienced felt sense of somatasensory processing pioneered by Eugene Gendlin in his work on Focusing. With Focusing, we feel into the events that are happening in the dream and experience them in our bodies. As we attend to our bodies, our felt sense can shift, and we find different responses. By interacting with the dream characters and objects, we also gain the ability to change the events that took place in the original dream when we work from the inside. That is, we come into the time/space of the dream itself, and then are able to make changes in the dream and in the outcome.

This is part of the essence of Carl Jung's active imagination, one of the two main principles upon which the GAIA method is based.

Active Imagination

Active imagination itself can be defined as dropping down into the dream landscape in order to interact with the dream and the characters therein. It is a tool for transformation. We can use it to interact with and freely imagine the thoughts, feelings, and alternative actions that our dream characters may take. When we meet a dragon in the dream during our active imagination, we can talk with it and hear how it answers us. In utilizing active imagination, we maintain the connections with our waking consciousness, with our dreamed characters, and then add the active transformational possibilities that emerge when we merge these two states of consciousness to create a third new option or form.

It encourages our conscious and our unconscious minds to communicate with each other by directing our attention and focus on that part of ourselves, our dreaming and unconscious self, that does not usually benefit from this direct attention. In active imagination, we have the opportunity to go back and interact with dream characters. I added the ability of the dreamer to interact with the dream objects, with landscapes, and with our own somatic responses to Jung's original formulation, and in doing so have the ability to change the actions that took place in the original dream by interacting with all the elements of the dream. We can go back and engage with various elements of the dream to dream it forward to a safer and more satisfactory conclusion.

Wired for Healing

My orientation to the healing of loss and trauma is that our own body/mind/spirit self-being is wired for healing, that it naturally wants to come into stasis and order. Connecting this to Lovelock's Gaia theory of the earth as a vast self-regulating organism, the underlying premise of deep healing both from nightmares and from what generated them is founded on the AEDP principle (Accelerated Experiential Dynamic Psychotherapy) that we all have innate capacities for healing. Diana Fosha's AEDP approach uses moment to moment tracking of emotion and body sensation help to engage the attachment system that has been disrupted through traumatic experiences. This is also why we pay exquisite close attention to embodiment, movement, and the movement of emotion as we work through our dreams. Both the tracking and the attention are part of the healing matrix we create.

The AEDP system itself is a therapeutic method also predicated on a safe and empathic relationship with a therapist. The principles of working with a connected and caring other, including a close friend or caring companion, can re-create the conditions needed for healing. The caring other can also be our own best and highest Self as we gently explore other parts of ourselves that have been hurt. There is always a part of us that the trauma never touched: our spirit, our soul, our connection with the Divine. This is a key principle as well for healing. When Elaine was setting up a safe place imagery prior to doing dreamwork, at first she said, "I can't imagine any place at all that is safe to be in my body." Finally, after much thought and negotiation, she was able to imagine a part of herself, her Witness or Spirit Self, watching out for her embodied Self as it immersed in warm, shallow water filled with glowing phosphorescence to light her way. The two parts were then surrounded by a bubble of light to keep them connected.

No matter what happened in our environment or to our bodies, our soul remains pure and whole. This idea itself can be hard for a long-term sufferer to fully grasp, but once grasped, we reclaim this birthright. We seize upon and highlight areas of health and hope in this method of dreamwork to fan the flames of generativity that are always present, even if buried. We also look for the Bright Ones in or around our dreams and inside ourselves to highlight hope and healing. In addition to a potential legacy burden of trauma from our ancestors, we also can find in them a legacy of healing and strength. These nurturing and guiding ancestors then are our Bright Ones, to borrow Tirzah Firestone's phrase, that we can tap into. Or as Mr. Rogers tells us, we need to look for the helpers. This forms the core of the GAIA method of nightmare work. We will revisit this later as we work with spontaneous visitation dreams and invited dream visitors.

How might this style of attention to movement and emotional tracking look in dreamwork? In addition to the story lines and images, we attend to the movement patterns and emotions. The act of bringing our attention to the movement and the emotion in and of itself allows us to have a different perspective. Some dreamers have a plethora of easily available resources; others will need more help in generating them, which then becomes the Guided part of this method. Here's an example of this process. Ericka dreams:

> I have taken a Zodiac boat out into the water, but it has sprung a leak and I am frantically bailing out the water. I wonder if I would be able to swim to shore if need be. I feel somewhat panicky and a bit helpless.

There are many ways to work with and approach this dream, but if we begin with tracking movement, here is what happened. First, I ask Ericka if she needed any resources before re-inhabiting this dream, a core principle of Stage 1 of the GAIA method. Because she is a good swimmer, she said no, she could "jump right in." I notice out loud (tracking) that she used the word "jump," an active and empowering word. That attention to her offhand comment allowed her to feel more self-agency. Here is a resource that is already contained within her dream that she didn't notice at first. I then invite her to pay attention to what it felt like to "jump right in" and she tuned into a feeling of strength and energy in her legs. Once in the boat, I ask her to really notice what it felt like to be bailing it out—the main part of the dream, and the most active part. We have learned that the main part of a dream can also be referred to as the CI or Central Image, and often contains the core energy of the dream.

As she tunes into her body, I invite her to physically show me how one bails out a boat, and what muscles she needs to do this. She begins to dip her imaginary bucket into the water in the boat and demonstrates dumping it over the side. I ask what it feels like to do this, to really notice what parts of her body are engaged. She first focused on her hands and arms, noticing how they were getting tired. I then ask her to put her attention on other parts of her body as well. Now Ericka says that if she "puts her back into it" and uses her larger back and core stomach muscles, that she is less tired and has more energy to bail harder. When I remind her of her strong jumping-in legs, she adds those leg muscles to her back and core, and now feels that she has plenty of energy to bail out the boat.

As I track with her both her movements and her facial expressions, I remark that she has a very determined look on her face now, as opposed to the panicky one she had earlier. I ask if this is true, as I don't want to assume or superimpose my opinion (it's her dream), but she agrees and smiles. Finally, at this point in the work, I ask if she notices anything else now that she was such a strong bailer, and she replies, "Now that you mention it, I seem to have gotten enough water out of the Zodiac to see that it is really just a little hole, and I can stuff my plastic rain poncho into it to plug it up until I get back to shore to repair it." Oh—a poncho!—here's another resource that she found inside of the dream that wasn't visible or available to her at first. While Ericka was able to generate internal resources pretty much on her own, with just a few questions to get her in touch with her innate strength and resourcefulness, many nightmare sufferers are not able to do so.

In this piece of dreamwork, with what started out to be a nightmare (using the definition of nightmare as a dream that contains upsetting, unpleasant emotions that are not resolved before waking), Ericka was able to transform it. By tuning into her body and her sensations, she was able to generate the internal resources she needed to feel assured that she had the strength to get to safety and be able to repair the boat. She transformed the original feelings of panic and helplessness into a connection with a more whole-body strength and creativity as she found a solution to patching the hole that was not originally available to her in her dream. In Ericka's case she had all the resources she needed right inside herself, and just needed some guidance to find and access them. Tracking her progress physically and emotionally helped to sort out the narrative trajectory and move it toward repair—such a nice metaphor. By the end of this piece of dreamwork, she was confident that she could get to shore and repair her boat. What this metaphor means in her life might be her next step of the dreamwork.

Sometimes this is as far as you or the dreamer needs or wants to go. Once the dilemma is solved inside the dream, you or they may not have a need or interest to make the bridge to waking life that generated it. Healing at one level of our being can transmute and carry over into other levels with or without our conscious awareness or connections. This is part of what makes dreamwork so powerful. Following the cybernetics principle that a change in the part generates a change in the whole, sometimes we are done right there at level three of the PARDES system, keeping the dreamwork focused on the metaphor of the dream story. Other times, especially if it is a recurring nightmare, we need to continue to make the connections directly to our current and past life (or lives) to be able to generate the reparative actions needed in the physical word as well. Robert Moss has called this subsequent step the Bridge to Life.

To explore this dream from another active imagination angle, that of interacting with the objects in the dream, I ask her to talk to the boat itself. In essence Ericka creates a dialogue with the boat and then speaks from the point of view of the boat itself. When Ericka enters into the dream she asks the boat, *"Who and what are you?"* and it responds, *"I am a small inflatable boat. I am named after the astrological configuration of stars in the sky known as the Zodiac. I think I am an Aquarius boat. I seem to be sinking. I am filling up with water and can't carry out my purpose of transporting Ericka to the other side. I feel ashamed and embarrassed to have sprung a leak."*

This insight from the point of view of the boat gives us a whole new direction to explore. What is the boat part of her that has not been able to fulfill its purpose and is feeling ashamed and embarrassed? And is she an Aquarius (born in late January or February)? Whether or not that is her sign, what does she associate with Aquarius? I think right away about the astrological symbol of Aquarius: the water carrier. Most icons of this sign depict a figure carrying a jug of water and pouring it out. Here's what I found when I Googled it and then shared it with her:

The sign of Aquarius is represented by the water bearer. She is the mystical healer who bestows water or life upon the land. Accordingly, Aquarius is often depicted as the most humanitarian astrological sign. These revolutionary thinkers fervently support empowerment of all people, aspiring to change the world through radical social progress.

This immediately resonated with Ericka; her career path is one of social justice reform. The new information takes us in yet another direction: The purpose that the Zodiac boat speaks about refers to both a career path and a larger mythical and transpersonal goal of somehow offering life-giving water. But she can only get there if her means of transportation is solid and intact. The message that Ericka now gets is that she needs to attend more carefully to how she is moving toward achieving her goal. Her dream takeaway thought is that next time she will examine her boat more carefully before setting out. In other words, to take her time and prepare carefully to avoid potential mishaps and the need to turn back for repairs once having set out.

When Erika first worked on the dream she was very creative when the boat began to fill with water and used her rain poncho to plug up the hole. So, we already know that she didn't go down with the ship. As she thought about how her dream connected to her life, she confessed that she knew that she tended to be impulsive and "jump into things" (there's that word *jump* again with a different meaning this time). Here was a bridge to life for her. Moving more slowly and "checking for leaks" before jumping into a project would help move her career forward into more of the managerial position that she sought. That would allow her to have more power to make change and "get to the other side" as in her dream. Checking her documents for typos before hitting send was just one small real-world example of checking for leaks before getting into the boat next time.

The GAIA Protocol Roots in Trauma Treatment and "Safety First"

Before moving into the engaged dreamwork of a more frightening nightmare, we need to feel safe enough to interact with the dream without feeling triggered. This is the first step in all good trauma treatment approaches. The following brief background of the creation of the mental health category of PTSD gives us the framework for understanding the need for a nightmare protocol that emphasizes safety as a precursor to exploratory work.

Originally, traumatic stress was identified as a phenomenon in soldiers on the battlefield and was referred to as shell shock. The treatment, if you can call it that, was to simply send the soldiers back to the front lines as soon as possible to "get over it." This direct exposure technique was the gold standard for many years, and while it did serve to get the soldiers back to the front, and sometimes allowed them to be able to function after discharge, it did nothing for their long-term health or mental health. Even though those soldiers may have been able to rejoin their comrades in battle, they still suffered nightmares, flashbacks, and other disruptions to their life long after the battle was over. In the 1960s and 70s this became classified as Vietnam Vet Syndrome.

In the 1970s there was also a surge in research and innovation in trauma treatments that coincided with the women's movement. Now other forms of trauma, specifically those of rape and sexual assault, were also categorized as traumatic events that created similar post-trauma responses as the soldiers had. Rape Trauma Syndrome was thus added to this categorization. The new diagnosis of PTSD was added to the *Diagnostic and Statistical Manual of Mental Disorders* (*DSM*) in 1980. The creation of the category of PTSD is unique in the framing of psychological disorders because it places the spotlight squarely on the external traumatic stressor rather than an internal factor of biology, neurology, or neurotic thought processes. This landmark change from blaming the victim for their own distress, to the recognition that the cause of the symptoms suffered lay in the external events that created the responses in the first place, generated a sea change in the understanding and treatment approaches.

At this time, Dr. Judith Herman outlined a protocol for treating survivors of abuse in her classic book *Trauma and Recovery*. She articulated three stages:

1. Establishing safety and stabilization

2. Remembrance and mourning (which includes telling the story of the traumatic event)

3. Reconnection and integration

These are not meant to be strictly linear stages, much as grief work or dreamwork do not follow a neat, linear path. Rather they are to be revisited and reinforced in a spiraling mobius strip as new material emerges and new life challenges are met. The reestablishment of safety addressed in stage one needs to be periodically revisited in the face of new information or new stressors in therapy, in dreamwork, and in life. Safety includes having the ability to tolerate, regulate, and manage strong emotions that show up in both waking and dreaming life. Trauma survivors may feel unsafe in their own bodies and in relationships with others as well as in the world at large.

Somatic therapist Babette Rothschild offers us a metaphor for creating safety. She tells us that the experience of emotional overwhelm is similar to that of a shaken bottle of soda. Inside the bottle is a tremendous amount of pressure. The safest way to release the pressure is to open and close the cap in a slow, cautious, and intentional manner so as to prevent an explosion.[29] Given that trauma can create unspeakable terror, we also need to attend to using nonverbal methods of creating safety until the words that can also slowly open the cap are once again available. Mindfulness, somatic practices like chi gung, acupuncture, yoga, and breathwork can all contribute to

---

29. Babette Rothschild, *The Body Remembers: The Psychophysiology of Trauma and Trauma Treatment* (New York: W. W. Norton & Company, 2010), 78–79.

creating a sense of safety in the body. We can use and access these in our Stage 1 of creating safety in our dreamwork before entering the stormy depths of a nightmare.

Herman's second stage of remembrance and mourning includes putting the power of words and language to the memories as much as is feasible, for using words allows us to be better able to mourn the losses with the company and understanding of others on the same journey. Words also allow us to access the more cognitive parts of our brains that help us to get distance and perspective from our more primitive sensory-only memories. We may certainly also recall and mourn through somatic practices like interpretive dance and art that allow us to tell the story without words. While still attending to safety, here the work is to integrate the trauma, the events, and the emotions so that they become metabolized and do not remain static. Attention to timing and pacing are crucial to avoid dysregulation.

Finally, the goal in stage three of reconnection and integration is to fully reclaim life, to create a new sense of self and life purpose that includes making meaning out of pain, having meaningful relationships, and no longer defining oneself by the story of the trauma. Empowerment of self, and possibly using one's own hero's journey out of trauma and suffering to help others, becomes the defining life narrative. Viktor Frankl titled his post-Holocaust book *Man's Search For Meaning*. The ability to make meaning even out of an experience as horrible as concentration camp life allows for the possibility of redemption. A psychiatrist himself, he mined his experiences in the camps in the service of helping to heal others in the world. Post-traumatic spiritual growth is often recognized in this phase of the work.

We keep Herman's stages of recovery in mind while working with traumatic nightmares. Stage 1 of the GAIA protocol focuses on the establishment of safety, and in Stage 2, as we work through the dream to a resolution, we also attend to the recognition of what happened to generate the nightmare, even if it is couched in metaphor. Moving forward to integration and connection with all the parts of the self may be the ultimate goal in resolving PTSDreams, as well as claiming our birthright of a peaceful night's sleep.

The GAIA Protocol

Here is the protocol to use when using the GAIA method. Please make it your own and adapt the wording as needed for your dreamer and yourself. After walking you through the stages, I will share an example of highly stressful repetitive nightmare work with Jay's nightmares using this method.

GAIA Stage 1

After the dreamer tells you that they had a dream, ask them if they want to *tell* you their dream. Sometimes the dreamer just wants to say, "I had a horrible nightmare," but not tell the details of the dream story. We respect the timing and the pacing of the dreamer to move forward at their own pace, something that did not happen during trauma. Sometimes with very scary dreams, the initial dreamwork is simply to say to the dreamer, "I'm so sorry that you had such a scary dream. Let me know if you want to talk more about it or share it." The empathy with which you greet the nightmare is healing in and of itself. It may take some time to unpack a particularly frightening dream or series of dreams, so we can go back to it as many times as is necessary to carefully explore it. It may take weeks, months, or sometimes years to come to the fullness of understanding all the layers, but we can continue to harvest the gifts of the loam-rich dark each time we work on it.

If they want to share the dream, ask them if they are ready to tell it now, or if they need to do anything else before they share it. While this level of incrementally slow proceeding is not necessary in most dreamwork, it is immensely comforting to someone who has been terrified by their nightmare and/or their trauma experiences. Some dreamers need to gather in ways to feel safe even before they tell the dream, but in my experience most will be ready to share their dream once they have told you that they had one, and then need to establish their protections before working on it or entering into it.

This slow and careful approach is part of titrating the work. The word *titration* is used in trauma treatment, which in turn borrowed it from the field of pharmaceuticals. We use a medicine dropper to titrate drop by drop the correct dosage of a medicine. Drop by drop, we inch into the nightmare with our dreamer and check the response before adding more to the mix.

Once they have shared the dream, we want to respond empathically to both the emotional narrative and to the story line content, as we learned about in chapter 1, and then to set the stage for the healing work. It is useful here to share with the dreamer the orientation that all dreams come bearing gifts, even the really frightening ones. This bit of wisdom comes from the Talmud, one of the holy books that serves to explicate and expand on the Bible. By sharing this orientation now, we are both setting the stage for our search for the diamonds buried in the chaos and rubble of the nightmare, but also making what is called in NLP (Neuro-Linguistic Programming) a presupposition. This presupposition of a gift to come through presupposes that there will be some learning or healing or wisdom in the dream but does not presuppose what exactly that will be. The discovery of the hidden gifts is part of the dreamer's journey, but we can start out orienting ourselves to seek out the buried treasure; be it in the form of insight, advice, memory, direction, a meaningful object, a guide, or an action. This begins the gentle guiding of the active imagination process.

Title and Re-Title

Next, we can ask the dreamer to give the dream a title if they haven't already. I encourage the dreamer to let the title just arise spontaneously from their gut and not think about it too much. If they are surprised by it, so much the better, for that means it emerged into their consciousness from a previously unconscious place. The title frequently contains the core of the dream and its center of energy and power. Allowing it to surface early on in the dreamwork process can be a shortcut to the core of the dreamwork and a signpost pointing us in an important direction. In addition, after we complete a piece of dreamwork, we can then ask if there is a new title. We will often find a profound title change, which provides a practical and concrete way for the dreamer to see the progress they are making as the titles shift and change. The original title often contains a negative belief or some emotional distress, and the new title will then hopefully be in contrast after the healing dreamwork.

I call this technique *"Title and Re-Title."* While working on dreams in my dream circle on one occasion, a member who shared her dream titled it *Everything Is So Dark and Unclear*. After we worked on it in the group for a while, my friend Marcia asked, "So, would you give it a different title now?" Sure enough, the title had changed from *Everything Is So Dark and Unclear* to *Deep Diving*. The feelings in and about the dream changed too, from the initial feelings of, "I feel foggy, this doesn't feel so good, and I don't understand what it means" to "Oh, now I have a new perspective; I can dive down into that water and discover what is there for me." Excitement and curiosity had replaced anxiety and dread. Here are a few other examples of dream title changes from before working on a dream to afterward:

1. Original title: *Broken Glass*. New title after dreamwork: *Picking Up the Pieces*

2. Original title: *Earthquake*. New title after dreamwork: *Rebirth*

3. Original title: *Dark Energies*. New title after dreamwork: *Claiming My Power*

As these examples illustrate, the tone and energy of the titles all shifted from something that was originally dark, harsh, or frightening to something else that was clearer, positive, or hopeful.

After getting the title of the dream, we use the SUDS method we encountered earlier to rate the level of upset or emotional distress it causes the dreamer, with zero being calm and relaxed when sharing or thinking about the dream, and ten being the worst upset they can imagine. We hope to see this SUDS level go down after working through the dream.

The Ingathering of Allies and Resources

Now we are ready to gather the resources and allies together before moving into the dream per se. At this point I ask my dreamer who or what they need or want to feel safe and secure enough to engage with the dream. Clearly not everyone who has a nightmare will need this kind of slow and intricate work, but we err on the side of caution and check first. Some folks are shy or reluctant or defensively competent and may not be able to come up with ideas on their own. Some trauma survivors hold back from asking for help or feel they don't deserve it. I assure them that they deserve help and assistance even if they don't believe it themselves yet. ("Yet" is one of my favorite therapeutic words—it gives permission to be where you are and offers the potential for change in three little letters.) So, with these and other ways of priming the dream pump, we set out to engage a posse of helpers, guides, objects, energies, and places.

Starting out with people, I invite the dreamer to think about who they know who helps them feel safe and secure, that they would want with them to guard their back on a dark road or scary journey. I explicate that these can be people from their current life or from their childhood; they can be alive in this world or already passed to the other side. They can be people who they know or know of, or fantasy figures or characters from a book or movie. They can also be mythical or spiritual beings: gods, angels, guides, or shamans. I invite them to tune into their own deepest wisdom to locate these guides, but if they get stuck and can't come up with a list that feels sufficient, I may make suggestions. Sometimes this participatory co-creation of the list adds a felt sense of safety to the process. We write them down and ascertain where they want these allies to stand—beside, behind, or in front of the dreamer—before entering the dreamwork.

Invited guests and protectors over the years have included Gandalf the white wizard from *Lord of the Rings*; the more contemporary Dumbledore, Harry Potter's wizard mentor; Marmee, the mother from *Little Women*; and Jesus, Buddah, Moses, and angels of all kinds. One of the children I worked with invited Mary Poppins as her ultimate magical and caretaking protector.

Back to angels and spiritual beings, there is a lovely bedtime lullaby that invites the angels to surround us before we drift off to sleep. The song names in turn Archangel Michael on our right side, Gabriel on our left, Uriel in front of us, Raphael behind us, and Shechinah, the feminine indwelling presence of maternal love, hovering and sheltering us over our heads. Each angel's name contains specific meaning. The word "El" is a name for God, so the angel's purpose is reflected in their names as follows: Micha-el is the one who is like God (God's right-hand person); Gabri-el is the strength, might, or protection of God (the root letters G. B. R. mean strong or boundaried in Hebrew); Uri-el is the light of God (Ur means light), (s)he is lighting the path before us); and Rapha-el is the healer of God (Ropheh means healer and also doctor in modern Hebrew). I like to think about Raphael, the healer who's got my back.

My friend Patricia finds great comfort in St. Bridgid, a patron saint of animals and children, and St. Anthony, the recoverer of lost objects. It is easy to see why these two saints might be of particular comfort to a survivor of childhood trauma, to protect the children and to recover the lost parts of oneself. I confess that when my friend told me that St. Anthony also helps find parking spaces (the lost space?), I have since invoked him for assistance in this endeavor to great success. She taught me to say, "St. Anthony, St. Anthony, please come 'round, something's been lost that must be found." I definitely find parking spots faster with his help!

While in the realm of spiritual or mystical protection, let's not forget the protective embrace of an egg or bubble of light to surround the dreamer and maybe their bed or room. Ask your dreamer what color or colors feel right to them. One of my colleagues, Fran, puts on her protective blue-light suit each time we ventured into the field of dreams. She zips it right up as she would zip up her sweatshirt. Adding the physical motion of zipping up helps her to feel it in her physical body as well as her spiritual body. Most of us also benefit from a physical gesture or movement to fully integrate it into our being. Inhabit and invite your body into the dreamwork—it will be happy you did.

We are not limited to people or spiritual beings; we can invite animal friends and bring talismans or objects as well. Many people fondly remember a childhood pet that was their main comfort and connection, and/or a current pet that provides the same service. During the time of the COVID-19 pandemic, many previously petless people adopted animals for companionship and comfort. I have at least three clients for whom I truly believe their pets played a large part in preserving their sanity during the dark times of isolation and quarantine. Again, the safety posse can include real animals or pets and/or imaginary ones. Dreamers may dream through a totem animal that provides comfort and protection. Animal spirits can be strong guides.

We then ask if the dreamer would also like to bring any objects with them before working on the dream. Objects that have made their way into the pantheon of protection include my client Tonya's warrior's shield, Mike's special stone, and religious talismans like a cross or a chamsa. A modern-day safety object as well as a means of connection was Valerie's cell phone with all the intact features of calling, texting, GPS, and flashlight for wayfinding in the dark dream. Meagan, an enterprising twenty-something, also made sure to bring her portable charger along with her cell phone into the dreamscape. Finally, we might also ask the dreamer how old they were in the dream and get safety and protection for the youngest parts there. That may be different from what the adult telling the dream needs. Our young parts might want a teddy bear or blankie, and when working with younger children, these may be the first items on their list.

Once we have created our list of helpers and resources, we want to get as thick a description as possible of them. Getting all the details of color, shape, size, texture, sound, smell, feel, etc., make them more real and therefore more available to the dreamer. Katherine brought her mother's silver charm bracelet. Jeremy described an old iron horseshoe that he once found while hiking. He had brought it home and hung it on the wall in his garage. It was fairly heavy, really solid, and a dull pewter color with spots of rust. These details are important in order to have the object be alive and available to the dreamer, and possibly of greater significance later on when doing the dreamwork.

And finally, to complete Stage 1, we just keep asking, "Anything else? Do you need anything else to feel as safe as possible and ready to address the dream?" until we get a clear no from the dreamer. This is a crucial step and is a hallmark of both dreamwork and trauma treatment. We often can't help but feel a bit uncomfortable when journeying thorough pain and fear, but we should not feel unsafe again. We want this to be a different experience than the traumatic events. *There are no extra brownie points for gratuitous suffering.* We back away from proceeding forward to Stage 2 until the light is green. Once it is, and our dreamer says, "Good to go," we go forward to the dream.

The Bridge: An In-Between Stage

An additional step that is a bridge between Stage 1 and Stage 2 is to invite the dreamer to peek inside the dream itself after completing the external gathering of resources and scan the landscape there. The purpose is to see if there is a resource that they may have missed noticing before or had neglected to mention that is already existing in the dream. Our wise unconscious and our dream source provide us with more than meets the eye at first glance. On a second look, the dreamer may find a safe resource already there, one that can provide an even greater level of comfort and mastery than bringing one in from the outside does. Ericka did this earlier when she discovered the poncho inside her Zodiac boat that she previously had not noticed. As Dr. Leslie Ellis reminded me, it affirms their own internal healing process to find something that already existed inside themselves. We might peek in from the outside of the dream, or step inside with our other resources and check out the scene from inside the dreamscape. We might find a source of comfort or solace in a small, soft animal hiding in the bushes; a calm, serene lake that reflects a moonlit sky; or a wise elder sitting so quietly that they seemed to blend into the trees before we looked more closely.

GAIA Stage 2: Working Directly with the Nightmare

There are two options for approaching the direct nightmare work: from outside the dream or from inside the dream. Working from outside the dream, we stand back and examine the dream around its edges, asking questions about the details of the dream, clarifying the sequence of events, asking the dreamer if they have any immediate associations to the dream, and looking for a bridge to life. Is this dream connected to anything that they can recall right now? There is an element of guidance here, to be sure, as we ask the dreamer (or ourselves if we are working on our own dream) these questions, but we are not yet engaging in the practice of active imagination. That practice will allow us to interact with the dream as if we were reliving it and have the power and ability to ask questions and make alternate choices as the dream itself moves forward. This can be done more easily with active imagination style methods and dream re-entry techniques, including image rehearsal therapy, gestalt work, shadow work, and re-dreaming, all of which we will explore in depth in subsequent chapters.

In general, in Stage 2 we invite the dreamer to gather up their resources from outside and inside the dream, and then find the best place to enter the dream to do the work. Sometimes we work a dream chronologically; other times we start at the place of either the least or the most energy, either the safest or the scariest part, depending on the dreamer's sensibilities. We continue to titrate the work, using a variety of methods, often simply asking, "What happens next?", or "What do you want to happen next if this is a stuck and scary spot?", or reminding the dreamer that this isn't where the dream ended, it is just where they woke up, so they can continue to dream it forward now with active imagination. We work the dream until the level of distress is gone or very low, and the dreamer reports feeling calm or neutral.

Dreams are alive; we are not just having a dream; we are having an experience in an alternate reality. As Dorothy told her Auntie Em upon her return to Kansas at the end of her journey to Oz, "Oh no, Auntie Em. It wasn't a dream—it was a real, truly live place." We know this too, whenever we have an emotional response in or about a dream. It moves us and we feel feelings, just as we do in waking life. Our dreams are real, truly live places both while we are inside of them and as we recall them upon awakening.

In some ways, the rest of this book is Stage 2 of the Guided Active Imagination Approach. Once we have set the stage to avoid abreaction (an uncontrolled negative emotional response) and avoid exceeding the boundaries of the dreamer's window of emotional tolerance for the exploration of dark places, we can prompt the dreamer to go forward toward or into the dream. A prompt now might be, "To learn what they need to learn to serve their highest and best purposes for healing." I will go through some guidelines and protocols here, and many of the specific nightmare healing methods will be described in greater detail in the next chapters.

Summary of the GAIA Method

Use these guidelines to frame your inquiry and feel free to use the wording that works best for you.

GAIA Protocol Stage 1: Pre-Dreamwork Safety Protocol

In keeping with attention to phase-oriented trauma treatment, we first address the safety needs of the dreamer before going into the dream or nightmare itself.

1. The dreamer tells you they have a dream. You first ask if they want to share it.

2. After they share it, you ask if they want to work on it.

3. Share with the dreamer that there is a gift to be found in every dream.

4. At this time, you can ask for the spontaneous working title of the dream and the SUDS level.

5. Ask, "What do you need to feel safe and protected enough to address this dream, or this part of the dream, or to go back inside the dream?"

6. Get the details of each resource. You are guiding their exploration with your questions, but not interfering in it.

7. Keep asking, "Is there anything else you need to feel perfectly safe?" I can't emphasize enough the importance of this preparatory work. It makes the difference between successful dreamwork and an experience that can be potentially re-traumatizing. Be cognizant of the difference between "unsafe" and "uncomfortable."

8. Find out how old the dreamer is in the dream, and how old they feel in the dream as they retell it—they may not be the same. Get the protection that the "youngest part of you that is present" needs.

The Bridge

Before diving inside of the dream, you may next want to invite the dreamer to peek into their dream and see if there is a resource there that they might not have noticed or mentioned before. Often, if they look around, they find a previously undiscovered, pre-existing resource hiding in plain sight inside of their dreamscape. This step can be done from outside the dream looking in, or by gathering up the resources generated in Stage 1 and entering the dream with them to look around in the dream before doing anything else.

GAIA Protocol Stage 2: Working Inside the Dream

After completing the pre-dream preparation in Stage 1, begin the process of dream re-entry by asking the following guiding questions and offering the following guidelines:

1. What is the best place to enter this dream?

2. Gather your safety people and objects and tell me when you are ready.

3. Go ahead and enter the dream and tell me when you are there.

4. Are you ready to continue?

5. What happens first? Next? What do you want to do/say? What do you need to stay safe? Anything else? Are you ready to continue?

6. Is there anything else you need to say or do to feel complete with this part? The guide can offer ideas or suggestions if the dreamer is stuck, being sure to give them the choice to accept or discard.

7. Is there any place in this dream or part where you still feel unsafe or unfinished? Check carefully.

8. Gather up the gifts you received from this dreamwork— the words, objects, writings, and learnings you now have.

9. As you prepare to leave this dreamscape, gather your learnings in a way that serves your highest purpose and is in the service of your growth and healing.

10. When the dreamer is out of the dreamscape, ask, "What have you discovered? What has changed? Is there anything else that feels incomplete or not safe? What is the SUDS now? Has the title of your dream changed? How will you incorporate these learnings into your life today?"

Jay's Story: Setting Up Stage 1 of GAIA

What follows is an example of using GAIA to heal from a traumatic event. We will follow Jay's nightmare healing journey through several chapters from Stage 1, setting up safety through Stage 2, working first outside the dreamscape, and finally progress to guided active imagination inside the dream itself and the concurrent and subsequent healing in his daily life that occurred. As an adult, Jay had been suffering ongoing nightmares in which he relived his experience of sexual assault in college. He had managed to put the memories of the assault behind him but was retriggered years later into a nightly nocturnal replay of this trauma after being near the finish line at the Boston Marathon bombing. Ernest Hartmann and Robert Stickgold's studies indicate that this kind of unsymbolized direct repetition of the trauma is more frequently seen when there have been acute and clear traumatic events. For example, studies of Vietnam veterans show that many of the intrusive nightmares that followed the war were scenes of bombs going off, body parts, explosions, and attempts to save buddies. Trauma expert Bessel van der Kolk discussed how many of the war veterans that he treated reported nightmares to him that contained the precise unadulterated images of faces and body parts they had encountered in battle. These dreams were so terrifying that many tried hard not to fall asleep.[30] Some reported sleeping for years with a gun under their bed, "just in case."

---

30. Bessel van der Kolk, *The Body Keeps the Score: Brain, Mind, and Body in the Healing of Trauma* (Westminster, London: Penguin Publishing Group, 2015), 8–12.

As is true for many triggers that stimulate recall, for Jay the current triggering event was not directly connected with what had happened to him in the past. However, there were enough similarities, particularly emotionally, to activate the memories of that time in his life again. The waking life similarities between his sexual assault and the marathon bombing were that they were both forms of attack, they were both unexpected, both involved two men as the perpetrators, and happened to innocent bystanders. Differences are that his own attack occurred at a private indoor party and was directed against him personally, while the marathon bombing took place on the backdrop of an enormous outdoor world stage sporting event with random bystanders as the target. His assault falls into the category of private trauma, while the Boston Marathon bombing was public trauma. But on the emotional level were the selfsame feelings of shock, vulnerability, helplessness, rage, and a sense of having been in the wrong place at the wrong time.

The intensity and frequency of his nightmares began to disrupt Jay's daily life as well as his dreams. Often haggard from lack of sleep, or from interrupted sleep and terrifying nightmares, his ability to focus on work and engage with his family began suffering as well. At this point he finally told his wife about it, the first person he ever told, and began therapy. The therapy helped him to get to the needed perspective that it was not his fault, and that he had been tricked into entering that bedroom at the house party under false pretenses. He got to a level of acceptance of this concept and his sense of self blame was greatly reduced and then he ended the treatment. The nightmares had reduced in frequency to once or twice a month at that point. Then more recently, after being retriggered by seeing a movie with a rape scene, the nightmares returned several times a week. This is when Jay sought out specialized dream therapy with me.

True to form with this type of nightmare, Jay was not able to tell me much in the beginning except, "That incident keeps replaying in my sleep." Following GAIA Stage 1 protocol, I asked him if he wanted to talk more about it. He said yes but was unable at the outset to do more than say he was sexually assaulted by two men, and that was what he kept dreaming about. As I could see that he was emotionally distressed, I suggested that we back up and first set up some safety parameters for him rather than go over the details of the dream so that we didn't re-create the anxiety, depression, and helplessness that he felt both at the time of the assault and in each of these repetitive dreams. Even the suggestion brought him considerable relief, and he took a big sigh and visibly relaxed. He said that even so many years later the content of the nightmares still felt so real and present-day.

Hearing this, I suggested that the first order of business was to set up some safety for him within which to explore his dream, and to start with, to have a clear and concrete reminder of the passage of time between then and now. This is a common characteristic of trauma and subsequent nightmares—that the past and the present have become entwined, and part of the work is to untangle them. The goal for the dreamer is to make it really clear "that was then, this is now" at an embodied and emotional level, not only at the cognitive level of understanding. To help with this goal, I used a technique with Jay called the Associational Cue for the Present. I asked him what concrete, tangible object or thing, ideally something small that he could touch or hold, reminds him that he is now fifty-eight years old, and not twenty. After a bit of thought he came up with his wedding ring, which he always had on, and the knowledge that he loved and trusted his wife. This was a terrific choice for him; it hit all the criteria for this exercise. Other good choices people have used include their car keys, their diploma, and their cell phone with today's date that shows up automatically whenever they look at it. One woman said, "My hands, because I can see that they are large adult hands now, not the hands of a child." Anything that helps to ground the dreamer in the here and now of their life and has a positive or neutral association.

We are carefully titrating the work; going very slowly so as not to re-create upset. After we did this exercise, I asked him what his SUDS level of upset was, and he said it was now about a 4. Before that, just thinking about the dream he said it was an 8 or 9. Clearly this event still had deep tentacles in him more than thirty years later. He was now able to title it, simply, *The Assault*. His homework assignment was to look at his wedding ring daily, and when doing so to remind himself consciously where and when and with who he was in current time and space. That was the extent of the dreamwork for that hour—quite enough for now.

Creating a Safe Space

The next time we met I continued the GAIA protocol with him, asking him what else he needed to feel safe before revisiting his dream. Somewhat of a loner, he couldn't come up with anyone or anything else, and offered that he often felt randomly ill at ease or unsafe in his life whenever he was in new situations, as well as just before falling asleep when he feared he would have the dream again. Therefore I switched gears just a bit and worked with him to create a safe space in his mind's eye that he could bring himself to whenever he needed to, including while preparing for sleep. This visualization technique is very similar to the part of the protocol of gathering people or objects, but here we are gathering in an actual space. Again, this safe space can be real or imaginary; a place they have been or seen a picture of or read about or seen in a movie.

Here Jay shone, and immediately remembered a place he had been to many times by the ocean north of the city. Here he sat on a large rock that seemed to have a seat carved into it by the wind. He named it his Armchair Rock. I encouraged him to give it the thick description from all his senses to make it come to life now with two goals in mind: 1) To have it be right there and immediately available for him to visualize and enter, and 2) To be at least if not more real than the nightmare images. With some prompting of, "And what else?" Jay described the sight and sound of the waves crashing gently over the shore, the gentle warmth of the autumn sunlight, his comfortable running clothes and well-fitting sneakers, the salty smell of the sea, and the comfort in being alone there with no demands or schedule, stress free.

We anchored this scene by another method of trauma work called pendulation. Like the swinging of a pendulum on a grandfather clock, we swing back and forth between upsetting images and safety images, or between neutral thoughts and safety and comfort, to embed and anchor the safe space. I first ask Jay to tell me about something neutral or just mildly irritating, like the phone call he had with a client yesterday, and then swing back to the Armchair Rock and tell me when he was there. After doing this three times, Jay could easily get himself back to his rock in two or three seconds. Now we were ready to work directly on the dream. Stay tuned for the next chapter.

EXERCISE

Practicing Stage 1 of the GAIA Protocol for Safe Work with Nightmares

Think about a dream or nightmare you have had. Do not pick your scariest one. If you are aware of or concerned that you may have an unresolved trauma history, or know that you could be easily triggered, please do this exercise with a therapist or guide. Practice doing Stage 1 of the GAIA protocol. Standing back from your dream, begin to think about what you need to feel completely safe and protected before engaging directly with the dream material. You may want to get some paper or write your list in your dream journal. You may not need all of the following resources: Use what feels right to you but be lavish—don't skimp! The supply is eternal.

Ask yourself, "What do I need to feel safe enough to work with this dream?" Begin your own list of resources, perhaps starting with the various categories of people you know or know of who are in your life today, or were ever in your life, real or imaginary, from a movie, book, or mythology figure. Be sure to check that they are completely safe and protective of you, and that you do not feel any hidden pockets of fear or uneasiness connected to them. You can ask yourself, "Is this being 100 percent safe for me? Is there any reason not to include them in my safety posse?" If they do not feel 100 percent safe to you—out they go! Pick someone else.

Next see if there are animals or pets or totem figures that are available, a current one or a pet from childhood, fantastic or imaginary creatures. If you have a pull toward a particular animal or animals, look up what their meaning and purpose is in totemic or shamanic cultures to see if there are special messages for you about this/these animals. Next go over objects: What, if anything, do you want to bring with you into the dream to be safe? Choose something symbolic or practical, whimsical or magical—the sky's the limit. It's your dream and you get to decide what feels right.

Finally, if you haven't already, see if there are divine, mystical, or angelic beings or guides to accompany you. Use the names of these beings that are right for you. Place them around you in just the right location for optimum peace and protection. Surround yourself or your bed or your room with light. Feel and see it in your mind's eye, sense its warmth, and using the skill of synesthesia, feel or taste the color, the warmth, the protection inside and outside of your being. You are now ready to go toward your dream!

SEVEN

· · · · · · · · · ·

ROUND AND ROUND WE GO

Getting Off the Merry-Go-Round of Recurring Dreams

Nothing ever goes away until it has taught us what we need to know.
—Pema Chodron

You have to face your nightmares, Jack. You have to unpack them like you would open up a gift. You must take your nightmares out of the box you've stuffed them into so you can learn what are lies and what is the truth.

—*Jacqueline Edgington*, Happy Jack

Remember the movie *Groundhog Day?* In it, weatherman Phil accidently gets trapped in a time loop and is doomed to repeat the same day over and over and over again. Once he realizes this, and that there are no consequences for his actions, he spends his days and nights in various forms of bad behavior. Eventually his friend, Rita, convinces him to think of this looping as a blessing instead of a curse, and to use his prescient knowledge of each day for good instead of bad. Once he is convinced to do so, he truly becomes a hero and helps the people of the town in innumerable ways.

Weatherman Phil was stuck looping in his waking nightmare, and it repeated endlessly because he was not learning what he needed to in order to break this particular spell: Namely, to do good instead of bad, and be of service to others. This has some wisdom for us as we think about how to resolve our own repeating nightmares. When we learn what we need to learn and start to do things differently in either our waking or dream life, it resonates through the layers of consciousness to make both dream life and waking life different. We can heal from the outside-in or the inside-out. A goal for many trauma survivors is to sufficiently heal from their own pain so they can help others. A survivor's mission is often a part of the healing process. That's when it changed for Phil the weatherman too.

Repeating Nightmares: The Message to Listen Up!

When traumatic events or a childhood filled with loss or pain are incompletely resolved, our wise unconscious keeps inviting us to examine it more closely. "Look here," it says to us, "You are not done with this yet. There is more for you to know or heal or do." Even if the source of the current nightmares was years ago, sometimes when our systems are ready and our life is settled enough to handle it, these voices from the past begin to emerge and call out. If we ignore these voices, they will get louder and louder, shriller, and more insistent. That is when our recurrent nightmares get more frequent or more upsetting—they are desperately trying to get our attention in any way possible. As uncomfortable as this is, it is also a sign that our system is trying to move toward growth and healing. Post-traumatic nightmares can be a sign of a vigorous life force pushing forward to bring in potential allies of deep, powerful inner strength and resilience that need to be brought forward into consciousness. Dreaming in and of itself is a healing process—it is one of our system's ways of digesting and processing information.

Dream researcher and author Kelly Bulkeley tells us that dreams that follow a crisis do not aim to simply return the dreamer to the status quo. These dreams aim to develop a whole new understanding of the self and the world that encompasses the trauma and help the dreamer to rise out of the ashes of their broken self to find new hope, structure, and meaning for their world. Post-traumatic dreams become spiritual growth dreams when this happens. Bulkeley's statements are in line with what trauma treatment experts tell us; that resolution of a trauma includes finding a way to incorporate what happened into a new source of meaning and healing for the survivor and perhaps for the world as well. Dreams are one of our most powerful sources of meaning-making.

Our dreams can be landmarks of our internal process and they are also a source of healing and solace. An additional tenant of AEDP (Accelerated Experiential Dynamic Psychotherapy) is that nothing that feels bad is ever the last step. I love this philosophy. It reminds me of what the proprietor of the hotel in the movie *The Best Exotic Marigold Hotel* also tells us: "Everything will be all right in the end and if it's not all right, then it's not yet the end."[31]

You may recall the previously introduced concept that the dream didn't necessarily end when the dreamer woke. Sleep specialist Guy Leschziner proposes that because of the extreme emotions of some dream experiences, people wake up during their dream before being able to finish it.[32] He too believes that in these instances the dreaming process was never truly completed, and therefore the emotional memory is never fully processed. Our waking job is to then purposefully dream it forward or dream it backward to complete the

---

31. "The Best Exotic Marigold Hotel Quotes," Rotten Tomatoes, https://www
.rottentomatoes.com/m/the_best_exotic_marigold_hotel_2012/quotes/
#:~:text=Sonny%20Kapoor%3A%20Everything%20will%20be,it's%20not
%20yet%20the%20end.

32. Guy Leschziner, *The Nocturnal Brain: Nightmares, Neuroscience, and the Secret World of Sleep* (New York: St. Martin's Press, 2019).

processing. As we work on it in our waking life, we also assist our unconscious dreaming self to do its Möbius strip loop the loop into our conscious mind and back again—a full circle of healing to counterbalance the insidious looping of trauma.

We can dream it forward, adding in the active imagination techniques of Stage 2 of the GAIA method to move the action along, and we can also add resources before, during, and after the dream that weren't there in the original dream or in the original trauma. When we thus reframe the dream and/or the trauma in our current life, we are on the road to making meaning out of pain and moving toward healing. This is the alchemical process of dreamwork where we turn straw or lead into gold as we shape and reshape our understanding. Let's go back to Jay's story and look at his dreamwork.

Jay's Story Continued: GAIA Stage 2 With Active Dreamwork Techniques

Now that we have built a solid safety platform for Jay to bring with him into the dream, and to fall back on if need be out of the dream, we are ready for the dreamwork itself. Originally Jay had the same repeating nightmare over and over that recreated the scene of his assault. It was as if his brain got stuck on replay and couldn't get off this merry-go-round. After gathering up all of his allies and supports, he was ready to share his dream:

I am twenty years old and at a college party. Two guys chat me up and tell me there is something they want to show me in the bedroom. I innocently follow them in, and then they close and lock the door. One of them holds me down face-down so I can't escape while the other sexually assaults me. I try to scream but I can't.

That was the dream. It was pretty much a replay of what happened over and over again, like in *Groundhog Day*. His SUDS level was usually a 9 or 10 in this dream. It seemed that there had not been any consolidation or digestion of this experience to help him move on or get some distance from it. Our first step in Stage 2 of GAIA was getting this dream/event spoken out loud. Now there were three people who knew about it: his wife, his first therapist, and me. We talked about why he never told anyone after it happened, and Jay said that he felt too ashamed and embarrassed, and thought that people wouldn't believe him. The secondary trauma of being alone and without support added insult to injury, which probably contributed to why it remained so entrenched years later and contributed to his suffering as well as his pain. At first I just stayed with Jay on the level of the dream itself and gave him support and kudos for his bravery for sharing it.

This is a great, and in this case literal, example of a dream where we know the dream hadn't ended when the dreamer woke up. The dreamed event was as alive as if he was still twenty years old, but we know that more than thirty years had passed since it happened. The next dreamwork step was to encourage him to dream it forward, to upgrade the operating system, if you will. Jay liked this metaphor; he is a computer guy. This is a form of image or dream rehearsal therapy, whereby we help the dreamer to add or subtract or change up some part of the original imagery, and then practice or rehearse it to embed the new images into the neural networks to replace the old ones.

"What happened next?" I asked. When Jay answered that nothing did, I reminded him that right here and now, he was not still in that room at the college party, so something must have happened after the assault. After touching his wedding ring (his associational cue for present time), thinking about his wife, and re-accessing his safe place of the Armchair Rock, he was slowly able to talk through the rest of that evening that was not contained in his original dream. Jay said that after the assault the men left the room, and then he got up and went out of the bedroom. He remembered feeling weird and spacey (he was probably dissociated) and left the party. I asked again, "And then what happened?" My goal with this simple question is to get him to retell the story onward without my interfering in his own sequencing until he finds himself in a safe space at the end. He replied, "I go back to my apartment and take a shower and go to bed." At this point I asked if he was now safe, and he said, "Yes." Okay, so now the dream has a different ending, one where he is safe in his apartment rather than the dream ending with him being assaulted as it had been for years. Checking now, his SUDS level was down to a 6. When I asked what that number signaled, he said that he felt more distant from the event now and that it helped to remember that he did get safely home that night. It had receded in his mind, but he still struggled with the feelings of isolation and shame.

Over the next weeks and months, we continued to work with this dream and with the practice of the image rehearsal therapy that had started giving him a new perspective on time. We added dream re-entry work using the Guided Active Imagination Approach, and now in the dreamwork Jay imagined himself yelling at the guys, "What do you think you're doing?", calling out for help, and getting a few good punches and kicks in before they left. He began to feel more empowered and less like a victim. Even his very logical mind, which initially said that it didn't really happen like that, got on board with the imagery work. So even though it didn't happen like that then, it does now, and that was helping him feel better. Go Jay! He also began to think about who he might have been able to tell then if he could have and came up with a good buddy that he trusted to believe him. Imagining telling this friend helped ease some of his aloneness and set the stage for him to actually start telling others in his current life. His isolation and his shame with this secret had been contributing to his being stuck in the trauma loop. Here was a chink in his armor to start opening his world.

At this point, in between his nightmares of this assault, Jay also began having other dreams as well. His nightmares of the assault lessened, and when he had nightmares, many were much more metaphoric, rather than a simple replay. This too was progress, as the event became more distanced for him. His dreaming brain also distanced it by now providing him with the event in metaphor fashion. One dream was of an evil, giant supercomputer brain that was sadistic with humans and saw them as lab rats to play with. (We can see the veiled metaphor here of the assault where sadistic beings played with him.) We stay inside the dream to do the work here and let the imagery and plot twists of the metaphor seep its way into the cracks in his psyche that they need to do their healing work. In my own mind's eye, I imagine rain gently falling on a parched desert, seeping into the cracks in the dry ground until they are moistened, nourished, and ready to support new life.

His goal in this new dream was to get the codes and the hard drive to make the evil super-computer brain stop. He explained the details of this to me in a much more technical manner that was, as I said to him, "beyond my pay grade," but I understood enough to get the gist of it. With this dream, in addition to connecting with his previous resources, Jay used more active imagination to add a top scientist engineer to his dreamscape. "A young hacker-type" was his choice, who headed up a hidden underground bunker to do the lab work to create new software that could be a counterforce. The underground bunker (much like underground dreamwork) provided the safety they needed to keep the counterterrorist work a secret until it was ready to launch.

Working through this dream in active imagination, Jay used his own strengths, organizational skills, and knowledge of computers to team up with this young hacker, insert the new program into some software, and disable the malware. Again, I don't understand all the details of how to do this, I am just reporting his work here, but the point is that *he* does. That's his own empowerment. At the end of this new waking version of his dream, Jay said that he programmed a special program that would keep looking for evil malware for infinity and shut it down before it could do any other damage in the future.

After this enormous piece of work, Jay gave a big sigh and said that he felt so much relief. What put a bow on it for him was the knowledge that he created a new world where he didn't have to do it all by himself—he could access and receive help. This was exactly in-line with healing his feelings of isolation, and he started talking about collaborating with others now. He decided that his waking dream task would be to seek out other men who were also survivors of sexual assault and join a support group. He was delighted when I told him that he had now joined the pantheon of heroes who save the world from evil, and a great smile crossed his usually taciturn face.

When elements of our trauma dreams begin to combine with other non-traumatic dream imagery, we know that deep change is at work. Some of Jay's subsequent dreams were other nightmares to work through, but some were not nightmares anymore. At first he was not writing those other dreams down, or even reporting them to me until I asked about it one day. He said that he thought that the goal was just to work on the nightmares. I replied that actually that was only half of the goal. If he was now having other dreams as well, particularly if they were not nightmares, that was a great sign that his system was processing the assault and healing. There was now some space for other things in his dreaming mind. This is a truth for all nightmare dreamers: Record not only your nightmares, but your non-nightmare dreams as well.

Tracking Your Progress with Recurring Nightmares

Catching our non-nightmare dreams as well as our nightmares is part of how we track our progress. The ability to mark our progress is one of the many reasons to keep an ongoing written record of our dreams. If we don't, we will miss these signs of movement toward healing and growth. And anything that lets us know we are making headway in our healing journey is worth celebrating. I encourage keeping a dream journal in writing, whether by hand or online. This allows you to better go back to review and catch the themes and signs of progress you may have missed had you not written the dream down and reread it.

I frequently ask my clients to notice the first small sign that something is different, or that they are responding to something differently. This micro-attention creates the building blocks for mindfulness and healing. We have to stop and quiet ourselves to notice the still small voice of spirit and light within, our unbreakable soul connection to the best parts of ourselves and the Divine, however we understand that concept. These first small signs can take the form of a thought, an emotion, or an action. The same stimuli may prompt a different action response, a different way of thinking about the event, or a different emotion. For example, Joan noticed that she no longer had such a big startle response when someone touched her. A survivor of childhood abuse, she had learned to be hyperalert to any unexpected touch. Both in her waking life and in her dreams, she began to gradually experience a sense of greater calm and centeredness. A landmark of progress for her was when she reported that when her partner touched her shoulder in her dream, instead of jumping and screaming as she usually did while both awake and asleep, this time she leaned into the touch and smiled.

Signs of healing to pause and give a round of applause for in our dreams and in our life include having fewer nightmares and experiencing less distress when we do have them. We want to appreciate when the SUDS level goes from an 8 or 10 to under 5, and eventually to 0 or 1. The change might be incremental or a sudden shift. The dreamer can also report feeling more distant from the events in their nightmares and moving from being an active character in the nightmare to the observer stance. That is from, "I am in the dream experiencing the events" to "I am watching the action take place in my dream rather than participating in it." This outside observer stance gives us more distance from the dream actions, something very desirable if it is a nightmare.

When the dream is a literal traumatic replay type of dream, like Jay had been having, a sign of progress is also to have the imagery move from a direct replication of the trauma to metaphorical representations, and to begin to have non-nightmare dreams about other topics that indicate feelings of strength, empowerment, safety, and delight. Sometimes this progression happens organically on its own, and other times you will need a guide or a group of dreamers or a therapist to offer suggestions, ideas, and prompt your waking self in the direction of healing as you do the waking dreamwork. As the title of this chapter indicates, you will then be able to get off this particular merry-go-round. When our creative dreaming produces safe images that are no longer fraught with fear, these new images begin to take hold in our brains and minds and begin to supplant the original fear-based memories. We are able to grow new neural networks in our brains to supplant the old ones—this is part of the essence of the concept of neuroplasticity. We used to think that our brains stopped growing in childhood; we now know that we can grow new connections and prune away old ones that no longer serve us throughout our lives.

Here are two of Jay's more recent dreams that indicate this healing trajectory, and then we'll look at some recurring dreams and themes of other dreamers.

> *I am running in an obstacle course event. The marshal tells us that the next part of the race is down in a subway. I enter, and it is dark and scary and there are two big holes to get past. Someone tells me to go through the smaller, narrower one, but I panic that I could get stuck in it. Instead, I decide to take the bigger one that I have to swing out on a rope over the platform to get to. It worked and I safely run up the stairs and feel good.*

Jay has several takeaways from this dream. First, even though he has to go down into the dark subway to complete his race (down into his dreams and psyche?), he is able to get safely out of this subterranean spot on his own before the dream ends. This dream contains an obstacle course race, and we remember that Jay's trigger to his dark memory place was that he was running in the Boston Marathon when it was attacked. The second takeaway is that he can trust his own judgment about which course of action to take and made the right choice for himself: Personal empowerment. He chose the route that seemed best to him, not what someone else told him to do. (Remembering his initial trauma where he innocently followed someone else's directive.) He felt almost giddy as he safely swung over the big hole. Third, he got out of the dark underground place and finished his race. We hadn't titled the dream at the outset, but his title after working it is *The Only Thing We Have to Fear is Fear Itself.* Nice.

The final dream of Jay's that we explore has a different tone altogether:

> *I am in a neighborhood where there is a lot of construction. After each day of work the builders organize pallets of the finds from tearing down the old structures first. I am going through the rubble; it is really cool to make these discoveries from another century. I want to remember them, so I call out loud the names of the things that I discover, then make signs for them, and describe it to someone else so I will better remember them. I am so excited to find an old butter churn.*

He titled it *Discovery.* This is a dream of a different color! Here are some of Jay's takeaways as we process his dream. Even though the neighborhood is getting stirred up, it is for a good purpose and the deconstruction is leading to new finds and new construction. He is rebuilding his neighborhood and his psyche. Each find is given a place by the builders on a pallet, on a safe resting place. In his dream Jay uses several skills and tools to remember things: naming them, having a tangible sign, and describing them out loud to another person. Dr. Daniel Siegel, trauma and mindfulness expert, tells us that to heal, "We need to name it to tame it."[33] The old butter churn he finds is a valuable and useful item. Finally, he reflects that even though there was a lot of construction, things are organized and in control and he finds value in going through the rubble. We didn't parse out what the rubble meant as a metaphor, nor who the build-

---

33. Bruce Freeman, "Name It to Tame It: Labelling Emotions to Reduce Stress & Anxiety," OralHealth, May 3, 2021, https://www.oralhealthgroup.com /features/name-it-to-tame-it-labelling-emotions-to-reduce-stress-anxiety/.

ers were. Staying inside of the dream lets us follow the story his psyche was telling him without overexplaining it. Same with the churn. Though it occurred to me later that his dreaming mind picked out such a great choice with this find within the rubble that was being organized and sorted through (great metaphor for therapy or dreamwork). Although things were being churned up in this work, and churning milk takes a fair amount of effort, the end result is sweet butter.

And finally, Jay reported to me last week that he had the dream of the assault again, but that he felt very far away from it as if it was happening to someone else. If you recall from the introduction, I asked and answered the rhetorical question, "How do we know when we have resolved the issues that are contributing to our nightmares? The short answer is: When the scary dreams stop, or we feel at such a great distance from them that they no longer have an upsetting emotional impact."

In this dream, Jay had the disembodied perspective of a witness, not an actor, and it had no emotional impact on him other than a bit of intra-dream lucidity where he realized that he was dreaming but it didn't upset him at all. We call this kind of dream a confirmatory dream, meaning pretty much just what it sounds like—a confirmation of healing.

Jay now articulates a waking life goal of helping other young men who are survivors by being a mentor, or at least an ear to hear their stories so that they are not alone. By churning up the dream rubble of his past hurt, he can now begin to pay it forward to help with the healing of others, churning up sweet butter. And not only is his SUDS level now a 0, but the emotions he reported with this dream are those of curiosity and excitement. Healing is also about finding purpose, often from the depths of the pain, and Jay's dreams helped lead him to a sense of purpose. He is living up to the dream healing goal we articulated earlier of making meaning out of chaos, hope out of despair, and a forward-moving life force out of the depths of darkness and sorrow.

Frequently Seen Nightmare Themes

There are many common themes in recurrent nightmares. Although the final meaning of the dream is always with the dreamers themselves; because we share DNA and we all have physical bodies that house our spirits, we also resonate similarly to certain life events. It can be comforting to know that when we wake with our hearts in our mouth that the dream we just had of falling or being buried or chased is a universal response to certain emotions, and not necessarily a premonition of our own imminent demise. I imagine that visceral reactions to traumatic events are cross-cultural as well, although the metaphors they are expressed in can vary according to social norms and languages.

For those of you who speak more than one language, think for a minute about how you might express the same idea in different languages. Do you dream in different languages? One of the hallmarks for learning a new language really well is the ability to dream in it. I'd love to see a study on this somewhere. Emotions are universal as well but may be expressed more or less overtly depending on the cultural context. For example, Mediterranean cultures typically are more emotionally expressive, while Northern European cultures are typically more emotionally contained. Dreams express our core concerns in both direct and metaphoric images. The following are some common nightmare themes in Western cultures. We will take a brief look at some of them here, and then expand on the themes in the context of the dreams of several other dreamers.

Dreams of Chase: We are running away from someone or something. Ofttimes the pursuer seems to be gaining on us. (Remember

Dina's dream of being chased by the giant?) We can ask questions of these dreams such as, "What are we running from in our life? What is chasing us?" The GAIA method teaches us to first ask who or what do we need to be safe enough to turn and face that which is chasing us to glean the messages they carry.

Dreams of Being Trapped: We are buried alive, or our leg is caught in a trap, or we can't move because something large is upon us, or we are imprisoned or drowning, as in my original dream of trying to swim up from underwater. Various forms of sleep paralysis are one aspect of this theme. Ask yourself where in your life you feel trapped, suffocated, or buried alive. We will examine Samantha's dreams shortly that contain these themes, as well as the next theme of wild animals.

Dreams of Animals: A dream of an animal may range from wonderous to terrifying. We may interact with our totem animal guide to the spirit world, our beloved pet, or be set upon by wild beasts. The wildness in us or in others may take the form of an animal, for better or worse. We can ask ourselves, "What is a tiger?" or "What is the tiger part of me that is chasing me?" Wildness might be a positive or a negative; we might need to slightly turn the dream kaleidoscope to see it in a different perspective. We can also turn to many resources on animals as metaphors or guides to see if the associations ring true for us. If, for example, you dream of being strangled by a boa constrictor, look first at your own experiences and associations for snakes, and boas in particular, and then see if shamanic, mythical, or biblical references ring true for you as well (e.g., snake as a rebirth image as it sheds its skin, as the tempter to evil in the Garden of Eden, or of infinity, like the ouroboros endlessly swallowing its own tail).

Violence in Dreams: Is someone you love, or you yourself, in danger of being hurt in the dream? Jennifer, a member of a dream circle, dreams over and over about children being hurt in a variety of ways: shot at, kidnapped, and strangled. Often she is charged with saving them in her dreams, and when she can't, it is her worst nightmare. How many parents among us can identify with that? And whether or not you are a parent, what is it about your inner child that needs rescuing or healing? Helene had a violent and gory dream of a mother who killed her children and held up a severed head, and then simultaneously stabbing and being stabbed by her husband.

Sickness or Injury: Dreams of various body parts being injured or diseased are common nightmare themes. A first course of action may be to get a good physical exam where you are sure to mention your dream concerns, even if you feel foolish. So many dreamers have reported that their dreams were their first order diagnosticians for a variety of illnesses that would have progressed had they not listened to their dreams, especially the reoccurring ones. By listening to them they caught the illness in an early stage. Once you have clarified, either with your medical provider or with your own inner wisdom, that this is not a diagnostic dream, look for the metaphors in your life. Attend to puns or plays on words, such as "choking on something" or "frozen in fear" or "brokenhearted" or "sick to my stomach."

Losing Things, Including Wallets, ID, Teeth: Loss is ubiquitous to life. To be alive means that we lose things small and large—our glasses, our car keys, our innocence, our identity, and ultimately our life and the lives of others we know and love. Dreaming of losing things can tap into this theme of loss. In your loss dreams, the emotions can range from mild annoyance to panic—one is an unpleasant dream, the other is a nightmare. Notice the emotional narrative that accompanies your dreams of loss to ascertain what it might be related to. What losses are you experiencing or anticipating in life?

One interesting note about the theme of losing teeth: It often seems to represent a developmental life passage, as we gain and lose teeth at nodal moments of change in our lives. (First growing our baby teeth and losing them as we enter latency years and grow our adult teeth; getting our wisdom teeth, usually in adolescence; and losing teeth again as we age.) Each movement forward in our development also contains inherent losses. Judith Viorst wrote a book with the powerful title *Necessary Losses* on this very theme.

Disaster or Apocalypse: This theme has always been with us, but it has risen to new heights of dream disaster with the Covid pandemic and the concomitant social and political unrest. Harvard researcher Deirdre Barrett collected a whole compendium of COVID-19 related dreams. Tore Nielsen, professor of psychiatry at University of Montreal, calls it a dream surge. Terms such as coronavirus dreams, COVID-19 dreams, and quarantine dreams have been regularly occurring on social media and in the press. Dreams of disaster and apocalypse tend to surface during times of global, national, or personal, persisting crises. As we learned in the PARDES method of dream layers, one or more layers of a dream may have to do with the collective psyche, not just our own. Dreams are multi-purpose—your disaster dreams may reflect both your own life, and what is happening in society around you.

Monsters, Vampires, Ghosts, and other Beings from the Beyond: We've heard the expression "the devil incarnate." Sometimes that devil or his ilk show up in our dreams as well. All kinds of supernatural and religious figures may haunt our dreams. Mostly they are our own biggest fears incarnate, not an actual devil or supernatural being. Ask yourself what is haunting you, sucking you dry, or even bedeviling you. In addition, you may be carrying the energies of some unfinished business of your ancestors whose stories are still haunting you either energetically or through your very DNA, as is the case in epigenetics.

Depending on who or what showed up, you may also want to examine your own spiritual belief systems, what you have been taught as a child, and whether or not those beliefs are still true for you now. If, for example, the "fear of God" was ingrained in your early upbringing, do you need to upgrade your belief systems now to see the Divine as a healer or nurturer or beloved, as the spiritual poets Rumi and Chefetz have done? Finally, whether you believe in being haunted by dark energies or not, having a ritual to clear the air and clear your dreams from them can be infinitely helpful and comforting. If these beings showed up in your nightmares, they need some kind of attention. We will examine a variety of rituals for clearing and healing in our final chapters, but for now, burning a bit of sage in the room, or lighting a candle with the intention to bring light to dark places and clearing out any unwanted energies that may be lurking can be a good start.

Recurring Dreams in Metaphor

Now let's look at several other recurring dreams that did not begin as replay of trauma but started out in their own metaphoric, dream-ish language.

Example 1: From Trapped to Loved

Samantha frequently dreams of being held down, trapped, stuck, or buried under something. Her dreams come in several variations of this metaphor. Let's look at three of these dreams:

> **Dream 1:** *I am trapped in a room with a large lion laying on top of me. It is terrifying. I need and want to get up and go, but I am afraid that if I move I will disturb the lion and he will attack me. So, I stay very still; it seems easier to just do that.*

Dream 2: *I am in a narrow, round space that is beneath ground—surrounded by dirt walls—almost like a vertical tunnel. It feels like some kind of kiva. I am on a ladder that reaches out of the space through a small opening where I can see the daylight from the sky above. It is the only way out of the cave. Above me on the ladder is another woman, and she is climbing very, very slowly. I start to feel claustrophobic; I am sweaty, feeling panic... I want her to move faster so I can climb to the top and get to the fresh air and light. My heart is racing. I am so mad that she won't move faster. I am terrified and uncomfortable and angry and feel out of control.*

Dream 3: *I am told that my daughter has to go to a psychiatric hospital without my knowledge or consent. When I protest, they say that I have to be hospitalized too. I try to protest, but they are not having it. When I start to take a walk around a beautiful pond that I see on the hospital grounds, they tell me that walking is not allowed, and I have to stay confined to one bench. I become very agitated at this point and start screaming ferociously and freaking out in a way that I never experienced in life. My body is shaking and sweating. I become aware that in the middle of this fury that it feels good to be so angry and I am actually impressed with my own ability to rage so loudly. I could stop if I wanted to at anytime, I am actually in control of it even if it doesn't look like it. Inside of the rage is a core of calmness. This feels like a big discovery. Then a staff person offers me use of a phone although it is against the rules. Her name is Pranja, which is the name of a friend of mine. This feels like a sign from the universe that things will work out okay. I give her a big, melting hug.*

In this series of nightmares, we see three differences from Jay's series of dreams. One, these are all metaphorical, not a replay of anything she literally experienced and two, they present a series of different images and narratives. Third, they occurred over a series of months, not years. For Jay, one of his biggest changes was when the replaying of the trauma dreams changed into metaphors, but with Samantha the dreams start out that way. While her dream stories are all different, the emotional story line is similar: Samantha is trapped underneath a lion, she is trapped again underground in a kiva. In the third dream she is not under a wild animal or underground, but she and her daughter are being held against their will and trapped at the hospital. In this final dream, she becomes enraged and feels some power in her anger. We can see her progress with this entrapment dilemma as the dreams unfold. In the first dream she is trapped, immobile, and frozen in fear under the lion. She chooses to simply stay there quietly, "because it just seems easier to do that." In her second dream she is no longer frozen, and at least attempts to get out of the underground kiva but doesn't succeed before waking up. In her final dream, the entrapment in the hospital is not physical, but real nonetheless, and now she rages against the injustice and feels some real power in her anger. By the end of this dream, she is even given the gift of contacting the outside world by a helper.

In this dream progression, Samantha's own psyche is moving to greater health and empowerment. In waking life, she is the mom of a teenage daughter. As everyone who has been in that position knows, it is all too common to feel like you are losing your sweet, little girl overnight as they hit about eleven or twelve years of age, and you begin to feel trapped by the hormonal beast that suddenly emerges in her stead. (If you are not a parent, can you remember how you felt about your mother at the age, complete with eye-rolling and embarrassment about how she dressed or ate or breathed?) Samantha also struggles with her daughter's very real health issues and how to respond to them, fearing that making the wrong move could evoke an even worse response (like under the lion where not moving felt the safest choice).

However, she also has a supportive community of friends, relatives, and professionals around her. Her hard wiring for healing is kicking in as the dreams progress. Her wise unconscious is strengthening her and offering options with each successive dream. She makes more and more progress and discovers hidden resources in herself with each dream. In Samantha's first dream, she is still trapped under that lion when she woke, frozen in fear, afraid to move or risk being attacked. We work with this dream with some strong embodied dreamwork in chapter 9. After doing this piece of dreamwork, in the second dream she is trying to get out from underground, but she is blocked by the Slow Woman. (We'll look at her again too. Shadow sides can show up in a variety of forms.) At least she is not frozen and immobile anymore and is trying to move up and out. By the end of the third dream, even though it is still clearly a nightmare, she is empowered by her own anger and is getting assistance from a caretaker who broke a rule in order to help her by offering her a phone to connect with the outside world. She also notices her "core of calmness" inside of the anger, a remarkable discovery that indicates to her greater control and an ability to think clearly on the inside even when her outsides were not calm. Samantha later told me that she looked up what *Pranja* meant, the name of the dream staff member, as well as her friend in waking life. It turned out to be a Buddhist word that translated as wisdom, intelligence, or understanding. What a lovely synchronicity. No coincidence here that her dream offered her this name-gift of a helper or ally to access the powers of using her own wisdom as well as the powers of connecting with others to get assistance.

An additional final dream in this series is as follows:

I am back in the kiva again. I am still trying to get out. That Slow Woman is still blocking my way. This time though I hear some music and the chant, "... You are loved, loved, loved by unending love..." I don't know if I actually hear the music from outside of me, or from within... the way a song pops into your head. But it literally feels as if the music is expanding my lungs, and the panic leaves my body. I very quickly feel expansive and calm. Nothing has changed, I am still in the cave, the woman is still ahead of me on the ladder... but I am relaxed and at peace and realize that I am fine as long as I keep singing that chant and remembering that I am protected and connected to infinite space, breath, and life force. In the dream I am aware of how amazing it is that the song can change everything, and I am now content to be where I am.

I trust that with this knowledge and the song of being loved, that Samantha will climb out of the kiva when the time is right and into the light that she glimpsed in her first kiva dream. For those who may not be familiar with the word, a *kiva* is a Hopi word for a circular ritual space dug out from underground. It is used for a variety of ceremonial purposes, and is often associated with rebirth, as the person re-emerges from underground having completed the rites. We could ask Samantha what she is being reborn from and into as she climbs out of this kiva. And since we know there are issues surrounding her daughter, how does that relate to her daughter's rebirth or issues in her life? How does the knowledge that she is loved by an "unending love" help in her own peace and comfort and her daughter's as well? This is one of those signs of PTSG— post-trauma spiritual growth. Samantha wrote at the end of her final dream of this series that she felt content to be where she was as long as she remembered that unending love. This speaks to trust as well, trusting in both the power of the universe as well as trust that things will come to completion in the fullness of time. Among her ways of working in the world, Samantha is a hospice worker, and has become more and more comfortable with the cycles of life and death as she helps to midwife souls over the divide. She recognizes what the fullness of time means in a different way with this work and knowledge.

Example 2: "I Don't Fit In and I'm Not Good Enough Anyway": Mothering the Child Within

We'll now look at another dreamer's recurring dreams. A colleague of mine, Bonnie, has repeating, bad dreams of being left out, marginalized, and unprepared. The heading here was her original dream title, *I Don't Fit In and I'm Not Good Enough Anyway*. In each of these dreams she feels that she doesn't know what to do, but that everyone else does. The dreams are always set in a professional conference or retreat setting and always contain the emotions of embarrassment and some level of shame. Although a good therapist, one of her main stumbling blocks is her lack of self-confidence. The dreams highlight her feelings of being unsure, less than, and inadequate compared to everyone else at the conferences.

> **Dream 1:** *I am at a conference held at a summer camp and learning a new therapy technique. Everyone seems to master it faster than I can. I am afraid that no one will want to work with me on it. I worry that I have paid good money for this, and if I can't get with the program quickly, I will lose out.*

> **Dream 2:** *I am at a retreat center in the woods. It is a spiritual retreat, but I can't focus or meditate and wonder what's wrong with me.*

When I asked her how long she had been having these kinds of dreams, she replied since middle school, about age eleven. That age clearly pre-dates her professional work, so it added another layer of information to the etiology of these dream themes. Her psyche has decided that now is the time to bring them forward to heal both from the more-recent feelings of inadequacy at work, as well as their deeper source in her childhood. The emotions of feeling left out were there since childhood, and the dreams of her younger self were also often set at summer camps. Bonnie then shared that she was sent away to overnight summer camp for an entire month at age eleven and felt left out the whole time there. "I was way too young for that," she reported. "It was all just too much for me." Her belief was that she was sent away to camp because things were getting so bad at home with her alcoholic parents, and that was when her mother "went off the deep end." How they picked this camp she'll never know, because she was a "northern, working-class girl brought up Catholic" and the camp was in Virginia and full of "rich, snobby southern girls" who rode horses and shot rifles, neither of which Bonnie had experience nor interest in.

Dream 3: *I am away at a professional conference site. I have been given a role in a play, but I am very nervous about performing. My best friend Mary Anne from college is there too, and she is a better actor than I am. I can't find her to eat lunch with though, so I have to eat alone and feel left out. After lunch I am given my costume of a pretty, flowing white gown. Then a young teenage girl who is also in the play is very upset. I give her a pep talk and help her put on some lipstick. It helps her feel better. Then the lipstick slips and leaves a big red splotch on my white gown. I try to get it out but can't. I am able to cover it up with another part of my costume though.*

I feel embarrassed that the gown isn't pure white anymore, but Mary Anne downplays my pain and is self-absorbed with her own role.

Bonnie titled this dream *Another Embarrassing Disaster* and her SUDS level of upset was a 7 out of 10. She said that it was "so typical" of her to mess up, or to have something go wrong with the physical details; that happened all the time. When I gently inquired about whether anyone had ever suggested that she had ADD, she responded, "Obviously, I can never finish anything." We worked on this dream for a while, and Bonnie said that her friend Mary Anne was very dramatic. While they were close, she also had a paradoxical relationship with her because both Mary Anne and Bonnie's mother were overly emotional and tended to hyperbole. Bonnie always sought her mother's approval but rarely got it, or even her attention. In the dream, Mary Anne was self-absorbed and ignored Bonnie's distress. There was an "aha" moment when Bonnie recognized that her friend was a stand-in for her mother, and that not having her mother's attention and approval was a constant source of pain in her life that interfered with her own sense of self-worth. That "I'm not good enough" theme had been following her since childhood.

After gently challenging this belief system, I pointed out that her true worth was not something anyone else could evaluate, and that her "off the deep end" alcoholic mother probably wasn't the best source of accurate feedback on her competency or skills anyhow. Using the GAIA method, I asked Bonnie who she might like to have on her support team to help shore up her sense of self-worth and stand up to Mary Anne in the dream. She replied that she'd like to have Marcel Proust and Albert Einstein. Interesting choices. She chose Proust because he was "a smart, deep thinker and excellent writer" and Einstein because "he was brilliant and went his own way even if others didn't understand his ideas, and because he kept God in the picture too." Bonnie's faith was important to her as well. She added that she would also include the best parts of her husband when he supported and encouraged her. With this support team, we went back to the dream.

I now notice with her that in the dream she helped the teenage girl who was so distressed. In both dreamwork and trauma work we work with parts of ourselves. Using the Gestalt perspective, every person, as well as everything in the dream, can be viewed as a part of ourself in dreamwork. A therapeutic technique designed by Richard Schwartz called IFS, Internal Family Systems, does much the same. It primarily focuses on the parts of ourselves that may have become separated out from our inner core of wholeness of Self with the capital "S." Dissociated or unwelcomed self-parts in this system are called exiles; they are frequently young child or adolescent parts that have been shunted away. Other parts of our psyche that show up to try to protect or defend us in some way are called managers (the parts that control or maybe keep others away) or firefighters. The firefighters are the big guns of addictions or self-harming behaviors whose parts believe there is always a conflagration to put out, so big firehoses of addiction or raging are called upon. This is a very simplified version of this system; the bibliography contains further reference. Bonnie is trained in this method, so she was right on board with examining the dream in this way.

In her dream, Bonnie's good mothering part could mother the teenage girl part of her, even though it meant giving up being perfect, having a perfectly unstained white dress. With this mother's strength and courage, we reframed the red stain from the lipstick into a badge of honor, a battle wound that she could wear with pride instead of shame. When I asked whether her title or SUDS level had changed, Bonnie said that she now saw the original title in an ironic or funny way instead of as devastating. Her new title is *This Is How You Learn*. The SUDS had gone down from a 7 to a 4. There is still more work to do for Bonnie to find her approval within instead of holding out for her mother's or a mother substitute, but this is good progress.

Example 3: Snippets of Silence:
Finding My Voice and Connecting the Past and the Present

To see how even a snippet of a dream can be repetitive and lend itself to healing, let's look at Robin's years of mouth dreams. These dreams centered on her mouth being stuffed up or gagged and/or her inability to use her voice. These recurring dreams began years ago, prior to her participation in the dream circle. When she could remember her dreams at all, she dreamt that her mouth was filled with taffy, and she couldn't speak or even swallow. Sometimes her tongue was literally tied in knots in her dream. How literal can we get? We can imagine even without too much information that she had difficulty speaking up for herself in her life and felt tongue-tied when she tried.

Later in the group Robin told us that she had grown up with a chronically depressed mother who was periodically hospitalized. Robin spent her childhood trying to be good and quiet to not upset her mother, while inside she was often seethed with anger, fear, and grief. As an adult, Robin was kind, polite, fairly soft spoken, and admitted to being conflict avoidant. She still kept her thoughts and feelings inside, not wanting to stir up potential trouble. In dream group, we explored with her possible connections between her tongue-tied dreams to both her current communication style and to this history with her mother. Both resonated with her as relevant.

Connecting the Past and the Present Through Dreamwork

This is one key form of dreamwork intervention: the creation of insight and connection between the dreams and life, both past and present. The bridge to life here connected Robin to her current relationships, especially to people in power, and her relationship with her depressed mother. These childhood patterns now manifest in adulthood. She recognized the ingrained pattern of keeping quiet as a child to protect her mother from upset, depression, and even hospitalization and her own conflict-avoidant stance as an adult in a variety of situations. The recurring dreams were of a gagged mouth, not being able to use her voice, or on occasion even open her mouth all the way. The taffy (a childhood candy) was blocking her way. Her "aha" was to understand the symbolic content of her repeating dream themes as connected to both past and current life.

Initially that was all she could remember of her dream life. The dream group spent weeks and months working with this snippet to try to help her pull out the taffy, freeze it so it would break into pieces that she could spit out, or try to chew or swallow it. During one meeting we had Robin use her hands to physically pull the imaginary dream taffy out of her mouth. When we asked her what she would say once she could speak again, she was still speechless, but said that she would probably just yell. At some point Robin started to tell us that she was doing just that—in her dreams. Her husband woke her up several times a week telling her that she was screaming out loud in her sleep. No words, he said, just a guttural kind of animal yelling. Although this was progress from being completely silenced, it did interfere with both her own and her husband's sleep.

One day Robin reported in group that she was betrayed by an old childhood friend. When Robin had to leave the friend's celebration early to go to a previous engagement on the same day, the friend wrote her a nasty breakup letter ending the years-long relationship. Robin was both hurt and enraged. She didn't remember any dream content after this event, just the feelings of the rage and betrayal that she knew were connected to this recent life event. She named these feelings out loud as she reported the story to us.

Soon Robin began to remember more of her dreams and didn't always tell us that she was only bringing "just a snippet" to group. She recounted to us a dream of her overbearing and pushy boss. In the dream her boss was asking her to perform a great many tasks way above and beyond her job description. In the dream, Robin felt angry, but only made some small peeps to protest. In dream circle, we asked her what she would have wanted to say to her boss in the dream conflict. Her first thought was that she wanted to say "F...k You" to her. Robin shocked herself but also enjoyed her out-of-character response, this time in waking life with forethought and malice! We helped her make the bridge to life after getting this off her chest by asking if there was anything slightly less inflammatory she might like to say in waking life the next time her boss made unreasonable demands on her beside a "little peep."

After several weeks of working on this dream theme, Robin reported two things: One, that she felt more empowered and safer to speak up at work, and two, that her husband told her recently that she has been waking him up at night not only screaming but also swearing in her dreams. From no voice to a big angry one, announcing in no uncertain terms another part of her processing. This became the next layer to address.

A few months ago, Robin made the enormous decision to retire early and leave her workplace of twenty years—a big "no" to feeling silenced and unappreciated. There were many things that she did like about her job; the work itself was a calling for her in life, and she had made close connections with many colleagues and families she worked with there. It took her several months of processing and thinking about it, but when she did leave, she was celebrated and appreciated for her years of service. In her appreciation for the dreamwork and the dream circle of support, she told us, "I couldn't have done it without you guys."

Example 4: Packing Up the Boxes

Finally, for our last dreams in this chapter, let's examine recurring dreams of boxes and drawers and packing. My client, Susan, has been having recurring anxiety dreams about boxes; packing and unpacking them. In her dreams she is sorting through what to keep and what to discard, but the boxes kept coming back in dream after dream. Every time she thought she was done, another box appeared to be dealt with. On one level these dreams were obvious: Susan was in the process of moving from her home of twenty years to take a new job in another state. She was moving from the city to the country as well. At sixty years old, this was to be her last big job, the pinnacle of her professional career. Susan was literally going through twenty-five years' worth of accumulated belongings and paperwork to prepare for the move. As she was doing so, she was also rereading her old journals, which were stirring up difficult childhood and teenage memories. As we talked about this, she realized that in both a literal and metaphoric sense she was reconfiguring her whole life now.

Her partner was joining her in this move. They had been having serious ups and downs for several years, but they both wanted to commit to this new lifestyle and to their relationship. In addition to the boxes of housewares, books, and clothing, Susan was sorting through old patterns of behavior that interfered with her relationship with her partner Karen. She had been identifying, working on, and trying to discard those reactions and responses that no longer served her, such as a quickness to anger and judgment, for quite some time.

At the time of the packing dreams, she had already figured out how the echoes of her childhood defense systems interfered in her relationship. For Susan, the fight part of the fight or flight syndrome had served as a protection not only at home but on the playground as well. That was her contribution, if you will, to some of the difficulties in her relationship. Her memories of these fraught periods of time in childhood were retriggered as she read through her old journals as she packed. Once this deeper layer of the dream boxes came to light (this was the Drash, the pursued layer of a deeper history), in her next dream she saw a pile of boxes taped up and on the curb, ready to be loaded into the moving truck. She was much clearer on what she was bringing with her, and what she was leaving behind. She could now sort out the time frame of "that was then, this is now" that is so crucial to healing from the pain of the past.

Not all recurring nightmares are trauma based, even though they are still upsetting. With the same images of packing and unpacking in her dreams, this time of dresser drawers, my friend Colleen came to a very different realization. Her recurrent nightmare healing process was pretty quick. She dreamt of trying to pack up her children's clothing and give it to them over and over. "Take this, don't forget this," she would call out to them in her dreams. She worried that they didn't have what they needed for whatever the outing in the dream was, whether it was rain boots or snowsuits or bathing suits. Her children were now adults, and she hadn't packed them up in a long time, so this was a conundrum to her. Her SUDS level was about a 4 or 5—upsetting, but not terrifying. With a few questions we figured out that her "baby," now 28 years old, had just moved out for what she thinks is the last time, and moved across the country from Boston to California to work in the hemp industry. He had been in and out of the house for a few years, but her sense was that this time she and her husband would really be empty nesters. No more packing up her children for her.

She practiced a few affirmations before going to sleep, such as "My children are safely grown and can care for themselves now" and "I have parented my children well and they are capable adults," which served to simply extinguish these nightmares in short order. For Colleen, there was not a deeper trauma to unravel here, rather a coming to terms with a normative life stage, albeit with its sense of loss. She could also look to the joys as well as the sadness in being done with this active stage of parenting. Colleen and her husband had been taking adventure trips without their kids for a few years now, and she is looking forward to just packing up her own bathing suit or skis more often as time goes on.

To review, our nightmares repeat like the revolving days in *Groundhog Day* when there is something recent, historical, or both that we have not yet understood, resolved, or transformed. Sometimes recent events also trigger past events, and the two time frames become entangled in the threads of the dreams. That is when we need to be sure to use the PARDES method or other ways of attending to the multiplicity of dream layers to dig deeply beneath more than one surface. Sometimes our nightmares reflect life-threatening events that happened to us ourselves, or life-threatening events we have witnessed happening to others, both part of the definition of trauma. Trauma is also subjective: What is experienced as traumatic to one person may not be experienced as traumatic to another. The reasons can be as varied as the availability of support systems, whether the survivor is able to access them, how others respond to the trauma, how old the person was when the event(s) occurred, their own personality and coping style, and their innate ability to make meaning and to take action after the trauma.

EXERCISE
Identifying and Tracking Recurrent Dreams and Themes

Take some time to sort through your dream journals to identify your own recurrent dreams and themes. You might decide to highlight or color code different themes or images to make them easier to find. What do you notice? Do you have the same dream over and over, or recurring images in different dreams? Are the dreams different but the emotions the same or similar? What are they? Take a moment and list the emotional narrative that repeats in your dream stories. Are your recurring dreams pleasant, anxious, or terrifying? Are you angry, sad, afraid, or frustrated in your dreams?

Once you have identified the images, people, landscapes, story lines, or emotions that recur, do you have any immediate associations to them? Is there a bridge to life that you can identify in your current life or in your history? Are you frequently dreaming of lost keys, lost wallets, lost passports? Is there a place or landscape where you feel anxious that keeps recurring? Do you notice, for example, that there is often a dark shadowy figure in your dreams that is threatening you, even though the specifics may vary from a strange woman dressed in black to a masked marauder to a man standing in the shade of a tree? What ties these three disparate images together for you? Is it your emotional response to them? When you are ready, take the dreamwork to the next step and ask yourself or your dreaming guides or dream sharing posse to help you to cast a wide net of associations to see what you may pull in. Cast this net wide at first. You can let the ideas that don't resonate sift out later, but don't discard anything that is connective until you've examined it.

Remember that repetitious bad dreams or nightmares are there for a reason; there is something you have not yet sufficiently resolved or understood. Getting to the bottom of it will not only give you more peace in the night (to say nothing of your partner if you are a dream screamer like Robin was), but also give you directions for healing the past traumas that pop up in your dreams so that you can find new meaning, take the right action steps, and make your own gold out of straw.

EIGHT

• • • • • • • • • •

SHADOW WORK, NIGHTMARE FIGURES, AND BEFRIENDING THE FEAR

People will do anything, no matter how absurd, in order to avoid facing their own souls. One does not become enlightened by imagining figures of light, but by making the darkness conscious.

—Carl Jung

We penetrated deeper and deeper into the heart of darkness.
—Joseph Conrad, Heart of Darkness

"Who knows what evil lurks in the hearts of men? The Shadow knows!" This is the memorable and somewhat-creepy tagline from a long-running crime series radio show in the 1930s and 40s hosted by Orson Welles. While I don't think that Orson Wells was a scholar of dreams or of Jung, I think he hit the nail right on the head with that tagline. The Shadow character on the show had the power to hypnotically cloud the minds of those near him to make himself invisible.

In dreamtime, our Shadow figures are often the parts of ourselves that we would rather not encounter or don't want to admit

163

to having—those that we have made invisible. These dissociated or shut off parts are invisible to the naked eye unless we have plumbed the depths of our psyche and examined our nightmare figures to find their bright sides. The flip side of a shadow is light. Only when the sun shines do we have a shadow, so in our work with the Shadow and scary figures in our dreams, we need to remember that behind them is a source of light and growth just waiting to be discovered.

When any powerful aspects of ourselves are not allowed expression, they may come through in our dreams as something that is pursuing us or endangering us in some way. While our personal shadow sides are not necessarily evil, they contain knowledge that is unintegrated, hard to own up to, and as Jung said, "The thing a person has no wish to be."[34] They may also represent from a more positive perspective our instinctive selves, our animal natures, and our creative impulses. Once we explore and find out what is hiding inside our shadow dream characters and give them voice, we can resurrect the value they hold.

In this chapter we will take a look at how the Shadow and other scary or dark figures show up in our dreams, where they may come from, and several ways to work with them. Our Shadow may also be the parts of ourselves that we were criticized for when we were children and have come to believe are unacceptable or wrong. If you were told that it was weak or unmanly to be gentle and nurturing, then you may have sent that soft side of yourself into the shadows. If you were told that your enthusiasm was too loud, or too much, then you may have sent your exuberance or passion into exile. These exiled parts then contain pieces of the essential and positive essence of who you are and will need to be integrated for you to feel whole.

34. Joana Bértholo, "The Shadow in Project Management," ScienceDirect, Elsevier, March 29, 2013, https://www.sciencedirect.com/science/article/pii/S1877042813004369.

If you were ever considered the black sheep in your family, then you probably have sent some of those parts underground in your psyche in order to try to fit in with your family. When strong or powerful aspects of yourself are squelched and not allowed expression, they often come through your dreams as something that is pursuing or immobilizing you. Healing can come from compassion and forgiveness first for yourself, and then with an additional understanding and compassion, for what your parents' and ancestors' traumas are that contributed to them silencing parts of you.

Jacob and the Angel: Shadow Wrestling

The failure to recognize these hidden parts of ourselves and the potential consequences for this have been in our world from time immemorial. Most cultures have sacred text, myth, or fairy tales of dark forces lurking, threatening to overtake us. In Western culture the Genesis story of Jacob wrestling with the angel is often understood as a Shadow encounter. Jacob, as we remember, is not only one of the esteemed patriarchs, but he has his own darker Shadow side as well. He cheats his brother Esau out of his birthright blessing as first son by lying to his father about his identity. He does this by covering himself in the mantle of a hairy goat (Esau was hairier) to trick his blind father into giving him the blessing. Later on, after this is discovered, he is on the run from the potential wrath of his brother when he has the encounter with the angel. In Hebrew, however, the word that usually gets translated here as angel is *"eesh,"* which simply means *man*. The identity of the angel is deliberately left ambiguous and is the subject of voluminous commentary. Jacob wrestles with the *eesh*/man/angel throughout the night, and as dawn breaks he receives from the angel a wounding, a blessing, and a new name: Israel, which means God-wrestler.

Was this night wrestling an encounter with an aspect of the Divine, or a dream? The idea of God-wrestling in the night is now a part of biblical scholarship and Western society. T. M. Lemos, a biblical scholar, hypothesizes that Jacob was afraid and wrestles with his personified fears all night long. Rabbi Klitsner, another biblical scholar wrote, "The things that you're wrestling with are the things you've relegated to darkness. You can wrestle with things in the dark, but when the rise of dawn comes, that enlightenment is the most threatening part of this…Our ways of prevaricating, of lying to ourselves or deceiving others don't withstand the light of day." Lemos adds, "[The story] gets at the difficulty of reaching transcendence and reaching understanding. It's not arrived at easily…And even in our moment of victory, we are just left limping toward transcendence. We are still wounded."[35] This work of wrestling with our own souls, or our darkness or a fallen angel is not easy. Shadow work can be challenging, and even leave us wounded (the wounded healer Chiron is a common archetype). But limping or not, reaching toward transcendence is a worthwhile struggle to engage in if we are reaching for our own fullness.

We can engage in this shadow work both with our own dark dreams and demons in the night as well as on the transpersonal and mythic level of society wrestling with its shadow. Sharing these struggles helps to heal the wounding and turn our faces toward the sun again. We are story-telling creatures, and telling our stories helps both us and others to understand and connect. Let's take a brief look at the societal or collective level before turning to the personal layers in our own dreams.

---

35. Sean Foley, "Jacob wrestling his 'angel' is our own struggle," CBC Radio, CBC, September 17, 2019, https://www.cbc.ca/radio/ideas/jacob-wrestling-his-angel-is-our-own-struggle-1.5285823.

The World Shadow

The unintegrated and projected hidden facets of ourselves account for much of the racism, xenophobia, antisemitism, and prejudice in our world. Our own dreams can reflect this layer of the world shadow, especially in the fourth layer of inquiry, the secret or "sod" layer in the PARDES system that we explored. This layer of buried secrets often reflects the transpersonal and larger societal layers of our dreaming psyche. When we do our own personal work, we are also lessening the likelihood of projecting our pain and suffering onto others. War, crusades, slavery, and violence in all forms have some of their roots in our collective unintegrated and unacknowledged shadow sides.

Some of the depths of the shadow as the Devil archetype on a transpersonal level can be witnessed as large-scale events such as Nazi Germany or the killing fields in Cambodia, and in America, the displacement and destruction of the Native American culture and the implementation of slavery and its maintenance with the Jim Crow laws. Looking at the rise of the Black Lives Matter and Me Too movements, we see society taking a look at its shadows of racism, sexism, and oppression. While the phrase "Me Too" was coined in 2006 by Tarana Burke, a social activist and community organizer, it really became known in 2017 as her hashtag took hold. Our society began to limp forward and take a closer look at its underbelly, naming the abuses, and making attempts to hold offenders accountable at a time when violence against oppressed or marginalized peoples was on a rise.

Sometimes the inner and outer shadow collide in our dreams. My friend Stefani accidently discovered several years ago while she was doing some ancestry searching that her family had a history as southern slave-owners. That new information provided her with an additional perspective on her years of dreams of entrapment, dark figures, and dream characters in chains. Stefani is very active in social activism and social justice, and I can always count on her to offer this perspective to the discussion of a dream. Recently she has had several dreams featuring coffins, one where a coffin was in her hotel room, and another where there was a narrow black rectangular box with five white balls inside of it. On exploration, it turned out that her father had five siblings, and that a few of the southern cousins were racist. One turn of the kaleidoscope on these dreams is that Stefani is working to put to rest the legacy that these five white balls from her family lineage represent. And while it is never comfortable to sleep in a room next to a coffin, there are epigenetic pieces from her history that she does not want to just banish or ignore. Since she didn't want to look away or ignore this history, it didn't feel right to her to remove the coffin from the room when this option was suggested while doing dreamwork. Instead, in group, we helped her to wrap the coffin in layers of energy protection, at least for the time being. Not out of sight or out of mind, she won't bury the coffin or the past, but will continue to address this side of her family history while staying protected by layers of light and energy.

The final association on these coffin images was that of another black box, in this case Pandora's. After Pandora opened it and loosed into the world all manner of evil, sickness, and pestilence, the thing that remained at the bottom after she slammed the lid back down was Hope. This part of the story often gets missed in modern retellings, but it is perhaps the most important part. Hope contains potential, options, and the possibility of redemption.

The Black Lives Matter movement exploded during a time of global pandemic. It seems that both as individuals and as a culture we try to ignore our darkness for as long as possible, often until the emergence of such times that the Shadow within collides into the Shadow without, and then it finally rears its head, roars, and demands to be seen and heard. As we explore shadow sides and dark characters in our dreams, it is important for us to remember that while the word "dark" has been misused as an insult, the word itself is neither good nor bad. It is just the other side of light, and we need both to be whole. We can reclaim it for the good in our shadow work and remember the necessity of seeds needing darkness to grow, and for the butterfly to emerge she must first spend time in the dark of the chrysalis. Because of our language and culture, we often don't dream in "politically correct" images. Honoring the personal and global work that is being pointed to when we dream of a dark or black character, Rumi tells us:

> "No matter how fast you run, your shadow
> keeps up. Sometimes it's in front!
> Only full overhead sun diminishes your shadow.
> But that shadow has been serving you.
> What hurts you, blesses you. Darkness is
> your candle. Your boundaries are your quest."[36]

When the sun is blocked, we get a shadow. The more the sun is blocked, the larger our shadow. But when we have a shadow, once we have examined it, we are free to turn and face the sun. Seeing our shadow gives us contrast and depth perspective. Without it, all is flat. With it we are able to better discern boundaries and contrast and edges.

Our Personal Shadow

Bridging the connection between Rumi's poem and a dream, let's return first to Jeanette's experience. We met her in chapter 3 as she struggled with the reactivation of the trauma of her child's suicide

---

36. Jalal ad-Din Rumi, *The Essential Rumi, trans. Coleman Barks* (San Francisco: HarperOne, 2004).

and her lack of family support while working in the ER during the Covid pandemic crisis. The negative belief systems she developed because of her personal traumas were that she was all alone and that no one would help her.

Using a form of EMDR, her therapist invited her to find an image where she was searching or looking for something or someone. After a period of silence, this rather left-brain and imagery-skeptical doctor said, "I am in a moonlit desert, alone, looking for something." When her therapist suggests that she look to see if there is any movement there in the desert, if can she see anything moving, Jeanette replies, "I can see my shadow. The moon is really bright, it is behind me now, and I can see my long and large shadow. Somehow seeing it helps me to feel more oriented, I can tell directions now and see which way to go."

Quite literally, her wise unconscious brought her this image of her Shadow. When she saw it, and faced it, she was more oriented even though she was still in the desert. Facing and addressing her shadow in this dreamwork allowed her to be more oriented to life than at any time since her daughter died. After this piece of waking dreamwork, Jeanette shared that several years ago she had driven alone through Death Valley in Nevada, contrary to the advice of her friends. Pointing out that she made it through the valley then, and therefore could now as well, was almost unnecessary. But articulating out loud what we are thinking or feeling is an important part of dreamwork, so naming that served to underline for her that she was now more oriented to moving forward. It also contained a wordplay to her ability to access faith, as in the reference to the lines from Psalm 23, "Yea, though I walk through the valley of the shadow of death, I fear no evil…"[37]

---

37. "Psalm 23," Bible, King James Version, BibleGateway, https://www.bible gateway.com/passage/?search=Psalm%2023&version=KJV.

The Bright Side of Darkness

Jungian dreamworker Richard Wilkerson recognizes that the Shadow can rob us of our strength and vitality and can show up in our nightmares as a frozen, speechless, or immobilized character as well as a pursuer. Sometimes that dark character who visits us in our dreams represents our negative disowned self-parts, but it may also be pointing the way to the glowing and positive parts of ourselves that we have become disconnected from. We need to reclaim these parts as well for our wholeness. As Rumi just told us, darkness can be our candle too. For example, in a recent dream of mine:

> *I am being kissed by a handsome, dark-skinned man at a party. We are both a little surprised and a little embarrassed but enjoying it. Later I learn that he is very smart but only has a formal education to fourth grade.*

In this dream, my "dark man" part is all about embracing my creativity and my passion, even my passion for writing about our nightmares. An important layer of our dreams, including our shadow dreams, usually reflects something that is going on in our waking life. When in doubt about the meaning of one of my dreams, an astute member of my dream circle always knows to inquire of me, "Could this dream be related to your writing?" and she is usually right. At an additional layer of this dream, I am being reminded to appreciate multiple intelligences and ways of being smart in the world.

One of my clients, Dannielle, who in her sixties and single by choice, dreams about lying in an embrace with a very dark-skinned man. She reported that she felt such a strong energetic connection with him that she was convinced that she had met her soul mate. Together we gave him the moniker of her "bright shadow" man. When she is struggling with her personal demons, remembering to re-embrace this bright shadow man in her mind's eye helps her to re-embrace those dark, bright shut-out parts of her soul that keep her connected to the world.

Shadow traits, then, are not equivalent to so-called bad traits. The shadow is the light, the dark, the left-behind, what is yet to come, or simply the unknown. The shadow may be a personification of everything about yourself that you have rejected, been embarrassed of, or denied about yourself, or perhaps never even knew was there. It is often more difficult to recognize the golden aspects of our shadow than it is to come to terms with our dark sides. We can get trapped in our shame and guilt, or conversely be terrified of our own magnificence.

Peter Pan takes the risk of being seen or even caught when he enters Wendy's room one night. He has inadvertently been separated from his shadow when the window was closed on it. (He was at the window in the first place to listen to bedtime stories. We really need to hear our own stories and the stories of others to be healed and whole.) Peter knows that he cannot live without his shadow and slips inside to reclaim it. He sadly finds that soap is not sufficient to stick it back, but after Wendy sews it on for him he is overjoyed to be reunited with it. He needs his shadow to be whole.

In one more mythic twist, all the main characters in *The Wizard of Oz* fear that they are missing a most valued part of themselves. Their shadows may be the fears of what they think they have lost. Each of them may also be representative of the parts of ourselves we need to be whole: our Scarecrow thinking self, our Tin Man feeling self, our Lion courageous or action self, and our Dorothy self that is always oriented toward returning home. Toto, perhaps representing our wise animal instincts, pulls back the curtain to reveal the meek little man standing behind it, pretending to be "The Great and Powerful Oz." His great and powerful blusterings from the throne that his projected visage sits on is revealed to be nothing more than that: a sound and light show with no real substance. The balloon-traveling professor got stuck in Oz too, and the wicked witch (another shadow figure) has prevented his return home. Like a seed underground, the shadow contains our potential. If neglected, our hopes, our dreams, and our capacities for creativity and growth can show up as shadow elements.

When the Family Shadow Intrudes

Sometimes it is old messages from childhood that cause us to disown or cut off a part of ourselves. "Nice girls keep their mouths shut and their legs crossed" was a message that Renee got from her mother and others in her family growing up. Consequently, she was not only fairly subservient in her marriage, but felt cut off from her sexuality and feminine power. This is what ultimately brought her into therapy. As her history unfolded, it emerged that her mother had been sexually abused as a child and passed on that legacy to her daughter in messages to be afraid of her womanliness. That shadow of her mother's trauma had been hanging over her head all her life. As we previously learned from trauma therapist Daniel Siegel, we "name it to tame it."[38] After naming this shadow from the past that was not her own experience, Renee began moving forward much more quickly in both in her dream life and in her waking life. This epigenetic piece of her mother's history had made it way under her own skin and needed to be compassionately banished.

Here are a few examples of some of the ways our shadow can show up in our dreams. We will then double back to look at various modes of working with them in the next piece. Joy has a two-dream miniseries: In the first dream she is shot by a shadowy male

---

38. Bruce Freeman, "Name It to Tame It: Labelling Emotions to Reduce Stress & Anxiety," OralHealth, May 3, 2021, https://www.oralhealthgroup.com /features/name-it-to-tame-it-labelling-emotions-to-reduce-stress-anxiety/.

figure outside on the porch; in the second she is shot at but not hit by her brother in the front yard. The following week Joy dreams a third dream of an epic battle with a dragon. She is not sure yet if the dragon is fighting with or against her.

Lorraine dreams that she is exploring outer space in a spaceship. When she peers through the telescope on the ship, she sees an enormous brown monster and is terrified. Upon questioning, she associates it with Sasquatch or Big Foot, a wild man monster from the snowy hills.

Helene has a bloody dream involving beheading; there are several shadow figures and dark ghosts in her dream.

Liza has recurring dreams about driving in pitch darkness without her lights on. In earlier dreams she is terrified and in danger, and in a subsequent dream she meets a guide. In Liza's dreams the shadow is not a dream character per se, but the darkness of the unlit night itself.

Previously in chapter 7 we met Samantha, who had recurring dreams of being trapped. In one dream, she was thwarted and prevented from emerging from the underground kiva by a very Slow Woman who was up on the ladder ahead of her. This Slow Woman, while neither dark nor particularly scary, is also a shadow figure that is preventing her from emerging from underground. Not coincidently, Samantha has a history of having difficulty making decisions. She has been slow to move forward or make decisions in parts of her life for fear of making the wrong choice. Her emerging power is around engaging with her anger and speeding things up. She had drifted in her life before, held back by this Slow Woman part, until now when her ability to access both her anger and her faith helped her to move forward more swiftly.

A dream colleague of mine, Jason, was haunted by a dark force of evil in his dreams off and on since childhood. When he consulted with a psychic about it he was told that it represented an old family curse about generations of tragic men in his lineage, as well as having some transpersonal connection with current events. (Here is another example of a multiplicity of dream layers being simultaneously true.) The psychic reading resonated strongly with him; that dark force that had seemingly attached itself to him had been around him for a very long time. He first met it while in middle school, and it returned on and off since then and felt quite threatening. There had been periods of time in his life where the Tragic Man archetype won out and he struggled with drinking and with much loss. We all look for Spirit however we can find it, and sometimes it seems that the only place we can find it is inside of a bottle. Jason has been doing his own "reverse the curse" work in dreamwork and personal work for some time now and is on a healing trajectory. When Luke Skywalker finally removes the mask of Darth Vader, he finds that behind the mask is his own father, his own ancestry. The masked or buried parts of ourselves can remain unconscious for years or even lifetimes until we are ready to turn and face them. They are a part of us though. Jason has been clear for a long time that, "The buck stops here."

After hearing Jason's dream story, I had a dream of my own that night about a dark force showing up.

> *I encounter a dark, evilly laughing entity. Luckily, I have some degree of lucidity and know that it is not my Darkness. I just keep sending it back to the light over and over again. Finally, I wrap myself in my rainbow tallit (prayer shawl) for protection and that seemed to do the trick for me. This time when I sent him away, he didn't come back.*

I later told Jason about my dream of his dream, and that for me the tallit was a symbol of being wrapped in protection. The rainbow is the sign of the Divine promise after the Great Flood that the world would never again be destroyed, a sign of redemption. I also let Jason know that I am happy to share my tallit with him! After I told him about my encounter with his dream shadow, at first he was worried about me; that his family curse would somehow attach itself to me. I was able to safely assure him that I didn't feel endangered or threatened by it, mostly intrigued by the clarity I had that this was not my dream. It was enough for me to be aware of keeping my own protections up. I think that it was our close connection around dreams and dreaming that had me resonate with his dream, and perhaps even to dream through some protective energy or options on his behalf. My version of his dream has not returned, so I feel that I am on the right track. We can remember what Jung tells us, "How can I be substantial if I do not cast a shadow? I must have a dark side also if I am to be whole."[39]

Befriending Our Shadow Parts

Now let's double back to the shadow dreams not yet parsed out and explore various ways of working with scary or shadowy figures in dreams. We'll start with Joy's dreams. In the first dream Joy reports:

There is a dark shadowy man standing at the sliding glass door on the back porch. He has a gun and fires at me, and I am shot.

She then wakes up feeling very anxious. Joy has done enough dreamwork over the years to begin to engage with this character on her own when she was not able to fall back to sleep. (Who could easily fall back to sleep after waking from a dream where they were shot?) Joy decides to use active imagination and engage with the

---

39. C.G. Jung, *Modern Man in Search of a Soul* (Eastford, CT: Martino Fine Books, 2017).

character to have a conversation and get more information. Here is what Joy wrote: "I can't go back to sleep, so I decide to have a conversation with the man to find out who he is. At first he tells me that he is my fear of death, but then he says he is Fear personified. I try to banish him from my home. He retreats as far as the porch, but he won't leave completely. I turn on all the lights and shut the door. I feel somewhat better knowing that the lights are on, and I have shut the door, even though he is still on the porch."

A few days later Joy brought the dream to her therapy. Together we use an energy therapy method called Boundary Balancing to strengthen her boundaries against Fear. It consists of tapping on the central meridian over the sternum while repeating out loud an affirmation of boundary strengthening. I will describe the method in detail in chapter 9. After doing this, Joy used the method each night before going to sleep and found that it "... transformed my relationship with Fear so that it is not so immediate."

Here is her second dream in the series, which is a week later:

I am in the kitchen and my brother is in the front yard. He has a gun and is shooting, but not at me. I am afraid that I may be hit by a stray bullet though. I see bullet holes all around me on the walls. Two of my oldest friends come over then and I say to them that there is a lot of anger in my brother to do that.

Joy reported that this dream was not as scary, nor as directly a personal threat. She compared the two, saying that in the first dream she was shot by a shadowy stranger, and in the second it was her brother, someone whom she knows and loves who was shooting blindly, but not at her. In addition, in the second dream she had two close friends show up as allies. The first dream was about raw fear personified, but she recognized that the second dream was more about anger. Joy said that it represented her own progress in dealing with her fears and anger about the rise in antisemitism, racism, and the existential crises of COVID-19. She moved from raw fear to outrage. We then figured out that the "brother part of her" in the dream was their shared anger at losing their sister at a young age to cancer. She still resonated with the feelings of how unfair it was that her sister died so young, and that she was also currently grieving for the losses from COVID-19 and violence against people of color or different religious belief systems. Her past and present grief is still there and still real, but not as threatening now. Dreamwork can't dissolve the pain of current real-life events, but it can give us tools and perspectives to deal with them.

When Joy works on her third dream the following week, the dragon dream, at first it seems to be a dangerous figure: a fire-breathing dragon. After engaging with it though, it becomes clear to her that rather than Fear personified, as in her first dream, this dragon is a new guide and ally for her, one that can breathe fire to protect her and her village. Her fear and anger of the first two dreams have been transformed from gunshots into a fire-breathing dragon ally that she can even ride on the back of. It told her that its name is Mirth, reminding her of this quality as a resource as well. How fitting that this dragon is a part of her as well—her own name is Joy. She can now be a protectress. Nightmares transformed can indeed become a source of healing and empowerment.

From Wild Man Monster to the Divine Feminine

Lorraine dreams of exploring outer space in a spaceship along with another woman, peering through a telescope and seeing a large brown monster like Sasquatch right outside the window of her spaceship. When she first looks through the telescope he seems big and hairy and quite scary. In reviewing her dream, she free associates to him from the safety of the ship and feels that he is more a wild man spirit animal than monster. When we look up the reference, we discover that the Sasquatch, or Yeti as it is also known by, is a symbol of courage to stand up for yourself, a truth discerner, and allying with him allows one to cloak oneself in invisibility when needed. If you follow in the footsteps of his big feet, it enables you to go outside of your comfort zone and walk in these big footsteps. These associations feel right to Lorraine as she is beginning to embark on her own exploration of the inner and outer space of her early life history of trauma, as well as the epigenetics of her family history. Her abusive and narcissistic grandparents, who suffered their own traumas escaping from violence in their country of origin, then parented their children—Lorraine's parents—from these broken and fearful parts of themselves. This is the emotional landscape she is moving more fully toward as she feels safe enough to navigate it.

What a great therapy dream—I loved the metaphor. She is safely ensconced in her spaceship, along with another woman (possibly her therapist?) exploring outer and inner space. As we continue with the dreamwork, I invite her to dream the dream onward in waking dreamtime, "... in any way that feels right to you." Lorraine decides to lie down on the floor at this point to meditate on the dream character. Through the magic of Zoom, I stay in touch with her as she peers through the dream telescope lens from the safety of the spaceship. I suggest that she could adjust the lens if she would like, to see if she gets any different perspective when doing so. To her surprise, after adjusting the lens, she reports that the monster is glad to see her. She then leaves the spaceship in her waking dream to follow in his big footsteps on a long trek to a cave set far away in the snowy mountains. When the going gets hard for her, the Sasquatch offers to carry her. He lifts her up in his arms and carries her to his cave. Once they safely arrive, Lorraine discovers that he is a she with large breasts as she offers to nurse and suckle her.

Here Lorraine encounters another part of her own shadow self—the cut-off Divine Feminine that can both nurture and be powerful in its own right. The Sasquatch then offers a gift to Lorraine, a glowing ball of light. She places it inside of her heart, saying that this was the light of her female self that she had shut out of her heart in the pursuit of her career. Together with Sasquatch, Lorraine walks about the womb-like cave, feeling that the vulnerable part of her is now protected with this internalized feminine light source within her heart. She tells me that she can feel a fierce protecting female strength that also allows her to have compassion for herself as well as her ancestors, and that she now feels much more ready to embark on the journey of uncovering her own traumatic past. As an aside, at the end of the session Lorraine tells me that she has been doing puzzles during the pandemic, and that she sees puzzle making as a great metaphor for attending to the little details that make up the big picture, just like deep dreamwork.

Blood and Gore: Step by Step to the Gift Within

In this chapter on nightmare Shadow figures, this next dream is perhaps the most graphic, so put on your seatbelt. In order to highlight this complex dream, I am sharing the dreamwork in dialogue form. I will also address my choices of dreamwork method so that you can distinguish the variable use of different methods at various choice points. Not a simple dream, this piece of dreamwork took up the whole of our therapy hour.

Helene dreams the following:

I am an evil mother married to an equally evil old man, and the two of us are at war with each other, killing off each other's children from previous marriages. I see sliced-up body parts all over and am holding up a bloody severed head. My husband and I are now entwined in an embrace while we stab at each other at the same time. He dies; I run, terrified. The maid stops me and holds up a video of me killing the children. I am enraged and chase her to try and get hold of the video.

Let's take a deep, cleansing breath after this dream. Here's the background information so you can contextualize the dream and the dreamwork we do on it. Helene's only brother was an addict who died in a car crash; she is now in her early thirties. As an adult, Helene struggled with her own addictions to alcohol but primarily to food. She is a beautiful and very large woman. She recognizes her own self-sabotage with her weight-loss struggles as she lives alone with her beloved cat, and so is solely responsible for bringing the wine and unhealthy food into the house. When she had this dream, she had recently ended abusive relationship with her alcoholic partner who punched holes into the wall when he was sufficiently drunk and angry.

In response to initial questions, here is what Helene had to say about her dream. She titled it *The Apartment* and said that the setting was her current apartment. She identified the worst part of the dream as the stabbing, and she said that she could still feel the dread and terror in the pit of her stomach when she recalled it. Working with the GAIA method, I ask her if she needed any additional resources on board before we deal with it. Helene responds, "No, I have you, and my mom. I just don't want to feel this way. I'm ready, all set."

Me: "Since you said that the stabbing part was the worst, do you want to start there or somewhere else?" (*Sometimes we start at the* *worst, and sometimes titrate the work and creep slowly up to the hardest parts with gentler aspects of the dream.)*

Helene: "Yes, there. Slicing into someone's body means that the death is not quick and painless."

Me: "Are you sure you don't need any other resources before going in here?" *(Never hurts to double-check, particularly with violent imagery!)*

H: "No, I'm ready." *(Okay, ready is ready. I also don't want to get in her way, so I trust her.)*

Me: "Does that sound or feel familiar to you in any way in your life, since it seems to be set in the present time in your current apartment? *(Attending to setting and time for the context of the dream.)* That sense of slicing into someone's body, even not with a knife?"

H: "Yes, the weight-loss issue. It feels like I would be losing parts of myself if I lost weight, even though I want to do it. It is certainly not quick or painless." *(Notice here that she repeats her exact wording as she connects the dream with the problem.)*

Me: "So, you associate the slicing/killing part of your dream with literally losing parts of yourself if you lose weight?"

H: "Yes. That's so gross, but I have been so overweight my whole life, so it's like a part of me now, like children are. It's not quite so bad when I think of the dream this way. Wow. *(She laughs.)* My imagination must be really active, probably because of all those Stephen King books I read."

Me: "Ready to move on?" *(We have an hour to get through as much as possible, so part of me is also monitoring the time.)*

H: "Yes."

Me: "What part next?" *(Note: I am trying to follow her lead with these questions, while at the same time checking in on her "window of tolerance" for the emotional aspects so as not to allow her to become overwhelmed by the narrative or the emotions.)*

H: "The man, the villain."

Me: "What are your associations to him?"

H: "He is like Tony Soprano, a mob boss, a sociopath, a gangster, a powerful alpha male who cheats on his wife. He's like my brother who cheated on us all with his addiction, and my ex who is even larger than I am and could be really scary when angry."

Me: "Wow, that's a lot right there. Does that description remind you of any parts of yourself as well?" *(I invite the Gestalt method in here to get the fullest picture, and also because she already identified that self-parts were an important aspect of this dream.)*

H: (Immediately.) "Yes, it's the addiction part of me too—I'm trying to kill off the addiction part of me and any future it could have in my life, like my children. Holy cow, I never thought of that!"

Me: "Good for you—that's a big insight. Where do you want to go next?"

H: "To deal with the maid. By the way, I just told my mom and three of my closest friends last week about my food addiction. It felt so good to finally name it out loud, but it is still new to me to name it at all. So, the maid is a servant, an underling; she sees everything but usually stays silent. She has this kind of quiet power and knows how to use it. In the dream she betrays me and caught me red-handed." *(Notice the double entendre here: red-handed also referring to bloody handed.)*

After a bit more discussion we move into some Gestalt work using two chairs. I ask Helene to invite the maid part to sit in the other chair while Helene dialogues with her. In response to her questions to this dream-maid, Helene tells us that the maid is the Scared part of herself, the part that is afraid to fail at losing weight. The tape that the maid has contains the evidence of her "misdeeds," like buying wine and junk food that she can't afford. I invite her to talk with this Scared part and invite her to also remember that she said that this maid part has, "A quiet power that she knows how to use." (*Here I am actively inviting in the light side of this shadow that she glimpsed in her telling about the maid part of the dream but isn't connecting with right now.*) Helene acknowledges that, and now adds that this was also the part of her that can't be bowed down, that is strong, courageous, able to confront power and addiction, and knows that she won't fail in the end.

H: "The tape contains the memories of my addiction to keep me on track with sobriety."

Me: "The memories of the way you've betrayed yourself in the past." (*Here I am jumping the gun a bit and making an active bridge to life connection for her since our time is almost up for the day.*)

H: "Yes, that's right."

Me: "So the maid's role is to keep you honest. She has it on tape so you can't lie to yourself. And a maid is here to serve you—she can help you with this issue. What is the gift that you take out of this dream?"

H: "The knowledge that my addiction is not in control anymore, it can't kill me. And that the tape is old school—we don't even use tapes like that anymore, so I can upgrade to a CD or streaming and let the tape be a thing of the past."

Me: "Powerful work here, Helene! The gift in a dream is not always fun or pleasant, but it has something to teach or remind us of a new resource for us to use."

Helene's parting statement of the day was, "This dreamwork is like giving birth—so much came out."

We covered a tremendous amount of ground in this hour, and the work continued in subsequent meetings as we used this dream as a springboard to also examine the multiple losses in her life. We also doubled back later to work on the image of the severed head, like the Gorgon Medusa from Greek mythology. Medusa, the snake-headed one, had the power to turn the viewer to stone. She was finally slain by Perseus who used his gift of Athena's shield to look at Medusa only in reflection, and thus be able to behead her. Helene could relate to having self-parts of both Medusa and Perseus. Her addiction froze her growth and turned her to stone, and she became immobilized in the face of it. Her strong persevering part (maybe that word has its root in Perseus?) could behead the monster with a creative non-direct attack, like Perseus' reflecting shield. Years later I got a birth announcement from Helene, letting me know that she had married the man she was dating when she ended therapy, had a new son, and had graduated with a counseling degree and was working in the field helping others. I was so glad to hear from her, and that her past was no longer killing off her present.

Light in the Darkness

For our last piece of dreamwork on the shadow, we move to Liza's dreams of driving in the dark. She has had repetitive dreams for the twenty years since her divorce of being in a black sedan, often in the back or the passenger seat, riding in pitch blackness. That car belonged to her ex-husband. In past dreams she fears that she will go over the cliff on the side of the road or crash into something and die. There has always been unresolved threat and fear in her past nightmares, and she wakes feeling out of control and in danger of dying. Her next dream is on the same theme, but with some significant differences.

> I am driving in the dark without lights and in danger because
> I can't see ahead of me. I know that I just have to make it
> around the curve in the road though and then I will be okay.
> I am driving, but I have no idea of where the car lights are
> or how to turn them on. I finally get to an intersection and

can't believe that I am not dead. A nice cop is there, and I am embarrassed to tell him that I don't know where my lights are. He is nice though and helps me and shows me how to turn them on.

To start with, here are the differences in this dream from her previous nightmares. This time she is in the driver's seat. She is still driving a black sedan, but it feels like her car this time, not her ex-husbands'. There is a curve in the road that she has to successfully traverse, and then she has a sense that things will be okay, even if it is still dark. No crashing or dying this time, and at the end she finds a helper, the nice policeman who shows her how to use her lights. Liza recognizes that she is finally out of the shadow of feeling completely disempowered by her divorce, "I'm driving again now." She had felt betrayed and like she was "going off a cliff" for years, but now is in a solid relationship with a new partner and all her adult kids are doing reasonably well.

The "curves in the road" that she has to traverse this time have more to do with her relationship with aging and illness than with her divorce. She is at an intersection in her life. Some of the same imagery comes through though—these dark and curvy roads with no lights are in a sense old friends to her psyche and dreaming mind. This particular type of darkness can't be avoided either. She is in her sixties, looking in the mirror at wrinkles and greying hair that weren't there before. (Even if she were to choose cosmetics, hair dye, or Botox, she would still be facing the shadow of aging by using those interventions.) This is part of her personal shadow side—her fears around the inexorable slide to old age and the inevitable death that ultimately awaits us all.

She is struggling to come to terms with her changing face and body as she ages. The policeman in this dream is a guide who helps her find and use her lights so that she can drive and navigate safely through the next chapters of her life. She reported that she felt surprisingly protected by the policeman/guide, that he was sort of a guardian angel who could keep her safely on the road. "The Dark" itself was the Shadow character in her dream. Threatening to envelope and possibly kill her without lights to guide her way, the dark night in and of itself is not a bad nor evil character. It is, however, a symbol of her aging, which becomes more visible to her in the light of day. (She even showed me the dark age spots on her hands and face as we talked out this dream.) Once she gets access to her car's lights, she can navigate the darkness, no matter where it leads. A final point here: Liza turns on the lights to her car from the inside, which then illuminate her road. We too can turn on our own inner light that can help us to navigate our own dark roads. The guide showed her where they were, but now she is empowered to light her own way as she continues.

EXERCISE
Finding Your Shadow Parts in Your Dreams

Take a good look at your dreams and nightmares, both your recent ones and those from over time. Are there any figures or landscapes that seem to contain a darkness or uncomfortable image for you? They may literally be black or dark, or simply feel uncomfortable in some way, or they are thwarting you somehow. Go back a few years if you can, or at least a few weeks or months and see if there is any pattern. Does anyone or anything seem to be following you, threatening you, or immobilizing you? Are there monsters, attackers, or ghosts of one sort or another? Make a list of both single and recurring images.

Then tune into your own felt sense as you consider these Shadow creatures, that body-based knowing that is more than words. It might be a wave of sensation, an "aha," or a tingle—some physical shift that you can notice, even if it is subtle. Ask yourself if this person or object is a shadow figure for you, and which one or more of the three categories of your dream shadow you are dealing with: Personal, Ancestral, and/or World Shadow. Once you have your allies and protections with you, see if you can begin to enter into a dialogue with this figure. You might ask it why it is following you, what it wants from you, if it has a message or even a gift for you, or any advice that it wants you to have. Write out both sides of this dialogue, listening within to your own small voice that contains the voice of the Other: the Demon or the Darkness, the Evil King, or the Slow Woman. Where are these images an aspect of yourself, and when are they there to warn or advise you about other beings or energies in your life?

Look too for the Bright Ones, the shining shadow parts you may have disowned or exiled that have returned to you so you can re-embrace them and welcome them into your life. Remember that you do not have to do this alone. Two, three, or more heads may be better than one at sussing out these human-sized, ancestral-ßsized, and global-sized shadows. Please be sure to engage with emotional safety places, people, and nature after doing this work.

NINE

· · · · · · · · ·

EMBODIED AND SPIRITUAL
DREAMWORK TO SOOTHE AND
RESOLVE YOUR NIGHTMARES

Awaken, arise to the wholeness of your being. Awaken, arise to the beauty of your soul.

—Hanna Tiferet Siegel

Dreams are alive. We are fully alive in their alternative world when we dream them. When we have bad dreams or nightmares, or any dream for that matter, our body / mind system does not differentiate between waking experiences and sleeping experiences. Whether we have a car crash, an assault, or a profound moral injury that attacks our values and beliefs in our waking life or in our sleeping life, we experience it in our bodies in the same way. Therefore, to bring the most complete healing to our nightmares, we must engage with them not only with our minds, but with our hearts, our bodies, and our souls.

Trauma responses are also embodied; we feel the fear, the anger, and the sadness in our tightly constricted throats or bellies, in our clenched jaws or fists, and in our heavy sagging shoulders or chronic fatigue. Emotions are called feelings because we feel them. Trauma expert Bessel van der Kolk titled his book *The Body Keeps the Score* for this reason—the imprint of what we experience in our lives, for better or for worse, is contained in our body. In addition to epigenetics, where we inherit our ancestors' experiences both in behavioral patterns and in methylation of DNA, we contain the imprints of what happened to us in our bodies as well. Have you ever had a massage or some body work, and all of a sudden you feel the urge to cry? I have. This emotional response to physical touch is the body releasing what is held in the muscles and tissues. We may or may not have a cognitive thought or understanding when this occurs to accompany the emotion. Full healing means we have to tap into the various ways that our bodies are reflecting the traumatic experiences and use healing strategies that include direct access to our bodies. Van der Kolk frequently recommends yoga, tai chi, and other somatic and body-mind methods of healing for trauma survivors.

Trauma affects not only the body, but the soul as well. It challenges our belief systems about safety for ourselves, our families, and our world. It can cause us to question or even lose complete faith in the North Star of a guiding spirit or higher power within or without that is a source of healing and comfort. Embodied and ensouled healing from the body and soul-shattering events of trauma and their manifestation in our nightmares is the subject of our inquiry in this chapter. Biochemist and energy psychology healer Judith Swack designed a multi-layered approach to mind/body/spiritual healing she calls *HBLU: Healing from the Body Level Up* that attends to all of these levels of healing in its protocols, including the use of applied kinesiology (muscle testing) as a means of accessing the body's deepest wisdom, much as we might do in dreamwork.

Psychologist and dreamworker Stephen Aizenstat teaches about the concept of an "ensouled world." In my book *Modern Dreamwork: New Tools for Decoding Your Soul's Wisdom*, I shared that this concept of an ensouled world is a key to the integration of our bodies, our minds, and our own souls with the All-Soul of what is larger than just us; with whatever your idea of the Divine or the Force or the Universe is. I also developed the Integrated Embodied Approach to dreamwork that is particularly well-suited to nightmare healing. This method of dreamwork invites us to apply somatic, body-oriented, energetic, and pan-spiritual approaches to dreamwork as well as the more common cognitive and associative styles that opens the doors to healing at all levels of being.

Tracking and Healing in the Dreaming Body

Two of my personal favorite body-oriented dreamers and healers are Eugene Gendlin and Robert Bosnak. Gendlin is the granddaddy of body-oriented work with his seminal book *Focusing*. It outlines his orientation to attending to the wisdom of the body through careful attunement to subtle physical signs in a state of awareness he called the *felt sense*. He defines felt sense as the body's physical experience of knowing or awareness. It is the physical manifestation of an inner knowing, the body's way of tapping into the essence of something.

Felt sense is both the location in which we find our Self and our location inside of our bodies, much in the way that we find ourselves and our location in the landscape of our dreams. It starts with a beyond-words knowing that we often then need to translate into words in order to fully understand it or to share it with someone else. We then track both the subtle and more obvious changes we notice in our bodies as we tune in and focus. Focusing in dreamwork allows us to tune into this wisdom of body-knowing to gain more information from our dream. Gendlin suggests that the element of surprise that can occur when engaging with this process lets us know that this is truly an active imagination process and not conscious wishful thinking. We can't be surprised when we are engaging in our own wishful thinking. The surprise of an "aha" moment is one of the most enjoyable aspects of dreamwork. Track what happens by simply asking yourself, "And what next?" each time you sense a shift.

EXERCISE
Focusing in Dreamwork

If you have a question, dilemma, or an upsetting feeling lingering from your nightmare, try holding still and bringing your attention into your body as you gently put your mind on the issue or emotion or the setting of the nightmare. Clear a quiet space for your inside and outside worlds for this practice. Then, just notice what happens as you hold the question gently in your mind as you simultaneously pay attention to your body. Allow the answers to well up from the inside. Don't rush; give it time. Maybe do a body scan, sweeping your attention slowly from head to toe, or toe to head. What do you notice? Does anything shift or change? Are there any spots of tension, ease, movement, or an image or memory that emerges as you scan? Now notice your breath: When do you sigh or exhale? A spontaneous sigh is often the signal of some kind of shift. Notice if you get a frisson, that sensibility of a wave, shiver, or "aha" of knowing that is beyond words, a slight change in your muscle tension or body temperature in one or more body parts. What do you then know when you attend to these small signs of somatic shift? What came through to your mind and heart from attending to the nightmare or problem with your body? Try it: Be gentle and patient with yourself and take your time, especially if this is new to you.

Gendlin himself compares the practice of Focusing to entering a dream state. When we sufficiently relax our striving and anxious monkey minds, we fall asleep. If we hold a question in our minds in a waking, relaxed state, and then consciously quiet our minds while tuning into our body sensations, we can have a waking or lucid dream experience. Gendlin believes that the setting is often a good place to start exploring a dream, because it brings the dreamer back into the dreamscape. I would add that it is also sometimes a more neutral place than where the action is occurring, and with nightmares we often need to start slowly and work our way into them. Gendlin also frequently uses Gestalt methods, where the dreamer becomes elements in the dream. Here's an example of the latter.

From "Fire and Ashes" to "Sparks and Soil": Entering Maura's Dreams of Healing

A client of mine, Maura, has a history of childhood trauma, of several marriages and divorces, and is now parenting an adult daughter who is struggling with bipolar disorder. In her dream she is watching a raw chicken breast being swiped by fire. It felt "very strange and somewhat uncomfortable." Using focusing, she became aware of a somewhat nauseous feeling in her center as she witnessed this. She then allowed herself to become the chicken breast. At first the word "raw" stood out for her; for her it felt connected to old, hurtful, and still-open wounds. She feels the tender rawness of the chicken breast on her own skin when she connects some aspects of her own childhood to her daughter's life. Her daughter struggles with both her own traumatic experiences and with carrying the legacy burdens from both her mom and from her father.

Maura next attends to the part of the dream where the chicken is swiped by fire and realizes, "That's what it needs to be available for human consumption." Her realization of this was accompanied by the frisson of knowing that came with the word "transformation." She said, "I am [as the raw chicken breast] being transformed by the alchemical process of fire into something that can now feed and nourish people." This embodied spiritual insight was congruent with what Maura was doing in her life today. In addition to her own healing journey, she has made herself available to assist her daughter. For the first time in her life she has been regularly cooking nourishing meals for the two of them. Rather than being burned by fire, she is now consciously using it to transform the rawness of her own life as well as her daughter's with love, care, and nourishing food. It was a chicken breast in her dream image, not a thigh or a wing. No coincidence there either—it is from her nourishing, mothering breast and heart that she is doing this work.

Maura's other two dreams lend themselves to paying attention to the setting. The first one was simply an image of a black rectangle: "a blank, black surface." Then someone else tells her that they saw two sparks of light in the rectangle. When Maura looks more closely, she sees two flickers of light as well, "like sparks coming from two eyes." The black rectangle itself was her setting.

In her second dream:

> I am walking outdoors, feeling vulnerable to an attacker...
> I find a door in a large, ugly building and open it to find a
> huge pile of grey ash. As I move inside to get away from the
> potential attacker, I see piles of ash as far as my eyes can see,
> and I know that I will not be able to get through it. I turn
> around and find that the door I came in is now at the top of

a steep pile of ash. I have to climb up hand over fist, and then looking down I see that what I thought was ash was really soil with specks of green growth that will be used to fill in the grass above ground. I worry that the door might have locked behind me, but I climbed the steep mountain of ash and turned the handle and the door opened.

When Maura turned her attention to these two dreams, the first thing that struck her were the eyes. In the first dream, those eyes flicker and shine out of the darkness "like sparks of light." In the second dream, at first there was ash "as far as my eyes could see" and then when she looks more closely at the ash pile she must climb, she sees specks of green growth. When she looks closely, first on someone else's suggestion in the black rectangle dream, and then on her own in the pile of ash dream, she sees light and growth that she hadn't noticed at first glance. For Maura, these are multi-layered dreams. Her transpersonal layer is associating the ash to the hundreds of thousands who have died of COVID-19. On the personal layer, she sees these dreams as very hopeful and spiritually uplifting. Seeing in or through the darkness is the theme of her first dream and seeing the green growth within the ash of the second dream reminds her of a phoenix rising from the ashes. My friend Lynda calls these divine sparks of life "Divine shrapnel," bits of which enter us to enliven us and help us to see with sacred eyesight. Maura reflects that there is no life without divine sparks first, and she is now "seeing with clearer eyes" how to help both herself and her daughter. The retitling of these dreams indicates how her orientation shifted by attending to the dreams: from *Fire and Ashes* to *Sparks and Soil*.

Integrated and Embodied Dreamwork

To create the integrated embodied approach, I borrowed and expanded on the idea of embodied imagination developed by Robert Bosnak.[40] He speaks of the science of phenomenology, which is the science of experience. As we have already noted, a dream or nightmare is an experience; you are convinced of the legitimacy of it when you awaken. In embodied imagination, Bosnak invites us to return to the dream and live in the perspective of the dream character of the self and the characters of others in the dream. In other words, to re-embody the point of view of self in your dream, and then to embody the point of view of others.

Start by knowing nothing with a beginner's mind. This can be particularly helpful with nightmares. Then allow yourself to be curious rather than afraid when the upset begins to occur. (Maura did this when her chicken was swiped by fire so that she would not panic and fear being burned.) When you experience distress in a dream, you may be able to find another character in the same dream who is not experiencing distress or has another perspective that you couldn't see out of your dream eyes. You may then get a resource you didn't know you had. It even works for a predator/prey nightmare. If we combine the energy of both the pursued and the pursuer, we may tap into an energy of a vibrant life force.

Jack dreams that he is being chased by a wild elephant. He feels it getting closer and closer until he feels its hot breath on his back. Jack feels his own legs running, his breath coming short and quick, and wonders if he will be able to escape before getting trampled or gored. He starts to panic. I invite him to slow down, to breathe, and to stand outside the dream in active imagination at the same time as

---

40. Robert Bosnak, *Tracks in the Wilderness of Dreaming* (New York: Delta Press, 1996), 30, 36, 159.

inhabiting it. He can tolerate the sensation this way and says that he likes the power of being in two places at once. I next invite him to step back out of the dream and then to inhabit the character of the elephant. He is intrigued by this idea and makes the emotional and physical adjustment by kind of shaking himself to move into the body of the elephant.

When I ask him what he is experiencing as the elephant, he replies, "Hey, I have such a tough hide. Almost nothing can penetrate it. My tusks are strong and can be lethal weapons. I am generally peaceful, and I love my family, but something has threatened us, and I have to protect them. I am powerful enough to do this." This is obviously a different perspective that might be useful in his life. I invite him to then put the two dream characters together, the Self in the dream and the Elephant Self, and experience that in his body. He then says, "I am tougher than I thought I was. I am fast and strong and can protect myself and my family."

Jack and his family had been the victims of a racially motivated attack a few weeks before he had this dream. Elephants are often seen as symbols of power and strength and are able to plow through challenges using their huge tusks. They are known to be highly intelligent herd animals and very protective of their young. The mantra of the elephant has been described as "family first." This set of elephant skills was a welcome addition for Jack at this time in his life, and he left feeling more empowered and able to think about next practical steps.

Body Knowledge in Our Dreams

Body-knowing or embodiment precedes cognitive knowing. As we continue working with various forms of embodied dreamwork, let us examine what Bosnak has to say about embodied imagination, and then look at another few examples of embodied dreamwork with both adults and children. Bosnak, along with Gendlin and Arnold

Mindell from the dreamwork world, and trauma experts, including van der Kolk, Peter Levine, and Babette Rothschild speak of this idea of sense memory and site or location-specific memory storage. We hold memory in the very tissues and structure of our bodies.

My friend David ate bananas because they were one of the few foods he could tolerate when he was nauseous while receiving chemotherapy. Decades later, in full health, he still gets nauseous when confronted by even the smell of bananas. His sense memory of the chemo-nausea gets triggered by the smell of a banana. Focusing tracks sensations within the body until they settle in a specific location, and then they are examined. Maura, with her sparks and ashes dreams, began her dreamwork by noticing the nauseous sensation in her belly that accompanied her telling of it.

The characters that show up in our dreams and nightmares, along with our emotional and physical resonance to them, can serve as landmarks or signposts on our journey to understanding and unpacking the dream, and ultimately to healing the upset both from the dream itself and the underlying causes. Like Aizenstat, Moss, and other dreamworkers, Bosnak also invites us to pay attention to place: *Where* we are in the dreamscape, as well as *who* we are in it adds to a total experience of embodiment in the context and the setting, and it connects us back to the environment of our waking lives. We are somewhere, in a place that is realer than real in our dreams. In PTSDreams, the landscape or setting is where the trauma occurs, so it is of added importance not to neglect this aspect of the dream.

Maura's dream landscapes of ash and dark streets and interiors provided the backdrop to her movement through that dreamscape. Her second dream setting was simply blackness: the black rectangle. In her third dream, the journey of traveling from an unsafe place that was barren and dead—just ash—to noticing the green specks of growth and life still embedded within, reflected for her the change in her internal environment that was mirroring the changes happening in her life. Bosnak also refers to a tipping point. Once we reach that threshold, things change. For Maura, the tipping point in the first dream was when she realized that the fire on the chicken breast was transformative rather than dangerous, and in the second dream when she was directed to see the bright flickers of light in the darkness like sparks from eyes. Her final tipping point was her ability to notice the green growth in the ashes of desolation, and the transformation of ash to good soil. Deep healing from our nightmares often contains transformative spiritual awakenings.

Active Imagination: Saving the Baby

We tune into the body for answers. We utilize the body in dreamwork through variations of Jung's active imagination work or through dream theater, where we physically act out the dream scenes. My client, Emily, has two dreams with a similar theme. Her first dream:

I am pregnant, and the baby is born prematurely; it is really small.

In her second dream, Emily dreams:

I have given birth to a baby in a hospital but somehow got separated from the baby. There are people who are blocking my way as I try to get back to my baby girl. I feel trapped. The most important thing is to get back to my baby.

She titled it *Separated* and said that her anxiety and distress level (SUDS) was a 6 or 7 out of 10. Here is Emily's relevant background. She did, in fact, give birth to her child prematurely four years ago. He had some pulmonary health complications as a result. Emily and her husband still panic whenever he catches a cold, because colds have turned into pneumonia that required hospitalization a few times in the past. However, this was not the case when she had the dream; he was currently healthy. Her immediate association on waking was that this dream had to do with her therapy practice—her other "baby." She has been debating for some time about changing to a self-pay system rather than an insurance-based one in order to have more freedom in the way she works. She is nervous about the financial risk of not being on insurance panels and feels a level of guilt about some clients not being able to afford self-pay. However, she is also burned out by all the paperwork and the lower fee that insurance pays her and thinks it might be worth the risk. With that context, here is the work she did with this anxiety dream.

I ask Emily what her goal in the dream is and she replies that it is to get her baby back "at all costs." I invite her back into the dream and ask, "What do you need to do now? How will you safely get the baby back?" Feeling blocked, her first thought is to pull the emergency alarm, but then feels flooded by guilt for contemplating pulling a false alarm. (Notice here the congruent emotion of guilt in the dream and guilt in contemplating changing her practice model. This feeling of guilt was also a part of her post-partem emotional roller coaster, the common "What if …" or "What did I do wrong?" questions many parents of preemies ask themselves.) I encourage Emily to look around the hospital in her dream for other options.

She then notices that there is actually only one woman blocking her at this point. Emily speaks with this woman who says to her, "It's not safe to go this way." When Emily asks why not, the woman replies, "It's dark and unknown that way—it's too risky." When Emily seems stymied for the moment, I ask her how she wants to reply to this. Emily says to the woman, "You need to let me try anyhow, because nothing is more important than getting back to the baby, and I am willing to take the risk." The woman reluctantly lets her by and Emily walks through dark and scary hospital halls until she finds a little lighted room with the baby. She picks it up and carries it out of the hospital into the sunlight feeling a sense of freedom that she is no longer trapped by the woman. Emily says that she can feel the sun warm on her face, and it feels like an opening up.

We might have been tempted to stop here, but I listened to my own dreamwork instincts as I joined her in the dream space and realized that we hadn't really dealt with the Blocking Woman; just got past her initial objections. Emily was willing to go back into the dream and this time embody and become that woman. In doing so, Emily says that she is big and strong and sturdy, but also tense. I asked Emily if she could invite the woman to join her to protect her, instead of blocking her way. The woman swiftly acquiesced and became her new Bodyguard, a strong and sturdy part of herself that could protect her and help her make these changes and life decisions. This Bodyguard was no longer tense once she had a job to do. By the end of the hour, Emily had set up a reasonable timeline in which to shift her practice, prepare her clients, and make plans for how to handle those of low income. Her title changed from *Separation* to *Union*. Her distress level was now down to a 2, which seems more than reasonable for making a large life change.

The dreamwork allowed her to recognize that this "baby" of her life's work and calling needed similar care and attention as her actual baby did, and that while it was a little "premature" to make these changes immediately, it was well worth the risk to make careful plans to switch over in the next several months. She felt a palpable sense of relief and openness with these plans. The highlights of the dream embodiment that helped her move forward were the sensation of the warm sun on her face that came with the emotion of freedom, and the full body feeling of sturdiness and strength from becoming and embodying the Blocking Woman.

This dream also shows us a spiritual side of embodied dreamwork. Part of what made this dream a post-trauma nightmare instead of a more straightforward anxiety dream is the contextual life history when we combine the information from the first dream of a premature baby. Emily and her husband had spent several years struggling with fertility treatments before finally getting pregnant, and then had to cope with complications of a premature birth as well. The whole experience together created traumatic stress, and the trauma of acute awareness of the fragility of life was again triggered each time their baby got sick. This was the backdrop for her anxiety when thinking about changing the way she approached her work, for anything that contained risk factors, the unknown, and related to health or mental health became loaded topics for her. It was no wonder that she had a Blocking Woman show up in her dream. The work on the dream of saving the baby in the hospital gave her several layers of healing. It showed her that with careful planning and support from the Light, the sunlight, and her own inner strength (the Blocking Woman transformed into the Bodyguard), she was prepared to take the calculated risk to work in the way that was more congruent with her current life and beliefs. It was set in a hospital, which gave another dimension to "saving the baby," for along with the metaphor of her clinical practice work as her new baby, she was reminded that she literally did save her own baby with good medical care in the hospital both before and after he was born.

Dream Theater: Trapped Under the Lion

Sometimes we embody the dream or dream it forward by continuing it with dream theater, acting out the parts ourselves or inviting others to take on characters if we are with a group. We met Samantha previously in this lion dream, and now we circle back to look at the way we worked with it. The following nightmare and dreamwork exemplifies a form of embodied dream theater. Samantha dreams the following:

I am trapped in a room under an enormous lion who is laying on top of me. I feel terrified. I want to get up and go but I am afraid that if I move, I will disturb the lion and he will attack me, and things would be even worse. So, I just stay still where I am.

She titled this dream *Trapped and Frozen*. When I asked her to describe her sensations, she said that she could feel the weight of the lion on top of her and that it felt heavy and warm. Her goal in the dream was to get the lion off of her but was afraid to move for fear of making matters worse. Her immediate association was to a health issue with her teenage daughter who was not on board with various medical and alternative options that Samantha was interested in trying. She was afraid of pushing too hard and triggering a firm refusal to participate from her daughter and was also afraid that if she did nothing that it could get worse. She was trapped under this lion of indecision and fear. We could have moved in the direction of exploring the metaphor and symbols of this dream and the waking life associations that she already had to it. Instead, because she already had a sense of what it was about, and the very physical nature of it, we decided to act it out. If her struggle was against immobilization and stuckness, movement seemed a good counter-choice. (Remembering also that one of the symptoms of PTSD is the freeze or the play-dead response.)

Tuning into how it felt to be trapped under the lion, she says that it is heavy and uncomfortable, but at the same time she feels warm and ironically safe in that do-nothing space. We notice the paradox of feeling warm and frozen at the same time—no wonder it is so hard for her to make a decision to move or try to move. Samantha is clear that this is not a permanent solution however, either in the dream or in her life. She knows that she periodically finds herself immobilized by indecision, though not always under a lion of this size. She now reconnects with her original goal of getting the lion off her back.

Before beginning the active phase of dream theater, I ask Samantha to add in resources to feel safe and protected enough to engage with a lion (in-line with the GAIA method). Using active imagination, she invites her mom, her grandmother, and some powerful women priestesses and shamans to join us in the room. After that I suggest to Samantha that she get into a crouching position in a runner's stance and ask her if it is okay if I put a heavy blanket over her to represent the lion. She laughs and says "yes." Our plan is that on the count of three, she will throw off the lion/blanket and run out the door. I count out loud for her: "One, two, three!" She throws off the blanket, runs out the door, into the waiting room, and into a big hug from me. She is both laughing, shaking, and a bit teary as she processes how much harder it was then she expected, and how relieved she felt to be able to do it. I asked her if once was enough, or if she wanted to do it another time for emphasis. She said, "No, that was really powerful. I can feel the strength in my body now and am clear that I don't have to stay under that lion even if it feels a little cozy. Hear my roar!" and she proceeded to give out a loud, strong roar.

I joined in with her for a good loud roar, we both laughed, and her body stopped its shaking. As Peter Levine teaches us, animals in the wild are attacked by predators frequently but they do not seem to ever get PTSD.[41] One of their innate strategies for moving on in life

---

41. Peter Levine, *Waking the Tiger: Healing Trauma* (Berkeley, CA: North Atlantic Books, 1987), 18, 30, 38.

is to "shake it off." He has film clips of a deer and a rabbit escaping a wolf attack, and in them we see the now-safe animal shake and quiver for a few moments and then bound away. Samantha was missing that shake-it-off strategy, so once she was free of the "lion," her body spontaneously knew what else it needed to do to release the trapped and stuck dream energy from her system. After her body finished shaking, she could brainstorm options for her daughter's care, including inviting her daughter to incubate dreams, record her own dreams, and work together to find some solutions that were amenable to both of them.

EXERCISE
An Introduction to Embodied Dreamwork Practices

There are many ways to incorporate somatic and embodied dreamwork into your nightmare healing practice. Some of the methods described in this chapter include active imagination, dream theater or sculpting, focusing, embodied attunement, and naming and tracking sensations.

★ ★ ★

EXERCISE
Body Sculpting and Body Talk

Here are some questions you can ask yourself and actions to try if you are comfortable doing so. Again, when working with very scary dreams or those that you know are PTSDreams, do them with a trusted friend or family member or teach them to your therapist to use with you. Safety first, both physically and emotionally. Take it slowly and return to a safe place if you get overly triggered.

- Notice where in your body you feel sensations when you put your attention on your dream. Are they pleasant, unpleasant, or neutral?

- How can you describe those sensations in words? Are they tight, tingly, jumpy, hot, cold, light-headed, achy? Do you get waves of sensation or are they stationary? What emotions accompany the sensations?

- If the sensation is unpleasant, what skills and techniques do you already have to move, change, or transform it or give it more space? Examples include breathwork, stretching, meditation, warm baths, or a walk in the woods.

- If you were to put your body into a pose that represents these feelings and sensations, what pose do you put yourself in? This is sometimes called dream sculpting. Can you try it now? What is that like? If it is uncomfortable (and it probably will be), try the next step.

- Now put your body into a pose that feels like the opposite of the unpleasant one. For example, if the emotion from your dream was anxiety and the sensation was feeling small and weak, you might put your body into a crouched, curled-up position. To counter that, if the opposite might be feelings of empowerment and calm, you might move your body so you stand up straight, arms lifted up and wide, your chest open, and a firm, grounded stance to your legs, maybe planting them a little more than shoulder width apart. Make any adjustments you need to be just right. Then, enhance this pose and make it even bigger—exaggerate it. You are re-embodying and recreating a new positional memory for your neural networks to learn. Practice this new pose daily. Bring this into your dream as well.

- If your dreambody could talk, what would it say?
- Try movement: Act out a scene from your dream. Embody the characters, objects, and landscapes. If you are working with a group, give everyone a role. If you are trying this alone or with one other person, take turns embodying different parts of the dream.
- Try simple movements to shake it off if you are stuck in feelings from a nightmare. Stomp your feet, shake your arms, brush yourself off, stretch your mouth and make funny faces, jump up and down, shake all over, do a dance!

Kids (of All Ages), Art, and Nightmares

Artwork is a wonderful way to enhance nightmare healing for kids of all ages—that means toddlers, children, teenagers, and adults. Not only is a picture worth a thousand words, but dreams usually come in images. The image is the key to unlocking the secrets of most dreams. Getting them physically represented on paper or in 3D with

Play-Doh or clay brings the dream to life so we can intervene and add or subtract or change what the nightmare needs to be healed. When doing art dreamwork with kids of any age, I am careful to tell them that this is not art class—stick figures and chicken scratches are just fine. Most youngsters are pretty uninhibited about drawing; it is the teens and adults that are often shyer and more critical of their own art. Everyone can draw something, and if they are really too young, then the parent or guide can help with motor skills. Artwork is a form of movement too—whether it is drawing, painting, sculpting, or making collages, our hands and arms move as we create the artwork that represents the nightmare or offers healing solutions to it. Children are often willing to try outlandish solutions, and monsters can be caged, driven back, spoken with, and kids can become superheroes. Jean Campbell and Clare Johnson's collection of various authors on this subject is a wonderful resource, and several other dream and art books are listed in the bibliography.[42]

Ann Sayre Wiseman recommends that when we search for interventions and solutions to dealing with frightening nightmare figures that we don't use killing them off as a solution. She suggests that we don't want to use killing others to be our defense of choice, and we don't want to teach violence to our children. Kids will usually feel better if they can outsmart, contain, or negotiate with the monster; it is more empowering. In addition, as we have already learned, the bad guys and monsters in our dreams often have something to teach us or share with us, so we don't want to eliminate this source of knowledge and healing. Figuring out how to create dialogue, to befriend and get to know our monsters, is a more useful approach. Remember Sasquatch from chapter 8? He turned out to be an

---

42. Campbell, Jean and Clare Johnson, eds., *Dream Monsters and Superheroes: Empowering Children Through Creative Dreamplay* (Westport, CT: Praeger Publishers, 2016).

important ally and protector by the end of the dreamwork that would not have showed up if we had just vaporized or destroyed him. We want to look inside and around the nightmare for guides and helpers, for creative solutions, for safe containment, and for transformation opportunities.

Children tend to be both literal and imaginative. Their dreams are peopled with monsters and cataclysmic events, and young children frequently can't even tell the difference between a dream memory and real life. Sadly, on some occasions, there may not be a difference. One of my clients, Patricia, recounted that when she was a child the "mad tickler" would come into her room and her dreams at night and touch and tickle her unmercifully. She remembered trying to hold her arms tightly against her sides so prevent him from tickling her. Later on, in our work together, she recognized that what she thought was a nightmare was actually a dissociated memory of being molested by her father night after night. Once this became clarified, she could move forward into healing from this trauma. As long as the memory was dissociated and she thought it was "just a dream," she remained stuck in victimhood and passivity. Naming the reality of traumatic events that have occurred allows us to deal with them, to put them in their proper place in the past, and tame their effects on us in the present and the future.

Katie's Dreams: Jail and Jesus to the Rescue

Katie was seven years old when the Boston Marathon bombers set off explosive devices on the race route and killed and injured many runners and bystanders. She lived in the quiet suburban town where the second bomber hid under a boat until he was finally captured. During the search for him, the town was in lockdown and the streets were patrolled by armored tanks. It really looked like a war zone for a few days. After he was captured, the town and all of Massachusetts celebrated and life went on. Katie went back to school, but soon developed nightmares. In them she was being chased and attacked by a variety of bad guys and felt that intruders were breaking into her house.

Katie had most of the nightmares while at her mother's house, but when it was her and her sister's turn to sleep at their father's just a few blocks away, she rarely had them. When her mom brought her in for counseling, I interviewed the parents as well as meeting with Katie. On the practical level, it turned out that she and her sister each had separate rooms at mom's house, and they shared a bedroom when at their dad's. In addition, mom often had to work until six or seven o'clock and Katie spent a few hours alone after dark with her twelve-year-old sister several days a week. Dad worked at home though, and either he or their stepmom was always in the house when Katie was there. By sharing a bedroom with her sister and having an adult around most of the time at her dad's, we could see how one household felt safer to Katie than the other. We brainstormed options to help Katie feel safer at her mom's house as well as working on her nightmares directly.

With kids especially, but with adults as well, look for environmental and practical solutions as well as dreamwork methods to help soothe and protect. Mom's work hours were non-negotiable, but we set up that mom would call them each afternoon to check in and would also call just before leaving the office so they could be assured what time she would be getting home (with wiggle room for traffic delays). Dad agreed to be point person and confirmed that Katie could call him even if it was not their regular visitation day if she was not able to feel soothed with her sister until mom came home. I also discovered Katie had a favorite stuffed animal called Monkey that she slept with and that he traveled with her back and forth between the two households. I had her bring Monkey into the office one day, and I formally charged him with the job of keeping Katie safe, to which he quickly agreed. Using the magic wand that I keep in my office, we touched him with it and gave him some more magic powers to keep her safe. I suggested that since she slept with Monkey, he could also watch over her while she slept and help guard against her bad dreams—we gave him this job together.

The next steps were a combination of reality testing and active dreamwork using art. The reality testing had to do with connecting her nightmares to their source, and then checking on real world safety. When I asked Katie when her nightmares began, she was able to say, "last spring," which I knew was when the events of the bombing occurred. When I asked her if she thought it could be related to her nightmares, she was relieved to make that connection rather than having no rhyme or reason for them. The next step was reality testing about what occurred then, and what was true now. This is a wonderful trauma treatment strategy for all kinds of past traumatic events that are no longer occurring. We reviewed the events that happened both in Boston and in Watertown (her town) and confirmed that at the end of those fateful few days, one terrorist was killed, and the other was captured and was now in a very secure prison a long way from here. I opened up a map and showed her where the supermax prison he was incarcerated in Colorado was and where Boston was in comparison. Seeing this laid out on the map, calculating the distance, and affirming that he "couldn't get out" helped calm her fears that he could come back and endanger her and her family again. So now, one strategy was to talk back to her personified fears both in waking life and her dreams and say to them, "You are in jail. There are really strong bars and guards, and you can't get out."

We next got out the drawing materials, and Katie drew a series of pictures showing both the bomber himself, and several dream characters who had been chasing and threatening her. With a thick black marker, she drew a very strong jail cell with heavy bars around them. The dialogue boxes she added had the bad guys saying, "Help, I can't get out of here" while she added herself to the picture dressed as a prison guard and said, "That's right—you did a bad thing and now you have to stay in this strong jail." We did variations on this theme, drawing her nightmares week after week adding more bars and locks, adding superpowers that let her become invisible so they couldn't find her, and surrounding herself in her drawings with her protectors: Monkey, her mom and dad, her stepparents, and Jesus. One drawing showed her in the center of the circle surrounded by all of the above helpers with lines connecting her to each of them. The jailhouse in this picture was depicted as a tiny little cell way down in the corner of the page. We could see that the impact of the trauma was diminishing as the safety imagery grew and the danger imagery shrunk. Her nightmares began abating with the combination of practical aide from her parents, connecting the source of the nightmare to the real-world event that triggered it, creating a timeline of then and now to show that the actual danger was past, and using creative solutions with art and writing with the dream content to empower Katie. On our last meeting Katie said that when a bad guy dares to show up in her dreams anymore, which was infrequent at this point, she sends him to jail with the help of her protection posse and tells him to pray to Jesus for forgiveness.

Shawna's Dreams: When Home Is Not Safe

When there is a discrete event that triggers nightmares, the healing work is more straightforward. However, many children and adults live in chronic and ongoing distress, so the dreamwork with these nightmares needs to take a different direction. Shawna grew up in a household that was chronically stressful and felt unsafe. Her parents fought all the time. She remembers her mother saying, "Oh damn, he's home" whenever she heard her father's car pull into the driveway at the end of the day. Her father yelled a lot, was loud and angry, and Shawna felt that he disrupted the peace as soon as he got home. He was critical and she felt that she could never do anything right in his eyes. In retrospect, she realized that her mother contributed to the lack of harmony as well, but at the time she took her mother's side. Her siblings were not around much after school as they all had sports and other activities and she was a latchkey child.

Shawna recalled three recurring childhood nightmares:

Dream 1: House Abducted by Spaceship and Father

My house is lifted off the ground into a spaceship. Inside is a short man with dark hair and long fingernails. He is going to do bad things to me, and I am afraid. I was abducted and feel helpless. My mom might be with me too, and she is also in trouble and scared and angry at this man. I know that the dark-haired man is my father.

Dream 2: Fooling the Witch

I have to walk on some kind of a path in order to get home and to get through it I have to pass an old witch. The key to passing her was that you had to show that you weren't afraid. Other kids and my siblings can do it, but I don't think I can. I usually wake up feeling anxious before I pass her. Sometimes I might have passed her, but then had to run an even more complicated obstacle course with more scary things to face.

Dream 3: I Lost My House

I am walking home from school and when I get to my street all the houses are mixed up and different. I can't find my home and I walk around feeling lost, confused, helpless, and homeless.

My heart breaks for this poor child. There are few things worse than feeling like you have no home in the world, or that your home is unsafe. This is not a situation where we can say, "that was then and this is now" because even though she is now an adult, this was the fabric of her whole childhood. It still lives inside of her. We can work with dreams retrospectively, however; even though these were recurring childhood nightmares, they still have impact and energy today. If you recall from the introductory chapter, I worked on a repeating childhood nightmare fifty years later as an adult. Even though that nightmare was not still "haunting my midnight pillow" and did not have any remaining emotional punch for me, it was still a relief to get clarity around it and realize what it was about.

Shawna already knew that these dreams had to do with her home life as a child, and with that knowledge we were able to go back into the dreams themselves and add some resources and changes to create a new dream story. The beauty of dreamwork is that it is always now in the dream. So, when we add resources to old dreams, they too resonate as now in our psyche and serve as resources for us in the now of our lives and for the future. We did a type of dreamwork called *dream re-entry* with these dreams. With this active imagination method, we can go back inside the dream and add or subtract or change the outcome.

When I ask Shawna what she would like to do to help the child in the first dream who was abducted in a spaceship, Shawna replied that she wanted to get the spaceship back to Earth in a nice, safe place and get the scary man out of it. Using crayons and paper, she drew the spaceship getting pulled back to Earth by a force field, and then tethered to the ground with a strong rope made of rainbow light. She knew that she didn't want to live the rest of her life in a spaceship, she wanted a real house, but this was better than floating in space for now. She teamed up with her mom in the dream to present a united front against the scary man, pushed him out the door of the spaceship, and sealed the space lock on the door so he couldn't get back in.

A note about art materials: You are welcome to use anything that you like—markers, colored pencils, crayons, pastels, sculpy clay. I find that using simple child-friendly materials with kids and with adults who are working on their childhood nightmares and issues help to provide the child parts of ourselves the comfort and ease that they need to heal more readily. I keep several types of art supplies in my office. Shawna chose the crayons.

When Shawna focused on the second dream about passing the witch, she realized that the witch probably represented her suppressed feelings about her mother's role in the family dynamics. Her father was the scarier of her two parents, but as an adult Shawna recognized that her mother provoked him at times, and that she set up the anxiety of his return home daily whenever she said, "Damn, he's home now." The "rule" in the family was that Shawna and her siblings were supposed to take their mother's side, so any negative feelings about her needed to be hidden. Hence, the witch energy and not being permitted to get by her unless she hid her feelings. If Shawna did get by, "there was an even more complicated obstacle course" to get through. In other words, if you didn't support mom and act as if it was all dad's fault, there'd be hell to pay. With this dream, the acknowledgement of the metaphor seemed to be sufficient, and gave her both food for thought and ideas about her own life as a married adult parenting a child.

Finally, her last dream was the opposite of Dorothy's "There's no place like home." For Shawna, there was no place that was home: it couldn't be found. This is the crux of her life work—to find her sense of home—to learn to carry it inside herself or around her like the turtle or the snail. For these animals, home is always right where they are—they simply pull themselves inside their shell. She has been working on this for many years. We were able to add to her repertoire of home finding and home creating by working with this dream. The image and the felt sense of being lost in her own neighborhood was so profound. Her first picture of this dream simply showed a little girl wandering around a maze. I asked her to look at the picture and see what the girl needed to find her way out of the maze and back home. As we worked together, I remembered the lyrics to an old folk song sung by Lui Collins called "Baptism of Fire." The relevant lyrics of the chorus include the sentiment that there is no easy way out of a maze or a forest, and that the only way out is to go through it.

When I shared my association to this song lyric with her, we both had a frisson of recognition. Shawna said, "Oh my, that's it—I could have written that about my life!" It was comforting for her to know that others shared this experience. With guidance from the song lyrics, the next picture she drew was the little girl again in the maze, but this time holding and following the thread of goddess Ariadne (who helped Theseus out of the labyrinth/maze of the Minotaur with a thread to follow) through and out of the maze. She then drew a house up on a hill with a clear path to it from the maze, no witches or other scary things on it, and drew little stick figures that she said were her husband and daughter waiting for her there. She will come back to these images and pictures again and again as she builds a new solid sense of home in her adult life with her current family. She is now pursuing the advice of Hanna Tiferet Siegel from the top of this chapter as she seeks wholeness and a home for her body and her soul: "Awaken, arise to the wholeness of your being. Awaken, arise to the beauty of your soul."[43]

---

43. "#BlogElul 17: Awaken," Velveteen Rabbi, August 23, 2013, https://velveteenrabbi.blogs.com/blog/2013/08/blogelul-17-awaken.html.

Healing the Spirit in the Nightmare

In some ways, all deep dreamwork involves spiritual healing. The fourth layer of the PARDES method directs us to look for this layer of the work in each of our dreams. Many of the dreams we have examined have this spiritual layer to them, either overtly or as an underlying message. I frequently invite nightmare sufferers to consider the option of inviting in angels, guides, spiritual beings, and the souls of beloved departed relatives to protect them in the night. Shawna's house on a hill in her final image was reminiscent of a common spiritual theme of a hill or high place being the location to go to find the Divine in many biblical and mythical tales.

Jacob, for example, had to climb the mountain to where he had the encounter with the angels going up and down the ladder, prompting him to utter afterward, "Surely the Lord is in this place, and I did not know it."[44] Moses goes to the top of Mount Sinai to get the Ten Commandments. The Greek mythical heaven of Zeus and the other gods is found at the top of Mount Olympus. Oz is found by going up to the Emerald City. Going up implies healing and protection for many.

There are also dreams that more directly connect us to other dimensions in the fabric or theme of the dream itself. Dreams and nightmares for many peoples in ancient times were thought to be visitations from angels, demons, or ghosts. Dark forces may still people our dreams, as did Jason's dark evil entity that connected to his Tragic Man archetype. Demonic creatures called incubi or succubi, male and female demons respectively, who purportedly seduced the dreamer were a popular explanation at one time. Exorcism and similar rituals were utilized to free the nightmare sufferer from these attachments. Many practices to ward off evil spirits and

---

44. "Genesis 28:16," Bible Hub, https://biblehub.com/genesis/28-16.htm.

nightmares have been used through the ages, including hanging dreamcatchers and smudging a room with sage, used by many Native tribes. The chamsa or Hand of Fatima in Middle Eastern cultures is used by both Arabic Muslims and Sephardic Jews. Alaya Dannu tells us that the earliest translation of the Egyptian word for dream is *resut*, which translates as "awakening."[45] The hieroglyph for this is an open eye.

Clearly there is a lot of anxiety worldwide about going to sleep at night. The Talmud teaches that sleep is $1/60^{th}$ of death. Many prayers specifically ask for protection in the night. The bedtime Sh'ma, the prayer said before going to sleep in Judaism, has a section that specifically asks for protection against nightmares. It translates as:

> *"May it be Your will, Adonai my God and God of my ancestors, that you lay us down in peace and raise us up to peace. May my ideas, bad dreams, or evil fantasies not trouble me."*

A common nighttime prayer in Western cultures that many of us learned as a child goes:

> *Now I lay me down to sleep, I pray the Lord my soul to keep*
> *And if I die before I wake, I pray the Lord my soul to take.*

You may also find guidance and words of comfort and wisdom to guard against things that go bump in the night in your own spiritual traditions or other traditions. Trauma itself is often called a soul-shattering experience, so anything that helps us to restore our soul, to heal from the dark dreams, or provide a barrier or protection in the night is useful. My friend Teri tried a simple technique before going to sleep at night: to remind herself that she has the ability to handle anything that comes through in her dreams, and

---

45. Ayala Dannu, "Ancestral Dreaming and Why it Needs to be a Part of the Dream Studies Conversation," *DreamTime*, Fall 2019.

also to request that her dream source not give her more than she can handle. She said that since starting this practice, she has not had nightmares that were too upsetting. Promising to write down and work on whatever she does remember also helps.

Boundaries and Visits from Beyond the Grave

There are two kinds of people in the world according to dream-worker and psychiatrist Ernest Hartmann: thin-boundaried people and thick-boundaried people. It is not a hierarchy, just different types. Thick-boundaried people tend to be more left brain, more linear in their thinking, excel at logic, and have fewer experiences that we might call psychic or spiritual. Thin-boundaried folks are more right brain, more intuitive, excel in creative non-linear pursuits, and have more non-ordinary experiences. Not surprisingly, nightmare sufferers and vivid dreamers tend to be more thin-boundaried.

Sometimes our departed relatives come through our boundaries to visit us in the night. We may get dream visits where we say to the visitor, "Hello, nice to see you," or "Goodbye, go in peace," or "Go back to the light; you are done here." They may be welcome, loving visits or frightening ones, depending on the relationship you had with this relative in life. In our household, talking to our departed parents is par for the course. In fact, when my daughter has a dilemma, I often invite her to find out what Bubbe or Zayde have to say about that issue. She invariably comes back with some very good advice from my mom and dad who passed over several years ago.

We can practice boundarying ourselves against the nightmare visits in many ways. We can surround ourselves with an egg of protective light or invoke protectors to accompany that soul back to the light where it now belongs. This may also be an opportunity for some healing of your relationship with your night visitor, even beyond the grave. We can hold conversations with our departed, saying what we could not say in life, and hearing from them what they could not say in life.

One Family, Two Approaches to a Dream Visitation

Thomas and his sister Liz had an alcoholic father who kept all the children in terror during his lifetime. He molested several of the girls in the family and physically beat the boys. He was diagnosed with a mental illness before there were adequate diagnoses or treatments available, and he died some twenty years ago. Both Tom and Liz were periodically haunted by nightmares of him. Tom, a more thick-boundaried person, saw the world mostly in black and white and clung to his anger and rage at his father. For a long time he was not amenable to exploring his nightmares or the direction of understanding the mental illness and the potential effect on his father's behaviors in the service of, as we say, "explanation, not excuse." His nightmares of his father abated somewhat as he got stronger and more empowered in his own life, but they reappeared whenever he was under stress.

Liz is thin-boundaried and studies reiki and other spiritual practices. She was more amenable to the idea of dialoguing with her dead father the next time he showed up. When she opened the door in her mind to him the next time he appeared in her dream, she asked him on waking, "What do you want now? Why are you here?" To her amazement he replied to her, "I came to apologize. I lost control in my life and regret the harm I caused you and your siblings and your mom. I want to tell you that even though it didn't look like it at times, I always loved you and still do."

Liz felt a sense of peace come over her with this information. She replied to him, "I hear you, and appreciate the apology, but I first need to tell you about the harm you caused." Her father replied that he could listen, and she told him of the pain and suffering that she struggled with into her adulthood long after she left the house as a child. Her active imagination dialogue work included both listening to her father's voice and speaking her own mind to him. She confronted him for his wrongs, and then allowed the apology and forgiveness in ways that never happened in life. This is an optimal healing scenario for trauma survivors—to get a chance to safely confront their abuser, receive an apology, and an offer of amends is as good as it gets. It doesn't often happen this way in waking, earthbound lifetimes. How nice that we are not bound by the limitations of the flesh to get a chance to have this healing. Now when she speaks about her father, she can report that he is on her side and watching over her with love from the beyond.

Mom to the Rescue

In this nightmare, Joy is able to connect with the loving and protective embodied spirit of her mother who died when Joy was in her twenties. When Joy was in her forties she was diagnosed with a serious, life-threatening illness. She reported, "I was whisked away via ambulance to the ER and spent several hours alone and afraid for my life. At the time I thought I was all alone, but when I look back on the experience, I realize that my mother had been hovering over me in spirit. I knew she was looking out for me." The surgery was successful. Fast-forward another fifteen years, and Joy was re-triggered in her current life around issues of abandonment. A writer, Joy was experiencing a severe writer's block that contributed to her feeling abandoned by the Divine, her source of creativity. Her feelings of abandonment by her Muse were similar to those she felt when all alone in the ER, and also to those feelings of loss and abandonment that accompanied the death of her mother. Here is her dream:

My mother and I are standing on the edge of a cliff that drops off into a dark, bottomless chasm. A strong gust of wind blows me over the edge of the cliff, and I am suspended over the darkness. In terror, I call out to my mother and stretch out my hand to her. She reaches out to grab me, but our fingertips are just inches too far apart to reach. My long, flowing cloak is whipping around in the wind. Just as I'm sure that I will be blown even farther away and completely out of reach, my mother grabs the edge of my cloak and pulls me safely back down to the ground.

Joy said that this dream was terrifying and that she still had a visceral response of feeling choked up as she writes it down now, both for the fear and the relief of her mother reeling her into safety at the last moment. She later wrote a poem based on the nightmare to help resolve the writer's block. The poem, which she titled "My Psalm," was later published in an online spiritual magazine, breaking her writer's block, and getting something published to boot.

EXERCISE
A Somatic Dreamwork Practice

Take a look at your last several nightmares. What do you feel in your body now as you reread them? What are the emotions and the body sensations that you felt in your dream? Write these down. Check to see if what you feel and sense now is the same or different than when you had the nightmare originally. Do you feel better, worse, or the same?

Name the sensations and find the location in your body (e.g., I feel tingling in my hands, tight and choked up in my throat, hot and flushed in my face). If these sensations could speak, what would they be saying to you? Also, try some movement. Practice again the stationary dream sculpting, first of the negative emotional physical stance, and then put your body into the opposite positive emotional position. Finally, shake it off: Find the place of energy in the nightmare and move it out of your body—shake, stop, yell, or brush it off. Take stock of your dreambody when you are done.

TEN

DREAMWORK AND TRAUMA-BASED TREATMENT APPROACHES FOR HEALING NIGHTMARES

Let everything happen to you: beauty and terror. Just keep going. No feeling is final.

—*Rainer Maria Rilke*

Hope is being able to see that there is light despite all of the darkness.
—*Desmond Tutu*

Nightmares are one of the most intrusive and insidious effects of trauma. They can begin immediately in the aftermath of the traumatic events and persist for years and decades following the trauma as the survivor continues to deal with the long-term effects and with the triggers that directly or indirectly remind them of the trauma. Nightmares can be actual replays of the trauma, as Jay's were, or couched in metaphor and symbolism that echo the emotional fallout and the spiritual toll the trauma has taken. Because this book is geared to healing from trauma-based nightmares and dreams, this chapter will offer you healing techniques both from the world of dreamwork and from the world of trauma treatment. Many if not most of the methods have been mentioned in previous chapters, but here I will break them down for easier access and let you know which ones are perfectly safe to try on you own and others that you would be advised to engage the help of a friend or therapist.

Remember that you do not have to take this journey alone. That is part of the healing too—being able to be accompanied down the dark roads of trauma and nightmare is the essence of Stage 3 in Herman's three stages of healing from trauma: "reconnection." Judith Jordan, scholar from the Wellesley Centers for Women tells us that healing can happen when we can return to the pain of the past and find that this time we are no longer alone.[46]

The loss of control inherent in simply going to sleep at night can itself be a trigger for some trauma survivors. Being asleep is the equivalent of being unaware and unconscious of our surroundings, a scary proposition for those who feel the need to permanently keep their guard up for safety. Add to that those survivors whose traumatic events happened in a bed, or in a bedroom, or in the dark, and we have a perfect storm for terrors in the night. It is no wonder why some survivors even develop a phobia of going to sleep, adding chronic insomnia to their struggles to cope.

My friend Eve had PTSD and one year slept in the living room with the Christmas tree lights on for months to keep the darkness at bay. By March when her roommates said that was long enough to keep the tree up, she went to the store and bought a small artificial tree that she installed in her bedroom and lit the colorful lights nightly. When my daughter was young, she developed a fear of sleeping alone in her bedroom, as many children do at certain ages. Even though nightmares can be a normative part of development,

46. Judith V. Jordan, Alexandra G. Kaplan, Jean Baker Miller, Irene P. Stiver, and Janet L. Surrey, *Women's Growth in Connection: Writings from the Stone Center* (New York City: The Guilford Press, 1991).

they are still nightmares. We made her a little nest of folded blankets and pillows on the floor near our bed, and she slept in it for the better part of two years. This proximity to her parents gave her comfort and a sense of safety, as it does for most children suffering from nightmares. When she was ready, she transitioned back to her own bedroom with the aid of snuggle time together in her bed and transitional objects to carry over the safety and comfort from her parents' room. "Blankie" or "Monkey" or "Teddy" are strong protectors in the night for many children. When she went off to college, my daughter informed me that most of the young women in her dorm brought their stuffed animal or the equivalent with them as well. As we are more vulnerable to our fears during times of transition in our lives, it makes sense that college freshman with this big life transition would need some extra comfort in the night.

Write It Down

Finding and creating safety, protection, and comfort before going to sleep is one route of healing nightmares and their sources. Another crucial step is developing a practice of anchoring them down on paper in our dream journals or on recording devices to be able to pin down the thoughts, emotions, images, and stories that our dreaming brains create. We can then be better able to address, deal with, and re-story our dreams, the events that shaped them, and our lives. If we don't keep a record, we are much less likely to recognize the patterns in our dreaming, or to know when we are stuck or when we are making progress. In addition, seeing the nightmare in writing and/ or drawing helps us to gain some instant mastery over it by attaching it to paper rather than free-floating in our heads. We can more easily see an association or insight that pops out from the written words or pictures that we may not have noticed otherwise.

If you can, write your dreams down in the middle of the night as well. I recently found a wonderful little book light that clips right onto my journal and doesn't disturb a sleeping partner. By the way, this works great for creative inspiration or even to-do lists in the wee hours. I don't know about you, but I don't always trust that I will remember something in the morning if I don't write it down, so I will frequently jot a few words of my grocery list, an idea for a chapter heading, or a reminder to send that birthday card, and then I can go back to sleep without worrying that I will forget. As far as dreams go, if you wake knowing that you had a dream or nightmare, but can't remember any details, just write down the emotions you woke with, and/or the word "dream" or "nightmare" along with the date. This honors your dream muse and lets it know you are serious about your goal of healing.

EXERCISE
Write It Down!

Hopefully you have purchased a dream journal as encouraged at the beginning of *PTSDreams*, but not to worry if you haven't; it's never too late. It can be a colorful, bound writer's journal or a simple spiral notebook. Your choice, whatever will prompt you to write them down. And don't forget to also record your emotions as well as the narratives and images. Draw, sketch, make lists, give it a title, or even name your journal "Dream Healing Odyssey" or "Mastering Nightmares" or whatever rings true for you and points you in the direction you want to be going.

I have broken down the rest of this chapter into methods and techniques that you can use to feel protected in the night and to unpack the meaning and messages from your nightmares. There are three sections:

1. Things you can do before going to sleep,

2. Things you can do during or on the threshold of sleep, and

3. Things you can do after waking.

In addition, get into the practice of writing down whatever you remember as soon as you wake to capture the optimum information from your dream state. Keep the journal right next to your bed. It may be tempting to avoid recording your nightmares. After all, who wants to remember such scary things? Try to do it anyway; keeping the record is important. Be gentle with yourself if you forget or just can't do it sometimes. Honor your own process. If it was important for you to know, the messages in the dreams will come back. (This is the point of those repetitive dreams. They keep coming back in one form or another until we have learned what we need to learn and have made the life changes we need to make.) Honor your own pacing and extend compassion to yourself. Putting your dreams and nightmares down in writing also makes it easier to share them with others and engage helpers on the road back home to your clearest and most peaceful self.

Nightmare Interventions Set 1: Things to Do Before You Sleep to Reduce Nightmares

Starting from the ground up, so to speak, set the stage for safety in your entire house. Lock your doors and decide if you do or don't want to leave a light lit somewhere so that you don't wake into pitch dark. Make a clear transition from your day activities to your nighttime for restorative sleep. This is also good sleep hygiene to help with insomnia. After these activities, we will look at specific ways to feel safe in your bedroom and bed.

Turn off electronic devices at least an hour before sleep, as the computer lights stimulate our wakefulness. Titrate your media exposure. Don't watch scary movies or the latest horrible news story before bed. The last thing we need is more upset that could pass through the wake/sleep barrier just before turning in at night. Personally, I choose not to watch horror films at all—I know that I am too thin-boundaried. Negotiate with your partner or housemates about what the media diet will be in the evenings.

Have nighttime rituals. Take a soothing, warm shower or bath, and while you do think about rinsing or soaking off anything upsetting from the day. Don't wear the same clothes to bed that you wore during the day, using that as a transition as well. Years ago I learned from a trauma specialist to change my clothes immediately after work so that I wasn't inadvertently taking the stress and trauma of my clients with me into my private life. I still do a version of that, even with Zoom meetings during the pandemic and comfy pants— I'll change something, maybe my shirt or even my socks, just to have a ritual to mark the transition. It seems to work well—I almost never carry my client's issues with me into family time or dreamtime.

Once you have cleared the space in your household and your immediate presence, it's time to safeguard your bedroom and your dreaming space. Developing a ritual helps here too. Then you don't have to re-create the wheel every night, and it becomes a comfort. Adjust it as needed until you get it just right.

EXERCISES

Before You Sleep

1. *The Bubble of Light*

A common and very helpful ritual is to surround yourself and your bed with a bubble or egg of light. In your mind's eye, trace an oval around yourself, your bed, or your whole bedroom that is filled with a soft, glowing light. Pick the color or colors that are just right for you. You might use the same colors all the time or vary it according to your needs. Let yourself feel this sense of enveloping protection. If it fits in with your belief systems, you may name it the Light of Universal Protection, or the Light of God, or The Force—or just feel the warm, protective light with no particular name.

2. *Incubate the Dreams You Want*

While you can't control what comes through into your dreamscape, you can still make requests. This is what incubating a dream means. You can write a line or two in your journal or say out loud or repeat in your head that you would like dreams that "Come only in the service of my healing," or "Nothing more than I can easily handle without becoming dysregulated," or "That give me wisdom and insight into healing from this traumatic event or period of time," or "That bring me Guides and Helpers to keep me safe," or "That I can remember clearly so I can work on them." Whatever you want, you can ask for it. Repeat this a few times to really set it in your psyche. Try to have it be your last purposeful thought before falling asleep.

3. Just Say "No"

While this may not be the optimal or complete approach to addiction issues, it often works very well to safeguard us from nightmares that dysregulate our system. Imagine a portal between your waking world and your sleeping world and a door between the two that you can shut. Firmly close that door before going to sleep, and say, maybe out loud, or in writing, or at least strongly in your mind "No" to your nightmares or nightmare figures. Deceptively simple, it is actually quite powerful and easy for kids to do as well as adults.

4. Incubate Insights from Last Night's Dream or Nightmare

In addition to incubating safety, healing, or protection before you sleep, you can also ask for advice about your last night's dream. If you have worked through a nightmare, but still have some questions or an image that is a conundrum, or there is still some upset connected to the nightmare, write a line or two in your journal asking for more insight into the meaning, symbolism, or importance of that image. This is often the homework we give in dream circle, especially when there are several dreamers wanting some airtime and we don't have the time to investigate fully every image. You can simply write something like, "Send me a dream that more fully explains image X to me," or "What am I supposed to do with character Y?", or "How can I further reduce my level of upset or distress about this dream?"

5. "Polarity Hands" and Other Mudras

Sometimes healing and comfort is literally in the palm of our hands. Use your body to ease your mind. A wonderful hand posture from polarity therapy is to put one hand on your belly, and the other over your heart. This helps to balance the energetic and meridian systems. Just lay there quietly with your hands on your heart and belly. You can try switching hands, but I find that most people have a preferred side for each hand once they get the hang of it. Just breathe quietly and come into balance.

Another lovely hand/body pose is one hand on your heart, the other cupping your cheek. This makes the face-heart connection that Steven Porges, Deb Dana, and others speak about in Polyvagal Therapy. Face-to-face contact is so necessary for soothing and what is called *co-regulating*, where one person helps another to come into a state of calm. It stimulates our internal neuroception, that nonverbal internal somatic response from our bodies, a wordless experience of pure sensation, very similar to tuning in while focusing. This hand to cheek and heart pose stimulates a sense of compassion and befriending, one might imagine doing this with a beloved child. Try it now; you may be amazed at how sweet it feels. Let your head tip ever so slightly onto your hand as you cradle your cheek and feel that connection with your heart space.

From yoga, the classic meaning of a *mudra* is fingers touching and being held gently together to close an energetic circuit. Experiment with which feels best for you; thumb touching index finger, thumb touching middle finger, etc., and breathe quietly into this pose as you drift off to sleep.

6. The Power of Smell and Taste

From our earliest ancestors, herbal and plant medicine has been used to help us heal from a variety of physical and mental woes. Some plants that are particularly used to help with restful sleep are lavender, chamomile, valerian, and spearmint. Sleepytime Tea recently added valerian to their proprietary blend. You can make yourself a nice cup of any of these teas, have a moisture cream that contains the scent, or buy a diffuser and put a few drops of essential oil in it. I was pleasantly surprised at just how lovely the diffuser was when I walked into my acupuncturist's office a few weeks ago and he had one running with a mixture of the above herbs. For some, CBD oil or cream is just the thing, and some companies add lavender or other scents to it as well.

7. Lullabies and Other Music

Some of our coziest methods of easing our young ones into sleep is singing them lullabies at night. The combination of the soothing sound and presence of a trusted caregiver helps to create this bubble of safety and protection around our child. If you were lucky enough to have a parent or caregiver who sang to you, you can probably still remember exactly what they sang. We now know that music soothes the savage beast for adults as well, and a recent study shows that adults who listen to restful music before sleep (sorry, not Metallica or hard rock!) tend to sleep better and more peacefully. You might find a song with healing or inspiring words, or some classical or folk music that is calming to you.

8. Meditate and Breathe

With or without a guided meditation tape, guide yourself or let yourself be guided into a state of calm relaxation. You can use a body scan method, head to toe or toe to head, to sweep your body clean of stress and invite in comfort, calm, and compassion. (It is not cheating to use a CD or app.) Sometimes we all need that external voice to follow. Breathwork is part of this as well. Let your breath slow down and lengthen the time between the in breath and the out breath, "in-spire" with images of safety, protection, and healing, "ex-hale" with expelling what you do not want—stress, fear, anxiety, porousness to bad dreams. There are many suggestions from the yoga world for types of breathwork, as well as a type of yoga called *yoga nidra* that is specifically set up to ease you into restful sleep.

9. Boundary Balancing

This phrase *boundary balance* is both general and specific. In general, before going to sleep we can incubate (pre-program) the desire to have good boundaries between ourselves and anything that would cause us distress in the night. Setting up that egg of light or drawing a mental circle of protection around ourselves is a form of setting up good boundaries. There is also a specific boundary technique I learned from Judith Swack, creator of HBLU (Healing from the Body Level Up). This Boundary Balance, which was originally created by Mary Louise Mueller, invites us to attend to setting up 100 percent healthy working boundaries at all five levels of our being: the physical, the emotional, the cognitive, the spiritual, and the energetic. It then instructs us to have all five of the *functions* of our boundaries be in good working order—the functions of keeping things out, of letting things in, of keeping things in, of letting things out, and of communications with others. This is a useful technique to protect you from over-activation from nightmares as well. What follows is a step-by-step protocol of this balance.

The Boundary Balance Technique

To practice this boundary balance, it is useful to imagine the image of a cell for understanding the five functions of a boundary. Imagine the cell wall around any type of cell, say a bone cell. It might help you visualize this if you draw two little closed squiggly circles next to each other. These can represent the cells. Then with each of the functions, you can draw an arrow depicting the function within or between the two cells.

The cell wall is the equivalent of the boundary. It serves five functions:

1. It keeps things out. Anything that is not a bone cell, like brain or liver cells, toxins, or anything that threatens the cell.

2. It lets things in. Like food and nutrients and whatever the cell needs for growth.

3. It keeps things in. Everything that is an integral part of the cell itself stays inside the cell wall, like the nucleus, the mitochondria, the DNA strands, etc.

4. It lets things out. Waste products, energy, and damaged or injured parts of the cell.

5. It communicates with other bone cells, sharing information and function.

These are the five functions that our energy boundaries need to perform as well. We typically think of a boundary just as keeping something out; here we see that it is more complex than that. Both cell walls and human boundaries need to be permeable, opening and closing at the right time and with the right stimulus, letting things in and out, keeping things in and out, and communicating with others.

We also need to have 100 percent healthy working boundaries at all the levels of being for optimal functioning:

1. With our physical body: Who is physically there with us, and with our own sensations and physical integrity?

2. With our emotional body and our feelings.

3. With our cognitive body, including our thoughts and belief systems.

4. With our spiritual bodies, keeping our own spiritual beliefs intact and not overly influenced by other people or entities from other realms.

5. With our energetic bodies: Not being influenced or hijacked by other people's energies or giving away too much of our own. (An example of this is being in contact with energy vampires who seem to suck out our energy and life force.)

My colleague, Joy, reminded me that since we can use this balance specifically to boundary against nightmares, we can add a sixth level too:

6. With our dream bodies, to let in only the dreams and dream energy that serves us while keeping out the rest.

How This Works

Now let's apply this information to nightmares. We might need to be boundaried from other people, other people's energies, from our own feelings (maybe anxiety or worry), or our own thoughts (maybe negative self-talk or self-criticism). If you know muscle testing, also called applied kinesiology, you can muscle test to ascertain what level of intact boundaries you have at any given time. This is the method Joy used before going to sleep when she was having that series of nightmares about a shooter outside her home. It helped reduce her degree of upset and calm her emotional state both before going to sleep and upon waking.

If you don't know muscle testing, simply ask yourself, "Do I have 100 percent healthy working boundaries between myself and X?" and listen intuitively for the answer to arise. The "X" might be nightmares; a particular person, scene, or image from a nightmare; or uncontrolled upset or strong emotions from a nightmare. If you get a "no" response, you can either move right to the intervention to reestablish your boundaries or discern which of the five categories might have been breached. It might be one, several, or all.

Then ask yourself how many minutes of *tapping* or *feathering* you need to reestablish healthy boundaries. Again, listen in with your inner ear for the answer to arise. Most people seem to need between one and five minutes of the tapping protocol. Some have needed up to ten or fifteen minutes. Here's what you do now:

The Boundary Balance Protocol

1. Determine how long you need to tap, to tap and feather, or to bring in light with an angel.

2. If your system calls for an angel with light, invite the angel of your choice, who may or may not have a name,

to bring you Divine Light. Notice what color or colors you need, and then bring your hands up overhead, grab hold of the edges of the light shield, and bring it down around your body.

3. Tapping in this case means gently tapping with your fingertips of either hand on your sternum. Just feel into the right spot. (This corresponds with the central and governing meridians from acupuncture.)

4. Alternately, your body may also want to "feather." Then you take the hand that was tapping on your sternum, and gently move it up your chest and neck and out from under your chin releasing the fingers at the end of each round.

5. Repeat as needed, either just the tapping or the tapping and feathering until you have reached your allotted time.

6. While you are tapping, also say out loud, at least as a whisper so that your ears can hear what your mouth says, "I have 100 percent healthy working boundaries between myself and X" (your fear, dream monster, father, critical thoughts—whatever you need the right distance from).

7. When you finish your tapping and speaking, check to see if you now have 100 percent healthy working boundaries. If not, you can do a few more rounds.

Please know also that good boundary establishment is something we may need to do periodically or even regularly in our lives. It is not just one and done. If you have chronic nightmares, you may need to do it nightly for a while. If you have a difficult family member, you might need to do it each time before you see them. Parents can use it to avoid soaking up their children's angst and upset, and vice versa. With practice you can tune in more quicky to when you need this balance and tap your way into good boundaries more quickly.

Nightmare Interventions Set 2: Interventions During Dreams or Threshold Dream States

EXERCISES
During Sleep or Threshold States

1. Lucid Dreaming

The main form of intervention to do while you are asleep and dreaming is called lucid dreaming. In a nutshell, this means learning to become aware that you are asleep and dreaming while you are in your dream. This skill stretches what we think of as consciousness and makes the boundaries between conscious and unconscious more fluid than we might have supposed. The simplest method of teaching yourself to do this is by noticing "I am awake, I am not dreaming" periodically during the day, and then extending the intention to being able to make this same distinction while you are asleep. In addition, lucid dreamers recommend choosing something to become aware of in your dreams, like your hands for example, that will alert you to the fact that you are dreaming. Therefore, if you see your hands in your dream, you can have the thought, "Oh look, here are my hands so I must be dreaming."

If you are interested in learning more about lucid dreams, there are a number of excellent books available, including those by Robert Waggoner and by Clare

Johnson. Practiced in its purest form, "Oh look, I am dreaming" may be a wonderful relief for nightmare sufferers. It can bring a helpful sense of distance to the experience rather than fully feeling the emotions in the dream in their full living color and going through them without the meta-consciousness afforded by lucidity. I would encourage those with nightmares to be cautious about *intervening* too quickly in their dreams however, which is often the next step for lucid dreamers.

Lucid dreaming has become quite popular lately in dream communities. It can be great fun, and you can learn to become lucid and can then fly, swim underwater, have adventures, and in general change your dreams as you dream them. I can certainly appreciate the apparent advantage to this if you are having a nightmare. Who wants to be stuck in a nightmare if there is another choice? But I offer a caution here: We need to first know what our shadow holds. We can't heal from trauma if we are always flying away from it or changing up what is happening in dreams that have come to show us what we need to learn to heal. After all, if we cut off the head of the Hydra, then two more grow back in its place. Even Hercules needed a special cauterization technique to avoid this problem. We don't want two more nightmares to grow in place of the one we cut off too quickly.

If you do become lucid in a nightmare, rather than stopping it or interfering with its natural trajectory, instead you might be able to find helpers inside the dream or to bring some in to support you in dealing with whatever shows up. Try bringing in protection and guides to keep you safe, but without removing yourself from the story or changing the dream in midstream. That way you don't accidentally short circuit the encounters or beings or circumstances that you need to heal. If you have already established guides and protections that can assist you in waking life, go ahead and call these in to keep you safe. Invite in who or what you need for enough safety to be better able to listen to your shadows and monsters with less fear and no harm. Then stay with the nightmare to see how it organically unfolds.

If you do become lucid in a PTSDream or nightmare, I invite you primarily to notice, "Oh, I am dreaming" or "I am dreaming and therefore safe," but not to try to effect changes in the development of the dream itself no matter how tempting. Let the dream bring you the hidden gems buried in its dry desert sands, waves of the impending tsunami, or the jagged, rocky landscape without smoothing it over. Then, once you awake, notice everything. Come back to your body. Try GAIA, focusing, Integrated Embodied Dreamwork, or any of the other methods to unpack your dream from the next section. Once you have learned what you need to know, then you can feel freer to explore lucid dream interventions, or in the meantime, try Wilding.

2. W.I.L.D.ing

There is a variation on lucid dreaming called by the acronym *W.I.L.D: Waking Induced Lucid Dreaming*. Lucid dreaming itself refers to the state of being aware that you are dreaming while you are asleep, and then have the ability to move things around or change the course of the dream while you are having it. *W.I.L.D.*

is a semi-waking version of this. I can get behind this variation on lucid dreaming for nightmares more whole-heartedly without qualifications.

Wilding happens in that half-awake and half-asleep state when you are just waking up or falling asleep. Jung called these the hypnopompic and hypnogogic zones. In them you have some measure of choice or control over the dreamish images that come through to you. In this in-between place we temporarily have full access to many more parts of our brain, so we can make the most of it by engaging with the dream characters, land-scapes, and objects. Here we can purposefully direct ourselves and our healing attention to where we most need it to be, along with actively bringing in any protec-tions or resources that we need to safely do so. We can practice active imagination, spontaneous writing if we are awake enough, and dream re-entry without losing the basic integrity of the dream itself. I would invite the trauma dreamers that are interested in lucidity to prac-tice it before or after the dream in the hypnopompic or hypnogogic zones, but to allow the unconscious in its wisdom to first give you what you need to know while you are asleep.

Dreamwork and Trauma-Based Interventions to Use with Our Dreams After We Wake

The bulk of our work with dreams and nightmares will happen after the fact, that is, after we have experienced our dreams and woken up. The rest of this chapter is a sort of cookbook of dreamwork and trauma work interventions, many of which have been referred to earlier, and some of which are introduced here for the first time.

Sigmund Freud is often cited as the grandfather of dreamwork. He coined the phrase that dreams are the "royal road to the unconscious," and contributed greatly to the modern science of psychoanalytic theory. We owe our attention to puns and plays on words in dreamwork to him. In modern dreamwork however, most dreamworkers have moved past his unilateral approach to dreams as being symbolic of unexpressed sexual desires or complexes. Regarding trauma work in particular, Freud missed the mark. He was seeing many patients, particularly women, who were apparently having memory bursts while dreaming of having been victimized by sexual assault or incest. When he first published work on these dreams that he was hearing about, Victorian societal norms could not acknowledge this as truth, and his findings were not believed. He then backtracked and repositioned his interpretations of these dreams as purely symbolic rather than as memories of events that occurred and had been dissociated. This set trauma treatment back many decades until later in the 1970s when the nature of trauma, incest, and memory was more fully understood.

Rather than a Freudian approach, my dreamwork is more centered in Carl Jung's work, using active imagination and attention to the spiritual and the transpersonal as well as the personal elements of a dream. Jung invites us to use techniques such as *association, amplification*, and *projection* as we explore our dreams. Good dreamwork is the skill of making associations. This reminds me of that, and then following out the associations wherever they may lead. The technique of *amplification* means to enlarge, to make bigger, to expand the image, and give it more life to see what else it may hold. It can also include looking at the *a priori* meaning of a dream image; looking up, for example what is the nature and the characteristics of a saguaro cactus or a chickadee to see how their unique, real-life qualities may be relevant for your dream. *Projection* happens when aspects of ourselves become personified in other dream characters and we explore through our dreams "the X part of me"—the angry man part, the scared child part, the warrior woman part. This style is also used in Gestalt dreamwork and in IFS, Internal Family Systems therapies.

EXERCISES
After We Wake

1. *Dream On!*

One of my favorite dream interventions is to remind dreamers: "This isn't where the dream ended; this is just where you woke up." And this is not just wishful thinking, for we know that our cognitions exist within a continuum of consciousness that ranges from deeply sound asleep to full wide awake and present. In between these end states of consciousness, we have not only the hypnogogic or hypnopompic states at the edges of our dreaming, but we also have daydreaming, spacing out, musing, being in "flow" state, or in a trance. In the trauma realm, being triggered to feel that a past event is currently happening as well as the range of dissociative states are also alterations in consciousness. So, my comment is not just hyperbole when I invite people to dream it forward: "If this dream was to continue, what happens next? And next?" This creates an opportunity to engage in active imagination work in waking consciousness that engages the same brain muscles as our asleep dreaming does. Here we do have some control and get to dream a nightmare forward to a safer resolution and more desired ending than the one we woke up with.

According to neuroscientist Robert Stickgold, recent studies seem to show that deep REM sleep processes older, more distant memories, while the hypnopompic zone offers us images and memories from the previous day that are still in the process of being consolidated and associated. Both types of dreaming help us with the task of memory consolidation or reconsolidation and allow our brain to look more expansively and creatively into the future. Creatively continuing our sleeping dream or nightmare upon awakening allows us to access the best of all worlds in healing the distant past, the recent past, the present, and the potential future.

2. Active Imagination

I have used this Jungian phrase several times. In essence, it means to translate and assimilate the workings of our unconscious minds into images, narratives, and landscapes in our conscious minds through some form of self-expression. These can include associative imagining, writing, art, movement, and storytelling. It includes paying attention to both our personal and the collective unconscious and allowing images, feelings, sensations, and thoughts to freely spring forward without censorship. Jung invites us to first hold the image or nightmare in our attention. The very act of contemplating it will often begin to produce changes and alterations. The next step beyond observation is to engage with the images in a conscious act of participation. Jung invites us to differentiate these fantasies from ourselves by coming into relationship with them through personifying them, amplifying (enlarging) them, and/or engaging in dialogue with them.

Jung felt that this process begins with an unsettled problem that is creating psychic pressure on us. The engagement in active imagination helps to relieve the pressure and open up new possibilities of understanding and subsequent action. It deepens our experience and allows us to come into a different relationship with the monsters and demons that may inhabit our dreams. If we stay with the feelings and the images long enough to experience the raw energy of them, then we have created the opportunity for transformation and healing.

Here is an example of this process. Olivia dreams:

I am in a hotel room, not in my home. There is a large rattlesnake that has made a nest there. I am afraid of it, so I jump up on the bed.

The CI or Central Image in this dream is the snake. Also significant is that Olivia was not at home, a recurring theme for her. She grew up knowing that her mother never wanted to have children and treated them accordingly, meaning a lot of neglect and emotional abuse. Her father was gone at work for long hours every day. By engaging with the dream and the dream snake in active imagination, Olivia had the following associations after her initial fear in the dream:

"A snake can be dangerous or benign, or even helpful because it eats rodents. Some snakes have venom. If I am too vulnerable, I will get hurt or bit by the snake. The venom will poison me—oh, just like my mother's venom poisoned me." (She sits with this association for a moment, letting it sink in. Then I simply ask, "What else about a snake?") "Snakes shed their skin. Tara Brach said that a snake that does not shed its skin perishes. We have to take the exquisite risk of being vulnerable for a while in order to survive and grow. The snake is a symbol of transformation. Surviving the venom of the snakebite involves an alchemical process. The antidote is trust in Spirit, trust in inner knowledge, and in a knowing of myself that is stronger than the bite."

Olivia's free associations in the process of active imagination with the snake allowed her to not only understand the symbolism of the snake in her dream, but why she was so often not at home in a dream. Through her active imagination and free association, she discovered that the antidote to this kind of mother/snake venom is trust, inner knowledge, and the courage to risk being vulnerable in the world. And after all, she said, since the snake had already made a nest in her room, she needed to learn to live with it and get along with it and learn how to make a nest for herself in the world. She also decided to work with some sculpy clay to make an image of a healing snake in its nest.

3. GAIA: The Guided Active Imagination Approach

I created this method of dreamwork in response to nightmares. It has two steps based on a combination of Jung's active imagination work combined with good, solid trauma treatment knowledge and protocols. The first step, before moving into an active imagination free associative style, is to set up safety parameters for the dreamer to avoid abreaction. I had several dreamers who came to me for consultation after they had consulted with someone else who freaked them out about their dream or led them to believe that they were haunted by dark forces and needed an exorcism.

The first order of all healing is "do no harm." Hence, I set up the safety protocol as Stage 1 of this method, bringing in all the guides, protection, comfort, and safety that they need before moving on to deal directly with the monsters, bad guys, or Shadow in the nightmares. Titrating (a little bit at a time) and pendulating (moving back and forth between safety and provocative or upsetting material) in Stage 2 of this method allows the dreamer to conquer their nightmares without undue distress or becoming dysregulated. If the upset gets too great, we go back and reconnect with the safety elements or add additional ones before moving forward.

4. Back and Forth Between the Dream and the Waking Now

Some dreamers need to go into and out of doing the dreamwork to maintain grounding and safety. They need to return to the reality of the here and now in between pieces of dreamwork. One of my clients, Dana, found the flowers I keep in my office very soothing and grounding for her. So, whenever she approached her edge of the window of affect tolerance and was afraid she would get overwhelmed, she would shift gears and focus on the flowers. She would then describe them out loud in detail to reground herself in something beautiful and present before continuing with the difficult stuff. She would say, "Oh look, you have purple and yellow flowers today. They look like irises, I love irises. And see how you've added in some green fern fronds. That makes such a nice arrangement." In the beginning I helped her with this. Later she internalized the process and was able to make the shift to describing the flowers spontaneously on her own whenever she needed to stay present and get a little break from the hard work.

5. Using the SUDS Rating to Quantify Distress and Progress

Borrowing from a technique used in many body-mind trauma treatment therapies and energy medicine techniques, you can keep track of your progress in relieving distress in your nightmare work. Give the nightmare a rating on the Subjective Unit of Distress (SUDS) scale before you start work on it. You can then re-rate the level of upset when you are done working on it. This gives you a more objective measure (even though it is called subjective) of your progress on resolving a nightmare and the issue that underlies it. When you wake, as you write the nightmare down, give it a SUDS rating between 0 and 10, from no distress (0) to the worst you can imagine (10). Find where in your body you experience the sensations and emotions of fear, anxiety, sadness, anger, etc., and what it feels like there (e.g., "I feel anxiety in my stomach. It feels churning and tight, and I rate it a 7."). Then, once you have done some work on the dream, check to see if the distress level has gone down, and if the sensations have changed (e.g., "Okay, now my anxiety is at a 4, and my stomach feels a little queasy but not churning. I am also now aware of some sadness in my heart, and it feels heavy. I give the sadness a SUDS level of 5."). Not only can the level of distress change, but the type of emotions can shift and change as well as you move energy and healing to free up other layers of the dream and the trauma response.

6. Remember Your Dream Layers Through the PARDES (The Orchard of Dreams)

In chapter 5 I outlined a system of working through the layers of a dream or nightmare through the PARDES system, based on the four layers of reading from the Torah in Kabbalist tradition. Each layer has secrets to tell and buried in your scariest nightmares are additional layers of meaning and healing. Review chapter 5 for how to work with the dream material at each of the four layers. You may choose or have the time to work through all the layers at one sitting. If you don't, you can always go back to your dream or nightmare later and glean more insight.

7. Image Rehearsal Therapy

This is one of the gold standards to resolve nightmares. In short, once you have "dreamed it forward" or added resources to your dream or changed how it ended, you then practice this new dream several times, and write down the new ending or resolution. Practice makes perfect. We rehearse to gain permanence, like an actor rehearsing a new role until they embody it. This is the premise of method acting. It helps us to break old patterns of recurring nightmares or trauma-based responses in life and to develop new neural networks and new patterns that are neutral rather than stressful, and ultimately that are life-enhancing and life-affirming. We are trying to create new neural networks in our brains to override the old trauma-based ones. According to Krakow and Harris, IRT is a three-step process:

1. Write down your nightmare.

2. Think of a way you can change it. Use your intuition to come up with your best response of the moment. You can change it a little or a lot. Come up with a positive change.

3. Set aside five to twenty minutes each day to review this altered version of the dream and paint a mental picture of it.

I would add going into as much detail as possible with your new, nicer version to create as clear a picture as you can and use all of your senses to really bring the new version into life. The more sensory input you add, the more powerful your new story will be. So rather than simply changing the ending from "The monster got closer and closer and was about to grab me" to "I escaped from the monster," instead say something like this: "I have grown wings on my feet like Winged Mercury, and as the monster gets closer I activate my wings and start soaring into the air. I feel the liftoff and I am light and free, and the monster is left down on the ground helpless." Following image rehearsal, the changes in your nightmares may be gradual. You might not stop having the nightmares all at once, but they will begin to morph and lessen the level of distress, frequency, and power of the images. They may start to become more distant, and the difficult characters more neutral or even helpful.

Notice that I write the new image in the first person, as if it is happening now. This too strengthens our image rehearsal work as we bring it into the present tense. If you start writing in the past tense (as I often catch myself doing), catch yourself and change it from "that happened" to "this is happening now" and see how much more powerful it is.

8. Inside or Out

We can work from outside the dream or from inside the dream. Both are valid, just different styles of work and each may get you different insights. Working from the *outside* means that you are talking about your dream or nightmare, perhaps discussing possible symbolism, metaphors, or associations to your current or past life. Working from *inside* the dream means that you re-enter the dream and speak from the first person of your dream self or another dream character. Here, rather than associative work, you are working in the first person in the here and now. The difference is something like, "I had a dream of a large rabbit that was eating up all the vegetables I had planted in the garden. It reminded me of my boss at work who seemed to tear up any work that I put on his desk. He even has buckteeth." That would be working outside the dream. Working inside the dream would be something like, "I see this large rabbit approaching my garden where I have just planted lettuce and sugar snap peas, and I want to protect them from the rabbit. I say 'shoo, shoo' to the rabbit and then I get some fencing and some coyote urine, which I have heard helps, and sprinkle it around my plants." Both methods can get the dreamer some associations and ideas to save her dream vegetable garden and her waking associated "garden" at work.

9. Title and Re-title

For a quick check to see how you are doing on resolving the issues that your nightmares are highlighting, give it a title. Let it emerge from your gut; allow yourself to be surprised by it. This first title will usually reflect the CI, the Central Image or Central Issue the dream is bringing forth. Then do your work on the dream, using any and all resources at your disposal: dreamwork techniques, trauma-work interventions, your friends and dream posse, your therapist. Once you have taken as much off the charge of the dream as you can in the time you have, check to see if the title has changed. You may be pleasantly surprised at how the new title is more affirming and positive than the original one. Two examples of this include the change for six-year-old Sophia from *The Monster Behind the Door* to *My New Friend*, and for Amanda from *Darkest Depths* to *Diving for Treasure*.

10. Embodied and Gestalt Dreamwork

We have a whole chapter on this, so just a reminder here to embody your nightmares and dreams in any way that supports your healing and growth. Somatic Experiencing developed by Peter Levine and Sensorimotor Psychotherapy developed by Pat Ogden are two body/mind therapies often used in trauma treatment that have contributed to several of the methods and techniques used in embodied dreamwork. Use Gendlin's Focusing work to tune into the dream. Become a character or animal or object or a piece of the landscape in your dream, using the Gestalt approach that every element in our dream is a part of ourselves. If you can't conceptualize how to embody a piece of the landscape, it may help to recall the talking and apple-throwing trees in the *Wizard of Oz*. Speak from that point of view.

My friend, Liza, dreamt that her breast was sore and red. After the requisite check to make sure that she had a mammogram recently, we asked her if she could speak from the point of view of the breast. It said:

I am so sick and tired of being hauled out every day to feed and take care of people. I feel so sucked on. I just want to rest for a change!

Well, she wasn't breastfeeding anymore, but she sure was tired of being the first order caretaker for her kids and husband and hospital patients, and this dream image showed her just how much she needed a break.

You can create stationary images referred to as dream sculpting or act out the different characters and give them new dialogue, either taking all the parts yourself, or enlisting others to perform the scene with you. Pay attention to where in your body you feel an emotion: in your heart, throat, or feet, etc. See what that part of the body wants to say / do with that emotion. Then dance it, move it, shake it out. Use art, writing, clay, theater, or movement to bring the nightmare to life and add resources if you need them to the picture or scene. Jungian analyst Marion Woodman believes that dreams live in a universe free of time and space restrictions, and that only the fluidity of the arts—movement, poetry, myth, and art—truly carry their messages well to waking awareness. However, if we feed our dreams with our creativity and curiosity, they will nourish our understanding for days, even years.

11. Body/Mind Interventions from Trauma Treatment and Energy Psychology

Finally, there are a number of powerful methods developed in the last several decades from the world of trauma therapy. These body/mind interventions are based on some combination of the science of neurobiology, energy meridians from acupuncture, and a wholistic unified somatic approach to healing. They can all be used in conjunction with dreamwork while targeting the nightmare or the part of the nightmare you are working on. Three frequently used methods are EFT (Emotional Freedom Technique) known colloquially as "tapping," TAT (Tapas Acupressure Technique), and EMDR (Eye Movement Desensitization and Reprocessing).

EFT involves tapping on various meridian points on the body while simultaneously attending to the emotion or distress that you want to alleviate. There is a specific protocol that can be learned, and once learned it is generally safe to practice on your own with elements from your dream or your life. Lynne and Robert Hoss wrote a book integrating EFT and dreamwork.[47] The other two methods also involve a protocol that combines elements of cognitive, energetic, and somatic work. These methods are taught to trained professionals. They are powerful healing tools with research supporting them. TAT is also based in the understanding of meridians, using self-acupressure on specific points while following a cognitive protocol.

---

47. Lynne Hoss and Robert Hoss, *Dream to Freedom: A Handbook for Integrating Dreamwork and Energy Psychology* (Fulton, CA: Energy Psychology Press, 2013).

EMDR in particular is now recognized internationally by many mental health licensing bodies as a treatment of choice for trauma. My colleague Deborah Korn co-authored a book with a client that is written for the lay person called *Every Memory Deserves Respect: EMDR* that does a wonderful job describing the method from both the inside (client point of view) and the outside (therapist point of view). EMDR is premised on bilateral stimulation of the brain while using eye movements and/or auditory or somatic bilateral tapping while focusing on the upset or trauma to be healed. It has been hypothesized that perhaps by crossing the corpus callosum, the central bifurcating seam in the brain, we are better able to integrate information from both the right and the left parts of our brains. If you have a history of trauma in your life, finding a good practitioner who is also trained in one or more of these methods can accelerate the healing process, particularly when combined with active dreamwork that attends directly to nightmares. Find a good trauma practitioner, and then, if they aren't well versed in dreamwork, give them this book!

ELEVEN

FROM PTSD TO PTSG

Post-Trauma Spiritual Growth Through Dreamwork

Her genius lies in rebuking darkness, in maintaining light and in giving breath to hope; to synthesizing that hope, lyrically, down to its bare essentials. She urges listeners to "get up every morning" with a smile on their face. To exude love and receive beauty.

—**"Regarding Carole King"** *by Tanya Pearson*

The world breaks everyone, and afterwards many are strong at the broken places.

—*Ernest Hemingway*

Bad things do happen to good people. No one is immune from the slings and arrows of life, and yet we are able to overcome. We heal, we move on, and ideally we learn from our pain and sorrow and use the knowledge to help others. Often our dreams and nightmares are the catalyst for both our initial inquiry into our dark places and our movement into healing. The theme of this book from the beginning has been that we are oriented to healing, to moving forward, to overcoming or befriending our monsters and demons. We can then reach the fuller life that has room for both/and, and not only either/or. Room for the joy that follows the resolution of our nightmares, as well as the recognition of our grief.

Meditation teacher Tara Brach teaches us a mindfulness practice that uses her acronym R.A.I.N.: Recognize, Allow, Investigate, and Nurture. Applying this to dream and nightmare work, we *Recognize* the nightmare or dream and the emotions in it, we *Allow* ourselves to finally feel the feelings that we may have spent years trying to suppress or ignore, we *Investigate* the sources of our dreams and nightmares and the characters, images, and landscapes they inhabit, and then we *Nurture* ourselves and others as we find the connections, understanding, insight, and ultimately right action to move forward. Working through our nightmares, rather than ignoring or suppressing them, allows us to resolve them at their source, which is often found in traumatic events. We can heal from the inside out or from the outside in, and the beauty of addressing and resolving our nightmares often means that we are simultaneously addressing and resolving the trauma that seeded them. Deep dreamwork is the best way we have of direct access to our unconscious selves, with all its mystery and wisdom.

Recap and Review of Post-Trauma Dreams

In the introduction to *PTSDreams*, we explored the relationship between trauma and nightmares, both the big-T traumas and the small-t traumas, and found that the seeds of the healing are often paradoxically found within the terrors of the nightmare itself. Chapter 1 invited us to attend closely to the emotional narrative of the dream, for the feelings and emotions connected with our images and landscapes and story contain our deepest and most personal truths. So, in my dream, if the falling rain is accompanied by feelings of peace and tranquility, the dream may be about nurturing and growth. But if the same falling rain in your dream is accompanied by a sense of fear and panic that a flood will ensue, then we have two very different dreams with very different meanings.

Chapter 2 helped us to differentiate between nightmares generated by trauma and those generated by other life events or life stages,
while chapter 3 gave us a deep dive into understanding the nature of
trauma itself, including how nightmares are often connected to a
history of trauma. The effect of trauma in our own lives as well as
in the lives of our ancestors and others around us was explored as
we examined the science of epigenetics; the premise that we can be
traumatized by events that happened to others in our family line,
even before we were born. These can show up as both symbolic and
metaphoric representations of trauma in our nightmares, as well as
memory bursts of actual events that push through our consciousness via the medium of our dream states.

Chapter 4 took us even deeper into the examination of repressed
or suppressed traumatic material as we learned to understand the
coping mechanism of dissociation, how it may emerge in nightmares, and the necessity of re-integration of our fragmented self-
parts into a cohesive whole and cohesive life narrative to fully heal.
In Chapter 5 we explored the layers of a dream available to our
inquiry through the four-part system of the PARDES that lets us
look at a dream through its 1) literal story line, 2) through our initial
associations, 3) to its deeper metaphorical significance, 4) and to its
transpersonal and spiritual messages.

The remainder of PTSDreams gave us a template to work safely
and deeply with our nightmares, avoiding the traps of abreaction
or becoming dysregulated. Slow and careful preparation for work
with trauma-based nightmares is the premise for the GAIA method
of the Guided Active Imagination Approach, emphasizing the safety
protocols built into this method of dreamwork. Once we listen
and pay attention, our nightmares begin to shift and change to less
frightening images and no longer "haunt our midnight pillow" in
the same way. Chapter 8 took us down into the Shadow lands, to

finally confront those dark nights of the soul that show up in our darkest dreams and learn to vanquish or befriend the monsters and darkness. The terrifying figures that come to us in the night may be guides or helpers in disguise bearing hidden gifts once we have investigated and perhaps befriended them.

In addition to understanding cognitively and emotionally what is going on in our nightmares, chapter 9 oriented us to embodied and spiritual dreamwork, learning how to literally (somatically) move our dreams forward. In the spiritual realm, we examined interacting with beings from the other side, welcoming as guides and resources the relatives who came to connect with us, Finally, in chapter 10 we added more depth and skills to our dreamwork repertoire as we looked at dream interventions that we could use before, during, and after our dreams from the worlds of trauma treatment, energy psychology, and dreamwork.

So now what? What is the next step in the resolution of our fears and the integration of the dark and the light that help us to move from PTSDreams to PTSG—Post-Trauma Spiritual Growth?

Reaching for the Light and Finding Faith

On the winter solstice this year, I had the following dream:

> I am in a small, dark room like a cell. It is cold and dank in there, and I am crouched down against the wall, hugging my knees. Suddenly a beam of light comes through the bars of the window. I stand up, turn, and hold out my arms to it, and I am transported on the light beam up and out through the bars of the window into the world outside.

The winter solstice is the darkest day of the year and at the same time the day of returning to the light. From this moment in time forward every year, the days lengthen, and the light begins to increase a few minutes each day. A paradox of darkness and hope. In addition to the metaphor of finding solace in the solstice and the return of the light, my dream also reflects a growing hope in the promise of the vaccines becoming available to protect against COVID-19. Glad to say that within a month of this dream I got my first vaccine, and we were all on our way to greater face-to-face accessibility. (To say nothing of yearning for light, warmth, and spring in what is our coldest, darkest season here in New England.) Hopefully as you read this now, the virus is no longer wreaking havoc in our world. But it will long remain a warning sign and a metaphor for us as to just how out of balance we had become, much as the metaphor of a black plague is still a part of the language and imagery we conjure up when describing something truly awful.

In my dream the Light came through the bars toward me, and then I participated in the process by actively reaching out my arms, joining forces with it, and allowing myself to be lifted out of that cold and dark place. That feels like a good message for our dream-work with nightmares and traumatic experiences. Participate in the process. Do your own work, and trust in something larger than yourself to lift you up.

One definition of faith that I love is my mashup variation on a quote attributed to Patrick Overton: "When you have come to the edge of all the light you have known and are about to step off into the darkness of the unknown, faith is knowing that one of two things will happen: There will be someone there to catch you, or that you will learn to fly."[48] The original quote adds that you will step onto solid ground. I like that too, but the "someone there to catch you" aspect in my mashup adds and invokes the interconnectedness

---

48. Patrick Miles Overton, *The Leaning Tree* (Bloomington, MN: Bethany Press, 1975).

of healing with others and the importance of the relationships you can trust in the process. Having both the inner and the outer witness to our healing is one of the key elements to trauma recovery. Befriending ourselves and learning to live peacefully in our own bodies is necessary to no longer view our body as an enemy. This shift in self-awareness is aided by having a compassionate and caring other on the journey with you.

Inspirational writer Byron Katie tells us that to live well and fully in the world, we need to be able to trust in three things: 1) in ourselves, 2) in others, and 3) in the Divine or the Universe. This does not mean to trust without discernment, but to do so with all of our senses and good, strong vetting. Being able to trust others and Other as well as ourselves is to be empowered and connected in the world. Trust too in your dreams, for we know they contain messages for our growth and healing, maybe especially when they come clothed in nightmare form. Turn the nightmare inside out to find the gifts buried deep inside. When Deborah had her dream about sharp spiders in her mouth in chapter 4, as she worked with the image, they turned into Swarovski crystals. These crystals are compared to diamonds and are known for their clarity.

Following Both the Light and the Darkness

After paying your respects and facing up to your Shadow and your dark sides, look for the light. When in doubt, go toward the light in your dreams. If you feel stumped in working through a nightmare, go there. Seek it out. Find it coming through the bars of your cell, through the cracks in your walls, around the edges of your mind. Create or re-create it if it is not there at first blush. Seek out both your outer and your inner lights. Stay in connection with both the light within you and the light without, they are parts of the same whole. Follow the stars, the sun, the moon, the flame, the flare of the match, the Light from the Divine. Close your inner eyes and see your flame still burning on the candle within. Light the candle in your dream, for the light of even one candle banishes the darkness. See your own seeds of green emerging from the ashes pushing up to whatever light there is as Maura did in her dream, the seeds of healing your own pain and hurt and sorrow. Have a helper or guide bring you the light from inside or outside the dream if you need assistance. There are no penalties to asking for help.

There is a song/prayer whose lyrics contain the phrase, "Rolling light into darkness, and darkness into light." Day rolls on into night, we dream in the deep dark, and then the light returns out of the darkness. Know too that the darkness contains its own form of light. Close your eyes and see behind them the glimmers and sparkles of another kind of light that emerges only in the darkest of times. In addition to the contrast that we need in order to differentiate between dark and light, darkness can also have its own glow or shimmer. The soft dark of womb safety, of deepening, is also a truth. The Fertile Void is a concept used in many spiritual traditions to imply this dark Source of Life. If you close your eyes and look inside your eyelids, you may see these glimmers and sparkles and shimmers of light. For years as a child when I closed my eyes I saw both these glimmers and another eye looking back at me. I remember how it freaked me out at first, and I would quickly open my eyes when it happened. Later I came to associate it with the Eye of God, specifically with the Shechinah, the indwelling feminine Presence who was watching over me. It was surrounded by these shimmers of light, and I subsequently learned to seek it, not run from it.

Sometimes the Post-Trauma Spiritual Growth happens right inside the dream, and sometimes it happens afterward as we work it through. Here is an example of the latter. Andre, a yoga and Reiki teacher and spiritual guide, had been working on recognizing and integrating his dark and light sides for several years. He came in yesterday telling me about a liminal dream/vision that he has been having for a few months in the hypnogogic zone between sleep and waking. He prefaced the dream with saying, "This feels like it is about my Shadow side, but I don't know how yet. It feels like I am putting those parts of me that I thought were true, but now know are not true, into a little boat and sending them down the river in a ceremony like the Japanese lantern boat ceremony that honors the souls of the departed." What a lovely metaphor, even before we begin the work. He continued, "When it happens, I feel a sort of clap inside of myself, sort of like a door snapping shut and great pressure in my chest." Here is his repeating image:

> *I am standing at the edge of a mountain, and there is fire and boulders raining down around me. I am wearing long, grey robes and others who are also wearing robes are with me. I hear a voice saying "Not again" amidst the screams.*

When I asked Andre if he had any immediate associations to this, he said it felt like he was a member of a holy order witnessing the volcano at Pompei that destroyed the town and killed thousands of villagers. His ancestors are from Italy. He went on, "My biggest fear is to hurt someone, and I think this is my fault because we angered the gods with our rampant immorality and fornication." He then came out of his semi-trance state to look directly at me and said, "Wow—fornication—that's a strange word to use." A gay man, he went on, "That's what they called it then. No wonder I felt guilty." Name it to tame it, and knowledge binds anxiety—here was a piece to bind up already.

Next, I invited him to dream the dream forward. As we moved into some active embodied dreamwork, he noticed that he was facing the volcano, the source of the dark power in this dream, holding up his arms but cowering in the face of the lava flow. I invite him first to stand up tall and not cower, and then to turn around and see what it felt like to have this force of nature at his back instead of in his face. When he did this, Andre said, "When I looked straight at it, I was afraid of it, but as I turn around and raise my arms with the volcano at my back, I am now invoking the power, rather than being overwhelmed by it. I control it now. I was afraid of my power and my feminine side, but now I can use it to heal. I am sending the lava down to clear the landscape of debris, clearing the path for new growth."

For Andre, this was a process of alchemical transformation, transforming fear and destruction into healing and potential for growth in co-creation with the power of nature. He was able to articulate that he recognized his own soul mission in this life was the integration of the dark and the light first in himself, and then to assist others in this process, and to recognize that the dark too was a source of power when used carefully and wisely. He continued, "I was not and am not morally bad, and this was not my fault. I can integrate my feminine side and my masculine side for healing. My chest feels much lighter too, no more pressure there. And no matter what, they could never take my soul."

Andre now walks his walk and teaches the teachers how to walk this path of power. His willingness to face and engage with the dark parts of his Shadow side in his dreams and images allow him to transform the traumas associated with being stigmatized for his sexual identity. By moving forward and backward in time to include the family epigenetics of trauma and cultural stigma, he was able to use the fires of the volcano for spiritual growth and release the pressure inside of himself.

Making Meaning and Repair from Our Nightmares

Sisu is a Finnish word that has been defined as, "An extraordinary determination in the face of adversity." This may be one of the hidden gifts embedded in recovery from trauma and the nightmares generated by traumatic experiences. No one wants pain or trauma. Yet they are a part of life. What we do with these experiences, how we respond to what has occurred, gives us back our sense of choice and self-efficacy. By working to turn our suffering into healing, we can make our dreams and our lives into a blessing that can help others to heal as well. Martin Luther King Jr. said, "I have a dream..." and this phrase and his work has gone on to be a blessing long after his death.

Viktor Frankl, a psychiatrist who survived the Holocaust, afterward wrote his philosophy of life and the title of his book *Man's Search for Meaning*. In it he states two main principles of his psychological framework of logotherapy: first paraphrasing Nietzsche's quote, "He who has a why to live can bear with almost any how,"[49] and "Everything can be taken from a man but one thing: the last of the human freedoms—to choose one's attitude in any given set of circumstances, to choose one's own way."[50] Following trauma, we need to re-whole ourselves, and find new meaning and purpose in life. Dreamwork can help us to choose our way and help our community and our world. As we unpack our dreams and make meaning out of them, the dreamwork expands and we make meaning out of our lives as well. It can be as big as choosing our new identity. Rather than self-identify as a victim or even as a survivor to trauma, we can build up self-statements and self-identities that don't invoke

---

49. Friedrich Nietzsche, *Twilight of the Idols* (Indianapolis, IN: Hackett Publishing Co., 1997).

50. Viktor Frankl, *Man's Search for Meaning* (Boston, MA: Beacon Press, 1959, 2006), 75.

the trauma such as, "I am a strong and powerful person" or "My mission is to bring healing and light to the world." This then is truly re-storying ourselves through our dreams.

Our dreams can be landmarks of our internal process. They can be a source of healing and solace as we attend to them and use their generative powers to move forward, creating meaning out of chaos, hope out of despair, and a forward-moving life force out of the depths of darkness and sorrow. A hallmark of AEDP (Accelerated Experiential Dynamic Psychotherapy) has as some of its tenants that we are all wired for growth, that we all have the capacity to experience joy and delight, and that nothing that feels bad is ever the last step. I love these philosophies. They remind me of what Dev Patel, who played the proprietor of the hotel in the movie *The Best Exotic Marigold Hotel*, told us: "Everything will be all right in the end and if it's not all right, then it's not yet the end."[51]

So many post-trauma dreams come replete with images of brokenness, of shattering, of things that are destroyed or smashed or crushed. If we think back to some of the dreams and nightmares we have explored here in *PTSDreams*, we have seen themes and images of being chased by people or monsters, of near drowning, of being buried underground, of being trapped, injured, or lost in the dark in so many ways. It seems that our psyche has endless ways of alerting us to the need to attend to ourselves, to our healing, and to repairing ourselves and the world. One of the tenants of spiritual practice in Judaism is called *Tikkun Olam*, which means Repairing the World. We start with repairing ourselves, and from our own

---

51. "The Best Exotic Marigold Hotel Quotes," Rotten Tomatoes, https://www.rottentomatoes.com/m/the_best_exotic_marigold_hotel_2012/quotes/#:~:text=Sonny%20Kapoor%3A%20Everything%20will%20be,it's%20not%20yet%20the%20end.

wholeness or repaired brokenness we can then move that energy out to help others.

The option of repair is always available. The Japanese art of kintsugi exemplifies this concept of healing from our broken places, because as Hemingway told us, that is paradoxically where we are often most strong. In Kintsugi, a cracked piece of pottery is mended and repaired with gold filling in the cracks. It thus becomes more valuable for having been broken and then repaired than never having been broken at all. The brokenness and the repair now become part of the bowl itself, part of its new story in life, rather than something to hide or discard. One of my clients took this method to heart and found a kintsugi kit online. She bought it and repaired the broken cup that came with it with gold colored glue. It lives now on her mantel as a constant reminder. I did much the same when I came down to my office one morning and found that my little bell was on the ground in two pieces. Though never proven, my mischievous cats were the prime suspects. I, too, glued it back together, and then colored over the super glue with gold sharpie pen. Even better than new!

Post-Traumatic Spiritual Growth

According to psychology professor Richard Tedeschi, trauma can affect our physical well-being, our psychological integrity, create moral injury, and fragment our self-narrative. Moral injury arises when the trauma challenges our ethics and belief systems (for example, being forced to participate in harming others). Our own story of who we are, our self-narrative, gets fragmented by trauma into "before" and "after" the trauma, and the unified whole of our being becomes disrupted. One of the treatment goals then becomes to rebuild a cohesive self-narrative, a cohesive wholeness of being, and re-create a new story of ourselves and our world that includes both the before and the after of the traumatic experiences. Post-traumatic growth then can transport us beyond our previous limitations. Tedeschi and Lawrence Calhoun outline five domains where this growth can occur:[52]

1. Recognition of our personal courage and resilience. (If I could get through that, I can get through anything.)

2. Greater appreciation of life. (Enjoying simple pleasures, recognizing gratitude.)

3. Opening to new possibilities. (Dreamwork is particularly useful in entertaining multiple options and opportunities.)

4. Deepening valuing of relationships. (An acknowledgement of our mutual interconnectedness and the gift of connection with others.)

5. Enhanced spiritual development. (Increased ability to recognize patterns, see the bigger picture, reach actively for the light, and extending compassion to others.)

My friend Rina had a dream that exemplifies many of these five principles. In her dream:

My friend and I are being chased by evil men. They keep gaining on us, getting closer and closer. I weave in and out of rooms and alleyways, and finally find myself facing a tall wall and think, "This is it, a dead end. We are trapped." But somehow, at the last minute, he boosts me up to the top of the wall, and then I pull him up as well and we help each other up and over to safety. I then hear a voice, sort of a voiceover from the sky, that says, "We do make it up. We're going to make it down too, and here we are."

---

52. R.G. Tedeschi and L.G. Calhoun, "The Posttraumatic Growth Inventory: Measuring the positive legacy of trauma," *Journal of Traumatic Stress 9(3)*, (1996): 455–472. https://doi.org/10.1002/jts.2490090305.

In this dream we see the power of mutual aide, the importance of relationships, clearly some courage and strength, and finally the dream option of how to climb an unclimbable wall that her psyche came up with to solve the problem and get to safety. And in a somewhat unusual style for a dream, we get that voiceover that lets us know that everything works out. This surprising ending to what at first seemed like a very stressful dream clearly points to post-traumatic spiritual growth.

We as humans have trouble holding both sides of a paradox. We are much more comfortable with a stance of either/or than with a stance of both/and. Dreamwork helps us to hold multiple perspectives: To see the before, the during, and the after in our nightmares and our lives. Deep dreamwork is one of ways we get the closest to seeing with divine eyes, or as Rabbi Alan Ullman taught me, to see in sacred time. When we can do this, we are able to see the past, the present, and the future all at once. This is part of our legacy of nightmare healing, and our embedded potentiality to see around corners of time into a future we have a part in creating.

One of the core tenants of this book is that we are all hardwired for healing, and that our system actually prefers to be in a state of homeostasis and wholeness. Nightmares come, paradoxically, to let us know that we are out of balance and need to move back into wholeness. As we learned in chapter 7 on recurring dreams and themes, they alert us repeatedly if we ignore them, sometimes increasing their siren call until we simply must stop and pay attention.

Recognition of Past Trauma Through Dreamwork: Roberta's Dream

It almost goes without saying again that we can't fully heal from a trauma unless we have recognized and identified it. Almost, but not quite, so we will say it once again. Without naming it, we can't tame it, and are not yet free to find meaning or growth from the experience. Some of us have had events occur in our lives years ago that were difficult or painful, and that we think we have put out of our minds. Sometimes the events happened to us personally; sometimes we are still unconsciously carrying the pain of our ancestors. Ofttimes it was not even identified as a trauma, or as something that we must recover from, or that had any lasting effect on us. That was the case for Roberta. However, as these events are wont to do, it showed up in her dream years later under disguise. Here is the dream that emerged early in her therapy:

> *I am an adult in my dream, but I have a child-sized purse. It is broken. The handle has come off and I am desperately trying to reattach it.*

Looking first to the emotional narrative, her feelings in the dream were of anxiety escalating to the point of panic, much more than we might have expected from just the narrative content of the dream itself. Her SUDS level was a 9. Roberta started therapy when her daughter hit adolescence and this triggered some of her own struggles as a teen, especially with issues around sexuality and coming out as lesbian. She had a feeling that the dream had something to do with this but couldn't figure out what.

After a few false leads that didn't get traction, I mentioned to her that sometimes a purse shows up as a symbol of a woman's womb in a dream. This symbolism had immediate traction for her. This purse was child sized, so she felt it had something to do with her childhood. Roberta didn't have a history of sexual abuse as a child, which could be a potential meaning to the symbol of a broken purse/womb. Then Roberta recalled, "Oh yeah, when I was really little, maybe about six, I had been having a lot of urinary tract infections. I ended up being taken to a gynecologist for a painful procedure. For some reason my mother was not allowed in the room with me, so I was all alone in this sterile office and strapped down to a gurney. It was pretty awful. Do you think the dream could be related to this?"

I replied that it could be, and let her know that event certainly counts as a medical trauma, saying, "What a scary thing to have to go through, and alone too." The pain she had experienced before getting the procedure, the procedure itself, and the fact that she was forced to go through it alone without her mother were all connected to the traumatic nature of it. She said that no one had ever suggested such a thing as medical trauma to her before. Once she became aware that this existed, Roberta said that yes, the dream was most definitely connected to this experience. I shared with her some of my own sadness and outrage that she had been so callously treated. Good trauma therapy is not about the therapist always remaining neutral at all costs; her role in bearing witness to the reality of pain becomes part of the healing. Roberta then remembered that for the years after that, she beat up on her dolls and subjected them to various forms of invasive assaults. No one had ever put that together though till now.

Once we had connected the dots, I asked if she would like to go back into the dream and use the GAIA method to add some resources that could have helped her through that time. She was all for it and invited into her dream a strong best friend to hold her hand, me on the other side, and her favorite childhood superhero, Xena Warrior Princess. Powerful Xena galloped in on her large, white steed and told the doctors what for! This image became a touchstone for her and her healing. An artist, she then took her dreamwork home and made an art piece with an assemblage of various materials and images representing this journey that she called, "From Nightmare into Healing."

Paying It Forward: Healing Ourselves, Healing Others Through Dreamwork

Significantly, in the dream, she is trying to reattach the handle to the purse. That was one of the most difficult parts of her experience, that for some reason her attachment person, her mother, was not allowed to be there with her. Now she and I could both give comfort to her six-year-old self who went through that, and also put into context why the dream came up now, as her daughter was hitting puberty and her own matters of sexuality. Although Roberta wasn't sexually assaulted, her experience was an assault on that part of her anatomy. Carrying her dreamwork forward, she continues to show up, be present, and advocate for her own daughter over the years in ways that she missed when she was a child herself. Her psyche must like this image, since Roberta has had subsequent dreams about purses in various sizes, states of repair, and color over the years. They often show up at transitional points in her life such as when her daughter started dating, when her wife's mother died, and when Roberta herself hit menopause and her "purse" now carried different connotations.

Roberta was given permission to heal through the dreamwork by being able to recognize that her experience was in fact a trauma, and that her feelings were legitimate. One of the elements of healing from trauma is to be accompanied, to no longer be alone with it. Putting together the pieces from Roberta's dream with her past experience in connection with a caring other in a safe place helped Roberta truly put it to rest. She could pay her healing forward as she parents her daughter. Recently in a waking dream meditation Roberta found herself lovingly surrounded by the trunk of a tree and safely enclosed within. Surrounding her tree in a circle of protection were another ring of women, including her beloved Xena

Warrior Princess, actress Mariska Hargitay (as the strong woman Captain Olivia Benson on *Law & Order: SVU* who investigates sexual assault cases), and her circle of dreaming women friends.

Legacies and Bright Ones

We have also named the intergenerational nature of both trauma and healing. The science of epigenetics gives us hope that long past events can still receive closure. Vamık Volkan, an international psychoanalyst who studies the effects of war, terror, and displacement world-wide, offers us the phrase *image deposits*. He feels that the internalized images of traumatic experiences can be unconsciously deposited onto the life of subsequent generations and become a part of their story even though they themselves have not been through the original experience. It is mostly an unconscious process. Since our dreams come to us replete with images and allow us access to our unconscious selves in a way that little else does, deep dreamwork seems to be a good way to unearth these deposits, give them back to the ancestors for healing, and replace them with more life-affirming ones.

We also learned that in addition to recognizing a personal history that included trauma over the generations, we can also seek and find the ancestors who are the Bright Ones in our past. We can bring their spirits and their legacy with us into our lives today as we dream them forward and reattach to their bright lights. Here is a waking dream synchronicity followed by a sleeping dream example of dreaming that manifests not our shadow or dark sides, but our Bright Ones.

Last fall I was teaching a class on dreamwork and Kabbalah. In the first class we talked about the spiritual legacies we have inherited from our ancestors; those that we were aware of and those that came through in the dream state. I was teaching on Zoom and sitting in my dining room instead of my office space so I could use the bigger table to spread out my class notes. (I am very visual, and a big spread-er-outer.) Sitting on the buffet piece behind me is an array of family pictures. As I see myself in my little Zoom window, I see that right behind me on the buffet is the picture of my mom as a child with my grandparents beaming on either side of her. Grandma Molly and Grandpa Joey were right over my shoulder, guiding me the whole time. I was so delighted to notice this that I shared the picture with my class, one advantage of teaching on Zoom. My Grandma Molly was always one of the Bright Ones for me. She died when I was twelve, but not before she gave me storybook grandmothering experience. She remains a nurturing presence for me to this day.

A few weeks later I had this dream in the night:

> *I am in front of my grandparents' A-frame brick house, and then I am inside it, walking around room by room. Then for fun I climb out of the bedroom window that overhangs the roof of the balcony to slide down the pole out into the backyard and gardens. I remember that I actually did this as a kid, much to my secret delight.*

This sleeping dream kept the theme of my grandmother's presence and infused the memories with the very physical sense of their house, a second home to me, and the physicality of using the bones of the house as a secret jungle gym that I could enter and leave without being seen. There was great fun here, and the glee of then walking innocently back in through the front door after I had snuck out the window.

Part of healing from trauma is to find the spiritual opportunity for renewal. Through these two waking and sleeping dreams I was able to reconnect with my beloved grandmother and bring greater healing to this childhood loss. The loss of my Grandma Molly was a common life cycle loss, not a big trauma of violence or betrayal, but a loss just the same. Her death left a hole in my life. Having her now over my shoulder as I write and remembering her immense kindness and sense of fun is delightful. We named my daughter after her, a spiritual namesake, and that carries her life force forward as well. We have Grandma Molly's old brass candlesticks over our mantle. I use them each week on Shabbat. My mother gave them to me when I married, and my daughter knows that they will go to her as well one day. We are passing on the candlestick torch, making the choice to pass on this kind of epigenetics of light and life.

Re-Purposing Our Monsters

A spiritual reframe or re-association to negative images or nightmare figures can also be part of our healing from nightmares. If we dreamed of scary monsters or mythological beasts, how can we re-purpose them for our healing? With deep dreamwork they can become our allies rather than our enemies. A dragon in our dream, for example, may not only be a fire-breathing lizard/snake bent on attacking us, but also become our own source of power and flight and the fire in our bellies as we roar with strength and fearlessness as we embody the dragon. Dina in chapter 5 made friends with her giant and ended up dancing with him. In chapter 8, Lorraine discovered that Sasquatch, her space Yeti, was a nurturing mothering figure who took her to a womb/cave for healing. She now uses that cave as her safe place imagery when doing EMDR work.

Trauma expert Peter Levine tells us that, "The paradox of trauma is that it has both the power to destroy and the power to transform and resurrect."[53] He also tells us that trauma "resolved is a

---

53. Victoria McGee, "The Pandemic & Collective Trauma," Medium, April 18, 2020, https://medium.com/an-idea/the-pandemic-collective-trauma -ebf01c07d03.

blessing from a greater power."[54] Medusa is one of the mythological Gorgons who had snakes for hair. Snakes are one of our most multi-laden symbols, we will return to them in a moment. After Perseus slew her, he gave the head to Athena, his benefactor. Athena, the goddess of Wisdom, collected some blood and gave it to Asclepius the Healer. He used the blood from the left side of Medusa to take people's lives, and from her right side to raise people from the dead. Euripides wrote that one vial was a deadly poison, and the other a potent cure-all. The power to kill and the power to heal coming from two sides of the same monster, just as our trauma also contains the seeds of our renewal. Medusa's name means Guardian or Protectress in ancient Greek. Fittingly, I think.

An additional word here on snakes, perhaps one of the ultimate in symbols that can be reimaged and repurposed since it is such a complex image. The snake in the Garden of Eden is depicted as the great tempter, we have snake-haired Gorgons who can turn you to stone if you look them in the eye, and He-Who-Must-Not-Be-Named in *Harry Potter* is depicted in all his snakey evil powers. And yet, the Ouroboros is the snake who swallows his own tail and is the oldest allegorical symbol in alchemy of eternity and endless renewal. The symbol began in ancient Egypt and spans millennia and cultures from Greek to Norse to the Gnostics concept of the union of the Divine and the earthly in mankind. When Moses needs to free his people from the Pharaoh, his staff turns into a snake and swallows the lesser snake-staffs of Pharaoh's minions. Later, in the desert, his staff becomes entwined with a bronze snake that healed the people if they looked on it: a prototype of our modern symbol of the caduceus. Snakes shed their skin, constantly renewing themselves. As

---

54. Peter Levine, *Waking the Tiger: Healing Trauma* (Berkeley, CA: North Atlantic Books, 1987), 196.

such, they are a symbol of new life and healing. We too can review and renew our nightmare symbols and re-image them for healing.

As We End, "Choose Life, That You May Live"

I will leave you with this final dream:

A young man lost his necklace of the Hebrew letter Chai, which means Life. I found it and returned it to him, and he was very appreciative.

What does it mean to you to dream of losing and finding Life? (Life: Chai, like the celebratory phrase, L'Chaim, "To Life.") To dream of losing Life, and then having it found and returned to you? Of wearing this symbol of life over your heart on a chain? My hope for you is that the generosity and wisdom of the dreamers and nightmare sufferers who have been willing to share their journey with you contributes to your own reclamation of life, to your own healing journey, and your own dreams to contribute to healing the world.

Folksinger Lui Collins sings to us of moving through her pain and suffering, "...Like a great bell resurrected, ringing loud and true" and concludes that the only way out, is through. You too can move out through the bars of your cage, shattering the illusions that you thought were true as you do your dreamwork with your dreams and nightmares. As we delve into these dark and scary places, we sort through the images, the metaphors, the symbols, and the pops of memory that burst through in the night. Once we attend and befriend our nightmares and demons and our deepest selves, we make meaning out of mourning and find the bright messages buried in the rubble. On your journey through your dark dreams, remember that the light is still there. Even if the landscape is dark, even if it seems endless, there is a force within that continues to move us to wholeness, that shines a light in the dark, that allows healing to come in the morning. The phoenix rises, the life force emerges, the nightmare becomes transformed both for your own healing and for the healing of your family and for the world.

When someone dies, we say, "May their memory be for a blessing." May you move through all your nightmares and dark places with grace and vision into the fullness of being and be a blessing to the world. Wishing you powerful, healing, and transforming dreams.

Bibliography

Aizenstat, Stephen. *Dream Tending: Awakening to the Healing Power of Dreams*. New Orleans, LA: Spring Journal, 2011.

Amen, Daniel. *Change Your Brain, Change Your Life (Revised and Expanded): The Breakthrough Program for Conquering Anxiety, Depression, Obsessiveness, Lack of Focus, Anger, and Memory Problems*. New York: Harmony Press, 2015.

Andrews, Ted. *Animal Speak: The Spiritual and Magical Powers of Creatures Great and Small*. Woodbury, MN: Llewellyn Publications, 2001.

Barasch, Marc Ian. *Healing Dreams: Exploring the Dreams That Can Transform Your Life*. New York: Riverhead Books, 2000.

Barrett, Deirdre, ed. *Trauma and Dreams*. Cambridge, MA: Harvard University Press, 2001, 1986.

_____. *Pandemic Dreams*. Oneiroi Press, 2020.

Berry, Walter. *Drawn into the Dream: How Drawing Your Dreams Can Take You to the Land of Awes*. Brentwood, CA: Precocity Press, 2021.

Bértholo, Joana. "The Shadow in Project Management." ScienceDirect. Elsevier. March 29, 2013. https://www.sciencedirect.com/science/article/pii/S1877042813004369.

"The Best Exotic Marigold Hotel Quotes." Rotten Tomatoes. https://www.rottentomatoes.com/m/the_best_exotic_marigold_hotel_2012/quotes/#:~:text=Sonny%20Kapoor%3A%20Everything%20will%20be,it's%20not%20yet%20the%20end.

"#BlogElul 17: Awaken." Velveteen Rabbi. August 23, 2013. https://velveteenrabbi.blogs.com/blog/2013/08/blogelul-17-awaken.html.

"Boann (also Boand, Boyne, Boannan)." LiveJournal. October 18, 2004. https://the-goddesses.livejournal.com/9019.html.

Bosnak, Robert. *Tracks in the Wilderness of Dreaming*. New York: Delta Press, 1996.

_____. *Embodiment: Creative Imagination in Medicine, Art and Travel*. Oxfordshire, UK: Routledge Press, 2007.

Bulkeley, Kelly. *Dreams of Healing: Transforming Nightmares into Visions of Hope*. Mahwah, NJ: Paulist Press, 2003.

Burch, Wanda. *She Who Dreams: A Journey into Healing Through Dreamwork*. Novato, CA: New World Library, 2003.

Burk, Larry and Katherine O'Keefe-Kanavos. *Dreams that Can Save Your Life: Early Warning Signs of Cancer and Other Diseases*. Dyke, Scotland: Findhorn Press, 2018.

Campbell, Jean and Clare Johnson, eds. *Dream Monsters and Superheroes: Empowering Children Through Creative Dreamplay*. Westport, CT: Praeger Publishers, 2016.

Carr, Michelle. *Dream Factory: Deconstructing the Sleeping Brain*. Psychology Today, https://www.psychologytoday.com/us/blog/dream-factory.

Clement, J.A. "Goodreads," Goodreads.com, https://www.goodreads.com/quotes/419330-it-was-a-time-of-dark-dreams-they-washed-in.

Conforti, Michael. *Field, Form, and Fate: Patterns in Mind, Nature, and Psyche*. New Orleans, LA: Spring Journal, Inc., 2013.

Dana, Deb. *The Polyvagal Theory in Therapy*. New York: W. W. Norton & Company, 2018.

Dannu, Ayala. "Ancestral Dreaming and Why it Needs to be a Part of the Dream Studies Conversation." *DreamTime*, Fall 2019.

DeBord, J.M. *Dreams 1-2-3: Remember, Interpret, and Live Your Dreams*. Charlottesville, VA: Hampton Roads Press, 2013.

DeBord, J.M. Dream Interpretation with J.M. DeBord. https://www.reddit.com/r/RadOwl/.

Dunlea, Marian. *BodyDreaming in the Treatment of Developmental Trauma*. Oxfordshire, UK: Routledge, Press, 2019.

Duran, Eduardo. *Native American Dreamwork Traditions*. Keynote Speech, IASD International Conference, 2021.

Dyer, Wayne. *Change Your Thoughts, Change Your Life—Living the Wisdom of the Tao*. Read by Wayne Dyer. (Carlsbad, CA: Hay House, 2009). Audiobook recording, 9 hours and 9 minutes.

Ellis, Leslie. *A Clinician's Guide to Dream Therapy.* Oxfordshire, UK: Routledge, 2019.

_____."Focusing-Oriented Dreamwork: Embodying the Hidden Life Energy in Dreams." *DreamTime.* International Association for the Study of Dreams. Winter 2019.

Estés, Clarissa Pinkola. *Women Who Run with the Wolves: Myths and Stories of the Wild Woman Archetype.* New York: Ballantine Books, 1992.

Firestone, Tirzah. *Wounds into Wisdom: Healing Intergenerational Jewish Trauma.* Rhinebeck, NY: Monkfish Book Publishing Company, 2019.

Fisher, Janina. *Healing the Fragmented Selves of Trauma Survivors: Overcoming Internal Self-Alienation.* Oxfordshire, UK: Routledge, 2017.

Foley, Sean. "Jacob wrestling his 'angel' is our own struggle," CBC Radio. CBC, September 17, 2019. https://www.cbc.ca/radio/ideas /jacob-wrestling-his-angel-is-our-own-struggle-1.5285823.

Fosha, Diana. *The Transforming Power of Affect: A Model for Accelerated Change.* New York: Basic Books, 2001.

Fosha, Diana. "Nothing that feels bad is ever the last step: The role of positive emotions in experiential work with difficult emotional experiences." Special issue on Emotion, L. Greenberg (Ed.). *Clinical Psychology and Psychotherapy* 11, 2004. https://aedpinstitute.org /wp-content/uploads/2015/06/Fosha_Bad_Last_Step_2001.pdf.

Frankiel, Tamar and Judy Greenfield. *Entering the Temple of Dreams: Jewish Prayers, Movements, and Meditations for the End of the Day.* Woodstock, VT: Jewish Lights Publishing, 2000.

Frankel, Estelle. *The Wisdom of Not Knowing: Discovering a Life of Wonder While Embracing Uncertainty.* Boulder, CO: Shambhala Publications, 2017.

Frankl, Viktor. *Man's Search for Meaning.* Boston, MA: Beacon Press, 1959, 2006.

Freeman, Bruce. *"Name It to Tame It: Labelling Emotions to Reduce Stress & Anxiety."* OralHealth. May 3, 2021. https://www.oralhealth group.com/features/name-it-to-tame-it-labelling-emotions-to -reduce-stress-anxiety/.

Gendlin, Eugene. *Focusing*. New York: Bantam Books, 1978.

Gendlin, Eugene. *Let Your Body Interpret Your Dreams*. New York: Chiron Press, 1986.

"Genesis 28:16." Bible Hub. https://biblehub.com/genesis/28-16.htm.

Goldrich, Lori, "Active Imagination." Lori Goldrich, Ph.D., 2017, https://lorigoldrich.com/.

Greenwald, Rick, "Eye Movement Desensitization and Reprocessing (EMDR): A New Kind of Dreamwork?" *Dreaming*, no. 1, 1995.

Hartmann, Ernest. *Dreams and Nightmares: The New Theory on the Origin and Meaning of Dreams*. New York: Plenum Trade, 1998.

Herman, Judith. *Trauma and Recovery: The Aftermath of Violence-From Domestic Abuse to Political Terror*. New York: Basic Books, 1992.

Huhne, Kari. "Shadow." Café au Soul, 2020, https://www.cafeausoul.com/oracles/dream-dictionary/shadow.

Horowitz, Adam and Tony Cunningham, Pattie Maes, and Robert Stickgold. "Dormio: A Targeted Dream. Incubation Device." *Consciousness and Cognition*. National Library of Medicine. 83, (2020). https://pubmed.ncbi.nlm.nih.gov/32480292/.

Hoss, Lynne, and Robert Hoss. *Dream to Freedom: A Handbook for Integrating Dreamwork and Energy Psychology*. Fulton, CA: Energy Psychology Press, 2013.

Ingerman, Sandra and Llyn Roberts. *Speaking with Nature: Awakening to the Deep Wisdom of the Earth*. Rochester, VT: Bear & Company, 2015.

Jesamine. "The Shadow: What You Do Behind Your Own Back." Jungian Analysis & Counseling. https://counselinginzurich.com/the-shadow-carl-jung/.

Jordan, Judith V., Alexandra G. Kaplan, Jean Baker Miller, Irene P. Stiver, and Janet L. Surrey. *Women's Growth in Connection: Writings from the Stone Center*. New York City: The Guilford Press, 1991.

Jung, Carl. *Synchronicity: An Acausal Connecting Principle. (From Vol. 8. of the Collected Works of C. G. Jung)*. Edited by Sonu Shamdasani. Princeton, New Jersey: Princeton University Press, 2010.

_____. *Memories, Dreams, Reflections.* New York: Random House, 1961.

_____. *Modern Man in Search of a Soul.* Eastford, CT: Martino Fine Books, 2017.

Kalsched, Donald. *The Inner World of Trauma: Archetypal Defenses of the Personal Spirit World.* Oxfordshire, UK: Routledge Press, 2016.

Kaufman, Scott Barry. "Post-Traumatic Growth: Finding Meaning and Creativity in Adversity." Scientific American, April 20, 2020. https:// blogs.scientificamerican.com/beautiful-minds/post-traumatic -growth-finding-meaning-and-creativity-in-adversity/.

Kaufmann, Yoram. *The Way of the Image: The Orientational Approach to the Psyche.* New York: Zahav Books, 2009.

Korn, Deborah and Michael Baldwin. *Every Memory Deserves Respect.* New York: Workman Publishing Co., Inc., 2021.

Krakow, B, R Kellner, D Pathak, and L Lambert. "Image Rehearsal Treatment for Chronic Nightmares." *NIH: National Library of Medicine* 33, no.7 (1995): 837-43. doi: 10.1016/0005-7967(95)00009-m. https:// pubmed.ncbi.nlm.nih.gov/7677723/

Krakow, Barry and Anthonio Zadra. "Imagery Rehearsal Therapy: Principles and Practice." Elsevier. February 9, 2010. doi:10.1016/j. jsmc.2010.01.004. https://antoniozadra.com/sites/default/files /biblio/krakow_zadra.sleep_med_clinics.pdf.

Johnson, Clare. *The Art of Transforming Nightmares.* Woodbury, MN: Llewellyn Publications, 2021.

Leschziner, Guy. *The Nocturnal Brain: Nightmares, Neuroscience, and the Secret World of Sleep.* New York: St. Martin's Press, 2019.

Lewis, Jacquie and Stanley Krippner. *Working with Dreams and PTSD Nightmares.* Westport, CT: Praeger, 2016.

Levine, Peter. *Waking the Tiger: Healing Trauma.* Berkeley, CA: North Atlantic Books, 1987.

Levine, Peter. *Healing Trauma: Restoring the Wisdom of the Body.* Louisville, CO: Sounds True, 1999.

Lightbringer, Thalia. "Boann – The Goddess Who Gave Life To The River Boyne In Celtic Mythology." Ancient Pages. June 9, 2018. https://www.ancientpages.com/2018/06/09/boann-the-goddess-who-gave-life-to-the-river-boyne-in-celtic-mythology/.

Lomas, Tim. *Happiness Found in Translation.* New York: TarcherPerigree, 2019.

McGee, Victoria. "The Pandemic & Collective Trauma." Medium. April 18, 2020. https://medium.com/an-idea/the-pandemic-collective-trauma-ebf01c07d03.

Moore, Thomas. *Care of the Soul, 25th Anniversary Ed.* New York: Harper Perennial, 2016.

Murphy, Andye. "Greeting Goddess Gaia." Gaia. April 13, 2016. https://www.gaia.com/article/goddess-gaia.

Nagel, Sandra M., and Lyle K. Grant. "Tutorial 12: The Endocrine System." Introductory Biological Psychology Tutorials. https://psych.athabascau.ca/html/Psych289/Biotutorials/12/part1.shtml.

Naiman, Rubin. *Healing Sleep: Discover the Restorative Power of Sleep, Dreams, and Awakening.* New York: Three Rivers Press, 2014.

Naiman, Rubin. "In exile from the dreamscape." Aeon. Aeon Magazine. December 24, 2020. https://aeon.co/essays/we-live-in-a-wake-centric-world-losing-touch-with-our-dreams.

Nielsen, Tore. "The COVID-19 Pandemic Is Changing Our Dreams." Scientific American. October 1, 2020. https://www.scientificamerican.com/article/the-covid-19-pandemic-is-changing-our-dreams/.

_____. "Dream incubation: ancient techniques of dream influence, bodily methods of inducing spiritual presence." Montreal Center for the Study of Dreams. 3(3-4):6-10. http://www.dreamscience.ca/en/documents/New%20content/incubation/Incubation%20overview%20for%20website%20updated.pdf.

Nietzsche, Friedrich. *Twilight of the Idols.* Indianapolis, IN: Hackett Publishing Co., 1997.

Ogden, Pat and Janina Fisher. *Sensorimotor Psychotherapy*. New York: W. W. Norton & Company, 2019.

Oliver, Mary. *Red Bird*. Boston: Beacon Press, 2009.

Overton, Patrick Miles. *The Leaning Tree*. Bloomington, MN: Bethany Press, 1975.

Pearson, Tanya. "Fifty years later, 'Tapestry's' hope and optimism still resonates." *Washington Post*. February 26, 2021. https://www.washingtonpost.com/outlook/2021/02/26/fifty-years-later-tapestrys-hope-optimism-still-resonates/.

Perls, Frederick, S. *Gestalt Therapy Verbatim*. Highland, NY: The Gestalt Journal Press, 1969, 1992.

Perry, Christopher. "The Shadow." Society of Analytical Psychology. https://www.thesap.org.uk/articles-on-jungian-psychology-2/about-analysis-and-therapy/the-shadow/.

"Psalm 23." Bible. King James Version. BibleGateway. https://www.biblegateway.com/passage/?search=Psalm%2023&version=KJV.

Radford, Tim. "James Lovelock at 100: The Gaia Saga Continues." Nature. June 25, 2019. https://www.nature.com/articles/d41586-019-01969-y

Roland, David. "Suffering, Compassion, and Transformation." The Wise Brain Bulletin. Wellspring Institute for Neuroscience and Contemplative Wisdom. Volume 15.1. 2020. https://www.wisebrain.org/tools/wise-brain-bulletin/volume-15-1#suffering-compassion-and-transformation.

Rothschild, Babette. *The Body Remembers: The Psychophysiology of Trauma and Trauma Treatment*. New York: W. W. Norton & Company, 2010.

Rumi, Jalal ad-Din. *The Essential Rumi*. Translated by Coleman Barks. San Francisco: HarperOne, 2004.

Sacks, Jonathan. "The Future of the Past." December 2018. Covenant and Conversation, www.rabbisacks.org.

Schiller, Linda. "Moving Into Your Dreams: Embracing Embodied Dreamwork." *DreamTime*, Journal of International Association for the Study of Dreams. 2020. www.ASDreams.org.

_____. *Modern Dreamwork: New Tools for Decoding Your Soul's Wisdom.* Woodbury, MN: Llewelyn Worldwide Publishing, 2019.

_____. "Title and Re-Title: How Dreamwork Can Be Like EMDR." Awake to Your Dreams. June 8, 2012. https://lindayael schiller.com/title-re-title-dreamwork-emdr/.

_____. "Getting Unstuck: Using the GAIA Method." Awake to Your Dreams. https://www.awaketoyourdreams.com.

_____. *Integrative and Comprehensive Trauma Treatment*, 2010, Western Schools: Behavioral Health Series, www.westernschools.com.

Schwartz, Richard, and Martha Sweezy. *Internal Family Systems Therapy,* New York: Guilford Press, 2019.

Siegel, Allan and Sapru Hreday. Essential Neuroscience. Riverwoods, IL: Wolters Kluwer, 2019.

Siegel, Daniel, and Tina Payne Bryson. *The Whole-Brain Child: 12 Revolutionary Strategies to Nurture Your Child's Developing Mind.* London: Bantam, 2012.

Shapiro, Francine, and Margot Silk Forrest. *EMDR: The Breakthrough Therapy for Overcoming Anxiety, Stress, and Trauma.* New York: Basic Books, 2016.

_____. *Eye Movement Desensitization and Reprocessing (EMDR) Therapy: Basic Principles, Protocols, and Procedures, 3rd Edition.* New York: Guilford Press, 2018.

Swack, Judith A., Ph.D. "The Basic Structure of Loss and Violence Trauma Imprints." Anchor Point Magazine. March 1994: 3:3-23 https://hblu.org/wp-content/uploads/2010/06/Trauma_Article.pdf.

_____ "Healing From the Body Level Up." *Energy Psychology in Psychotherapy. Gallo, Fred, Ph.D., ed.,* New York: W. W. Norton & Company, 2001.

Szpakowska, K. "Through the Looking Glass: Dreams and Nightmares in Pharaonic Egypt." In Kelly Bulkeley (ed.) *Dreams: A Reader on the Religious, Cultural, and Psychological Dimensions of Dreaming*, Palgrave, 2001.

Taylor, Jeremy. "Dreamwork & Collective Trauma: Unconscious Elements in Public Debate." Dream Network. October 2001. https://dreamnetworkjournal.com/bcpov6ctraum/dreams-and-christianity.

Tedeschi R.G. and L.G. Calhoun. "The Posttraumatic Growth Inventory: Measuring the positive legacy of trauma." *Journal of Traumatic Stress* 9(3), (1996): 455–472. https://doi.org/10.1002/jts.2490090305.

"Tutorial 12: The Endocrine System." Introductory Biological Psychology Tutorials. https://psych.athabascau.ca/html/Psych289/Biotutorials/12/part1.shtml.

Volkan, V.D. *A Nazi Legacy: Depositing, Transgenerational Transmission, Dissociation, and Remembering Through Action*. Oxfordshire, UK: Routledge, 2015.

Van der Kolk, Bessel. *The Body Keeps the Score: Brain, Mind, and Body in the Healing of Trauma*. Westminster, London: Penguin Publishing Group, 2015.

Van de Castle, Robert. *Our Dreaming Mind*. New York: Ballantine Books, 1994.

Walker, Matthew. *Why We Sleep: Unlocking the Power of Sleep and Dreams*. New York: Scribner, 2017.

"What Are REM and Non-REM Sleep?" WebMD. October 16, 2020. https://www.webmd.com/sleep-disorders/sleep-101.

Wilkerson, Richard. Dream Network. https://dreamnetworkjournal.com/@richardwilkerson/.

Wiseman, Ann Sayre. *Nightmare Help: A Guide for Parents and Teachers*. Berkeley, CA: Ten Speed Press, 1989.

Wolynn, Mark. *It Didn't Start With You: How Inherited Family Trauma Shapes Who We Are and How to End the Cycle*. New York: Viking Random House Press, 2016.

Bibliography

Woodman, Marion and Jill Mellick. *Coming Home to Myself: Reflections for Nurturing a Woman's Body & Soul.* Newburyport, MA: Conari Press, 1998.

Zadra, Antonio. "Nightmares: We're Not at Their Mercy." The International Association for the Study of Dreams. 2018. http://www.asdreams.org/IASD/wp-content/uploads/2018/03/BAW_2018-03-13-am_Nightmares_Zadra-1.pdf

Zadra, Antonio and Robert Stickgold. *When Brains Dream: Exploring the Science and Mystery of Sleep.* New York: W. W. Norton & Company, 2021.

Zukav, Gary. *The Seat of the Soul.* New York: Simon & Schuster, 1989.

Recommended Reading and Resources

https://www.asdreams.org/—IASD – The International Association for the Study of Dreams.

This vibrant international community brings together dream experts, therapists, healers, scientists, artists, and interested dreamers to attend to all aspects of dreaming. It hosts an annual international conference as well as online forums and local events. It offers a forum for information sharing through two publications: *Dream-Time*, the tri-annual magazine, and *Dreaming*, the academic journal.

These international therapeutic organizations contain resources, information, and frequently a find-a-therapist page for help near you:

- **www.emdria.org**—Eye Movement Desensitization and Reprocessing, the EMDR International Association

- **https://www.isst-d.org/**—International Society for the Study of Trauma and Dissociation; *Also see*

- **https://www.nesttd-online.org/** for the New England chapter.

- **www.tatlife.com**—Tapas Acupressure Technique, TAT, designed by Tapas Flemming

- **https://eftinternational.org/**—Emotional Freedom Technique, EFT International

- **https://www.hblu.org**—Healing From the Body Level Up

- **www.malesurvivor.org/for-survivors**—Male Survivor

- **https://www.traumasurvivorsnetwork.org/pages/home**—Trauma Survivors Network

- **www.aedpinstitute.org**—Accelerated Experiential Dynamic Psychotherapy
- **www.trauma-recovery.ca**—Manitoba Trauma Information and Education Centre
- **www.psychologytoday.com/us**—Find a Therapist menu

To Write to the Author

If you wish to contact the author or would like more information about this book, please write to the author in care of Llewellyn Worldwide Ltd. and we will forward your request. Both the author and publisher appreciate hearing from you and learning of your enjoyment of this book and how it has helped you. Llewellyn Worldwide Ltd. cannot guarantee that every letter written to the author can be answered, but all will be forwarded. Please write to:

Linda Yael Schiller
℅ Llewellyn Worldwide
2143 Wooddale Drive
Woodbury, MN 55125-2989

Please enclose a self-addressed stamped envelope for reply,
or $1.00 to cover costs. If outside the U.S.A., enclose
an international postal reply coupon.

Many of Llewellyn's authors have websites with additional information and resources. For more information, please visit our website at http://www.llewellyn.com.